A NEW BIBLIOGRAPHY OF WRITINGS ON VARIETIES OF ENGLISH 1984-1992/93

Varieties of English Around the World

General Editor:
Manfred Görlach
Englisches Seminar
Universität zu Köln
Albertus-Magnus-Platz 1
D-50923 KÖLN
Germany

GENERAL SERIES
Volume 12

Beat Glauser, Edgar W. Schneider and Manfred Görlach
A New Bibliography of Writings on Varieties of English 1984-1992/93

A NEW BIBLIOGRAPHY OF WRITINGS ON VARIETIES OF ENGLISH 1984-1992/93

BEAT GLAUSER

EDGAR W. SCHNEIDER

MANFRED GÖRLACH

JOHN BENJAMINS PUBLISHING COMPANY
AMSTERDAM/PHILADELPHIA

1993

Library of Congress Cataloging-in-Publication Data

Glauser, Beat.

A new bibliography of writings on varieties of English 1984-1992/3 / Beat Glauser, Edgar W. Schneider, Manfred Görlach.

p. cm. -- (Varieties of English around the world, ISSN 0172-7362. General series; v. 12)

Includes index.

1. English language--Variation--Bibliography. 2. English language--Foreign countries--Bibliography. 3. English language--Dialects--Bibliography. I. Schneider, Edgar W. (Edgar Werner), 1954- . II. Görlach, Manfred. III. Title. IV Series.

Z2015.V27G58 1993

[PE1074.7]

016.42--dc20 93-41367

ISBN 90 272 4870 2 (Eur.)/1-55619-443-9 (US) (alk. paper) CIP

John Benjamins Publishing Co. · P.O. Box 75577 · 1070 AN Amsterdam · The Netherlands

John Benjamins North America · 821 Bethlehem Pike · Philadelphia, PA 19118 · USA

ENGLISHES. A SELECTIVE BIBLIOGRAPHY 1984 - 1992/93

BEAT GLAUSER, EDGAR W. SCHNEIDER, MANFRED GÖRLACH

The present bibliography is intended to complement the earlier reference work published as Viereck, Schneider & Görlach (1984). It covers the years 1984-1992/3, with the addition of a few earlier publications not included (or incompletely listed) in the previous book.

We have decided to arrange the titles in four sections; the second (by B. Glauser) covers Great Britain and Ireland, the third (by E.W. Schneider) the United States and Canada, and the fourth (by M. Görlach) the rest of the world. Works devoted to more general topics of English dialectology, sociolinguistics and varieties of English, as well as collections containing publications on themes treating more than one of the three areas or comparative studies cannot be easily accommodated in any of the three sections; we have therefore thought it best to collect these in a first, introductory section. Cross-references to this first section have the authors asterisked to permit easier identification; a few titles containing 'external' cross-references to parts II, III and IV have these numbers in superscript form.

Each of the four sections has a special introduction explaining the scope of the collection (and the exclusion of certain works from the list), but there is only one index covering the entries in all four parts.

Most of the major books in the field have been reviewed in *EWW*. Because of the close links between *EWW* and *VEAW* (and the fact that readers might well turn to *EWW* for more detailed information) we have indicated reviews in *EWW* (and only in *EWW*); for a similar reason, summaries of theses (re-)printed in *EWW* have also been indicated.

The predecessor volume covered twenty years of research and included some 4200 titles. We thought it best not to wait another twenty years, but to gather together what bibliographical evidence was available for a ten-year period on the same field as that covered in 1984, thus fulfilling one of the major aims of bibliographies, *viz*. to present information as recent as possible. The shorter timeframe has meant that the present collection with its 2800 entries is only 66% of the length of the earlier book. It includes everything we found and thought worthy of inclusion among publications out by April 1993 - and a few titles announced as forthcoming (fc.). We are aware of the risk - books may never appear, or change editors, titles or publishers during the period of preparation.

Last-minute additions are arranged alphabetically numbered a, b, etc.

No bibliography will ever be complete or error-free, but we have done our best to make the book as perfect as possible - for instance, by having each editor proofread and supplement the complete volume rather than his own section only. The final compilation, editing and computerization would have been impossible without the meticulous and patient work of Christoph Stephan at Köln.

Beat Glauser Edgar W. Schneider Manfred Görlach
Heidelberg Regensburg Köln

List of abbreviations

AJL	*Australian Journal of Linguistics*
AnL	*Anthropological Linguistics*
ANU	Australian National University
AppL	*Applied Linguistics*
ARAL	*Annual Review of Applied Linguistics*
AS	*American Speech*
AUMLA	*Journal of the Australasian Universities Language and Literature Association*
BACLA	*Bulletin de l'ACLA/Bulletin of the CAAL*
BASS	Bayreuth African Studies Series (University of Bayreuth)
BBES	Bamberger Beiträge zur Englischen Sprachwissenschaft
CIEFL	Central Institute of English and Foreign Languages (Hyderabad)
CJL	*Canadian Journal of Linguistics*
CMLR	*Canadian Modern Language Review*
DAI	Dissertation Abstracts International
ES	*English Studies*
ET	*English Today*
ETF	*English Teaching Forum*
EWW	*English World-Wide*
GURT	Georgetown University Round Table on Languages and Linguistics
IDEAL	*Issues and Developments in English and Applied Linguistics*
IJAL	*Indian Journal of Applied Linguistics*
IJSL	*International Journal of the Sociology of Language*
IRAL	*International Review of Applied Linguistics*
ITL	*ITL, Review of Applied Linguistics*
JEngL	*Journal of English Linguistics*
JESL	*Journal of English as a Second Language*
JIPA	*Journal of the International Phonetic Association*
JL	*Journal of Linguistics*
JLDS	*Journal of the Lancashire Dialect Society*
JLSP	*Journal of Language and Social Psychology*
JMMD	*Journal of Multilingual and Multicultural Development*
JPCL	*Journal of Pidgin and Creole Languages*
JPrag	*Journal of Pragmatics*
KanQ	*Kansas Quarterly*
L&C	*Language and Communication*
L&L	*Lore and Language*

LACUS	*The ... LACUS Forum* (Lake Bluff, Ill.)
LinS	*Language in Society*
LL	*Language Learning*
LPLP	*Language Problems & Language Planning*
LSE	*Leeds Studies in English*
LVC	*Language Variation and Change*
NADS	*Newsletter of the American Dialect Society*
NM	*Neuphilologische Mitteilungen*
NWIG	*New West Indian Guide/Nieuwe West Indische Gids*
PacL	Pacific Linguistics Series
PADS	Publications of the American Dialect Society
PHCC	*Proceedings of the Harvard Celtic Colloquium*
PSCL	*Papers and Studies in Contrastive Linguistics*
RELC	Regional English Language Centre (Singapore)
RFEA	*Revue Française d'Etudes Américaines*
RLS	*Regional Language Studies Newfoundland*
SAP	*Studia Anglica Posnaniensia*
SCL	Society for Caribbean Linguistics Occasional Papers
ScoL	*Scottish Language*
SECOLR	*The SECOL Review: Southeastern Conference on Linguistics*
SELL	Series in English Language and Literature
SL	*Studia Linguistica*
TBL	Tübinger Beiträge zur Linguistik
Teanga	*The Irish Yearbook of Applied Linguistics*
TeReo	*Journal of the Linguistic Society of New Zealand*
TESOLQ	*Teachers of English to Speakers of Other Languages Quarterly*
TPS	*Transactions of the Philological Society*
TSL	*Typological Studies in Language*
TYDS	*Transactions of the Yorkshire Dialect Society*
UP	University Press
VEAW	Varieties of English around the World
WE	*World Englishes*
WWays	*Word Ways: The Journal of Recreational Linguistics*
YPL	*York Papers in Linguistics*
ZAA	*Zeitschrift für Anglistik und Amerikanistik*
ZDL	*Zeitschrift für Dialektologie und Linguistik*

Part I: General entries

1 Aarts, F.G.A.M. 1985. "Linguistic variation in English: idealization, varieties and linguistic items". *ES* 65:59-73.

2 Adamson, H.D. 1988. *Variation Theory and Second Language Acquisition*. Washington, D.C.: Georgetown UP.

3 Adamson, Sylvia, *et al.*, eds. 1990. *Papers from the 5th International Conference on English Historical Linguistics, Cambridge, 6-9 April 1987*. Amsterdam: Benjamins. (Rev. in *EWW* 12:143-4).

4 Ahrens, Rüdiger, ed. 1989. *Anglistentag 1989. Würzburg*. Tübingen: Niemeyer.

5 Aijmer, Karin & Bengt Altenberg, eds. 1991. *Corpus Linguistics: Studies in Honour of Jan Svartvik*. London: Longman.

6 Aitchison, Jean. 1991. *Language Change - Progress or Decay?* 2nd ed. Cambridge: UP.

7 Alatis, James E. & John C. Staczek, eds. 1985. *Perspectives on Bilingualism and Bilingual Education*. Washington, D.C.: Georgetown UP.

8 Algeo, John. 1986. "The two streams: British and American English". *JEngL* 19:269-84.

9 ---. 1989. "Americanisms, Briticisms, and the standard: an essay at definition". *TSL* 31:139-57.

10 ---. 1990. "British and American English: Odi et Amo". In Adamson, *et al.*, 13-29.

11 Allen, Harold B. & Michael D. Linn, eds. 1986. *Dialect and Language Variation*. Orlando, Fla. & New York: Academic Press. (Rev. in *EWW* 8:154-6).

12 Altbach, P.G. & G.P. Kelly, eds. 1984. *Education and the Colonial Experience*. 2nd ed. New Brunswick, N.J.: Transaction Books.

13 Aman, Reinhold. 1992. "Ethnic, racial, religious and sexual slurs in an American and Australian dictionary". In [IV]Dutton, *et al.*, 41-7.

14 Ambert, Alba N., ed. 1991. *Bilingual Education and English as a Second Language: A Research Handbook, 1988-1990*. New York: Garland.

15 Ammon, Ulrich, ed. 1989. *Status and Function of Languages and Language Varieties*. Berlin & New York: Mouton de Gruyter. (Rev. in *EWW* 11:141-3).

16 --- & Jenny Cheshire, eds. 1989. *Dialect and School in the European Countries*. (Sociolinguistica, 3). Tübingen: Niemeyer. (Rev. in *EWW* 11:145-7).

17 ---, Norbert Dittmar & Klaus J. Mattheier, eds. 1987/88. *Sociolinguistics. Soziolinguistik. An International Handbook of the Science of Language and Society*. 2 vols. (Handbücher zur Sprach- und Kommunikationswissenschaft, 3.1 & 3.2). Berlin: Mouton de Gruyter. (Rev. in *EWW* 10:321-8).

18 Andersson, Lars & Peter Trudgill. 1990. *Bad Language*. Oxford: Blackwell.

19 Bahner, Werner, *et al*., eds. 1990. *Proceedings of the Fourteenth International Congress of Linguists. Berlin/GDR, August 10 - August 15, 1987*. 3 vols. Berlin: Akademie-Verlag.

20 Bailey, Guy, Natalie Maynor & Patricia Cukor-Avila, eds. 1991. *The Emergence of Black English: Text and Commentary*. Amsterdam: Benjamins. (Rev. in *EWW* 13:129-34).

21 Bailey, Richard W., ed. 1987. *Dictionaries of English: Prospects for the Record of Our Language*. Ann Arbor: University of Michigan Press. (Cambridge: UP, 1989). (Rev. in *EWW* 9:134-6).

22 ---. 1992. *Images of English. A Cultural History of the Language*. Ann Arbor: University of Michigan Press.

23 Baugh, A.C. & Thomas Cable. [4]1993. *A History of the English Language*. New York & London: Routledge. (Rev. in *EWW* 14:2).

24 Bédard, Edith & Jacques Maurais, eds. 1983. *La Norme Linguistique*. Québec: Conseil de la Langue Française; Paris: Le Robert.

25 Bell, Allan. 1984. "Language style as audience design". *LinS* 13:145-204.

26 ---. 1991. *The Language of News Media*. Oxford: Blackwell.

27 Berry, Reginald & James Acheson, eds. 1985. *Regionalism and National Identity: Multi-Disciplinary Essays on Canada, Australia, and New Zealand*. Christchurch, N.Z.: Association for Canadian Studies in Australia and New Zealand.

28 Bhatia, Tej K. 1992. "Discourse functions and pragmatics of mixing: advertising across cultures". In Smith & Sridhar, 195-215.

29 Biber, Douglas. 1987. "A textual comparison of British and American writing". *AS* 62:99-119.

30 ---. 1988. *Variation Across Speech and Writing*. Cambridge: UP. (Rev. in *EWW* 10:162-4).

31 Bickerton, Derek. 1984. "The language bioprogram hypothesis". *The Behavioral and Brain Sciences* 7:173-88.

32 ---. 1991. "On the supposed 'gradualness' of creole development". *JPCL* 6:25-58.

33 ---. 1992. "The sociohistorical matrix of creolization". *JPCL* 7:307-18.

34 Blank, Claudia, ed. 1992. *Language and Civilization: A Concerted Profusion of Essays and Studies in Honour of Otto Hietsch.* 2 vols. Frankfurt/M.: Lang. (Rev. in *EWW* 14:2).

35 Bolton, Kingsley & Helen Kwok, eds. 1991. *Sociolinguistics Today. International Perspectives.* London & New York: Routledge. (Rev. in *EWW* 13:145-7).

36 Breitborde, Lawrence B. 1983. "Levels of analysis in sociolinguistic explanation: bilingual codeswitching, social relations, and domain theory". *IJSL* 39:5-43.

37 British Council. 1988. *The Place of Grammar in the Teaching of English.* An International Conference held at the British Council, Nairobi.

38 Britton, James, Robert E. Shafer & Ken Watson, eds. 1990. *Teaching and Learning English Worldwide.* Clevedon: Multilingual Matters. (Rev. in *EWW* 11:308-9).

39 Burchfield, Robert W., ed. 1987. *Studies in Lexicography.* Oxford: Clarendon. (Rev. in *EWW* 9:136-7).

40 ---, ed. fc. *English in Britain and Overseas: Origins and Development.* Vol. V. *The Cambridge History of the English Language.* Cambridge: UP.

41 Butters, Ronald R. 1993. "Current issues in variation theory". In Viereck 1993a:3-36.

42 Byrne, Francis & Thom Huebner, eds., 1991. *Development and Structure of Creole Languages: Essays in Honor of Derek Bickerton.* Amsterdam: Benjamins.

43 --- & John Holm, eds. 1993. *Atlantic Meets Pacific. A Global View of Pidginization and Creolization.* Amsterdam & Philadelphia: Benjamins. (Rev. in *EWW* 14:2).

44 Callan, V.J., *et al.* 1983. "Evaluative reactions to accented English: ethnicity, sex role, and context". *Journal of Cross-Cultural Psychology* 14:407-26.

45 Cassidy, Frederic G. 1986. "Some similarities between Gullah and Caribbean Creoles". In [III]Montgomery & Bailey, 30-7.

46 Chambers, Jack K. 1992a. "Linguistic correlates of gender and sex". *EWW* 13:173-218.

47 ---. 1992b. "Dialect acquisition". *Language* 68:673-705. [= 981]

48 --- & Peter Trudgill. 1991a. "Non-finite verb forms in English dialects". In Trudgill & Chambers, 215-7.

49 --- & ---. 1991b. "Adverbials in English dialects". In Trudgill & Chambers, 261-6.

50 --- & ---. 1991c. "Dialect grammar: data and theory". In Trudgill & Chambers, 291-6.

51 Cheshire, Jenny L. 1987. "Syntactic variation, the linguistic variable, and sociolinguistic theory". *Linguistics* 25:257-82.

52 ---, ed. 1991a. *English Around the World. Sociolinguistic Perspectives*. Cambridge: UP. (Rev. in *EWW* 13:115-8).

53 ---. 1991b. "The UK and the USA". In Cheshire, 13-34.

54 Chevillet, François. 1991. *Les variétés de l'anglais*. Paris: Nathan.

55 Coates, Jennifer & Deborah Cameron, eds. 1988. *Women in Their Speech Communities: New Perspectives on Language and Sex*. London: Longman.

56 Coelho, Elizabeth. 1991. *Caribbean Students in Canadian Schools, Book 2*. Markham, Ont.: Pippin Publishing.

57 Collinge, N.E., ed. 1990. *An Encyclopedia of Language*. London & New York: Routledge. (Rev. in *EWW* 14:145-6).

58 Cooper, Robert L., ed. 1982. *Language Spread: Studies in Diffusion and Social Change*. Bloomington, Ind.: Indiana UP/ Washington, D.C.: Center for Applied Linguistics. (Rev. in *EWW* 5:275-80).

59 Corson, David. 1989. "Adolescent lexical differences in Australia and England by social group". *Journal of Educational Research* 82:146-57.

60 Coulmas, Florian. 1992. *Language and Economy*. Oxford: Blackwell. (Rev. in *EWW* 14:2).

61 Crozier, Alan. 1984. "The Scotch-Irish influence on American English". *AS* 59:310-31.

62 Crystal, David. 1985. "How many millions? The statistics of English today". *ET* 1:7-9.

63 ---. 1987. *The Cambridge Encyclopedia of Language*. Cambridge: UP. (Rev. in *EWW* 14:141-4).

64 ---. 1988. *The English Language*. London: Penguin.

65 Davis, Lawrence M. 1990. *Statistics in Dialectology*. Tuscaloosa: University of Alabama Press.

66 Delbridge, Arthur. 1989. "Usage and style: implications for lexicography". In Gregory James, ed. *Lexicographers and their Works*. Exeter: University, 66-73.

67 Denning, Keith, ed. 1987. *Variation in Language: NWAV-XV at Stanford*. Stanford, Calif.: Department of Linguistics, Stanford University.

68 Dingxu, Shi. 1992. "On the etymology of *pidgin*". *JPCL* 7:343-6.

69 Duncan-Rose, Carolina & Theo Vennemann, eds. 1988. *On Language: Rhetorica, Phonologica, Syntactica: a Festschrift for Robert P. Stockwell from his Friends and Colleagues*. London: Routledge.

70 Durrell, Martin. 1990. "Language as geography". In Collinge, 917-55.

71 Eastman, Carol M. 1983. *Language Planning: An Introduction.* San Francisco: Chandler & Sharp.

72 Eaton, Roger, *et al.*, eds. 1985. *Papers from the Fourth International Conference on English Historical Linguistics, Amsterdam, 10-13 April 1985*. Amsterdam: Benjamins.

73 Eckert, Penelope, ed. 1991. *New Ways of Analyzing Sound Change*. San Diego: Academic Press.

74 Edmondson, Jerold A. 1983. *Research Papers of the Texas SIL: Pilot Studies in Sociolinguistics: Variation, Use and Attitudes*. Dallas: Summer Institute of Linguistics.

75 ---, Crawford Feagin & Peter Mühlhäusler, eds. 1990. *Development and Diversity. Linguistic Variation across Time and Space. A Festschrift for Charles-James N. Bailey*. Dallas: Summer Institute of Linguistics & University of Texas at Arlington. (Rev. in *EWW* 12:317-9).

76 Edwards, John R., ed. 1984. *Linguistic Minorities, Policies and Pluralism*. London: Academic Press.

77 ---. 1985. *Language, Society and Identity*. Oxford: Blackwell.

78 Edwards, Vivian K. 1983. *Language in Multicultural Classrooms*. London: Batsford. (Rev. in *EWW* 4:324-5).

79 ---. 1987. "The notion of 'competence' and the Patois speaker". In Rod Ellis, ed. *Second Language Acquisition in Context*. Englewood Cliffs, N.J.: Prentice-Hall, 149-58.

80 Edwards, Walter F. 1991. "A comparative description of Guyanese Creole and Black English preverbal marker *don*". In Edwards & Winford, 240-55.

81 --- & Donald Winford, eds. 1991. *Verb Phrase Patterns in Black English and Creole*. Detroit: Wayne State UP.

82 Enninger, Werner & Lilith Haynes, eds. 1984. *Studies in Linguistic Ecology*. Wiesbaden: Steiner. (Rev. in *EWW* 5:299-300).

83 --- & Thomas Stolz, eds. 1987. *Beiträge zum 3. Essener Kolloquium über Sprachwandel und seine bestimmenden Faktoren vom 30.9.-2.10.1987 an der Universität Essen*. Bochum: Brockmeyer.

84 Fabian, Johannes. 1986. *Language and Colonial Power*. Cambridge: UP.

85 Fasold, Ralph W., ed. 1983. *Variation in the Form and Use of Language: A Sociolinguistic Reader*. Washington, D.C.: Georgetown UP.

86 --- & Deborah Schiffrin, eds. 1989. *Language Change and Variation.* (Current Issues in Linguistic Theory, 52). Amsterdam: Benjamins.

87 Fennell, B.A. 1986. "Nurturing the difference". *Verbatim* 12:7-8.

88 Fishman, Joshua A. 1989. *Language and Ethnicity in Minority Sociolinguistic Perspective.* Clevedon: Multilingual Matters. (Rev. in *EWW* 11:115-7).

89 ---, *et al.* 1985. *The Rise and Fall of the Ethnic Revival: Perspectives on Language and Ethnicity.* Berlin: Mouton de Gruyter.

90 Fisiak, Jacek, ed. 1984. *Contrastive Linguistics. Prospects and Problems.* (Trends in Linguistics, Studies and Monographs, 22). Berlin: Mouton de Gruyter. (Rev. in *EWW* 5:305).

91 ---, ed. 1986. *Papers from the 6th International Conference on Historical Linguistics.* Amsterdam: Benjamins & Poznan: Adam Mickiewicz University.

92 ---, ed. 1988. *Historical Dialectology, Regional and Social.* (Trends in Linguistics, Studies and Monographs, 37). Berlin: Mouton de Gruyter. (Rev. in *EWW* 10:158-60).

93 Fluck, Hans-Rüdiger. 1985. *Fachsprachen. Einführung und Bibliographie.* (3rd enlarged and revised ed.). Tübingen: Francke.

94 Frajzyngier, Zygmunt. 1984. "On the origin of *say* and *se* as complementizers in Black English and English-based creoles". *AS* 59:207-10.

95 Freeborn, Dennis, with J. Peter French and David Langford. 1986. *Varieties of English: An Introduction to the Study of Language.* London: Macmillan.

96 Fries, Udo & Martin Heusser, eds. 1989. *Meaning and Beyond. Ernst Leisi zum 70. Geburtstag.* Tübingen: Narr.

97 Garcia, Erica C. 1985. "Shifting variation". *Lingua* 67:189-224.

98 Garcia, Eugene E. & Raymond V. Padilla, eds. 1985. *Advances in Bilingual Education Research.* Tucson: University of Arizona Press.

99 García, Ofelia & Ricardo Otheguy, eds. 1989. *English across Cultures, Cultures across English. A Reader in Cross-cultural Communication.* Berlin: Mouton de Gruyter. (Rev. in *EWW* 11:117-21).

100 Gardner, Meredith Knox. 1984. "Kad existas usana lingvo?". *Ido-Vivo* 3(7):18-21.

101 Gilbert, Glenn C., ed. 1987. *Pidgin and Creole Languages. Essays in Memory of John E. Reinecke.* Honululu: University of Hawaii Press. (Rev. in *EWW* 9:149-51).

102 Gläser, Rosemarie. 1990. *Fachtextsorten im Englischen.* (Forum für Fachsprachen, 13). Tübingen: Narr.

103 ---, ed. 1992. *Aktuelle Probleme der anglistischen Fachtextanalyse.* (Leipziger Fachsprachen-Studien, 5). Frankfurt/M.: Lang.

104 Glauser, Beat. 1985. "Linguistic atlases and generative phonology". In [II]Kirk, *et al.*, 113-29.

105 Goebl, Hans, ed. 1984. *Dialectology*. (Quantitative Linguistics, 21). Bochum: Brockmeyer.

106 Görlach, Manfred, ed. 1986. *Wilhelm Busch: Max and Moritz in English Dialects and Creoles*. Hamburg: Buske.

107 ---. 1987. "Colonial lag? The alleged conservative character of American English and other 'colonial' varieties". *EWW* 8:41-60. (Reprinted in Görlach 1991:90-107).

108 ---. 1988. "*Varietas delectat*: forms and functions of English around the world". In Nixon & Honey, 167-208. (Reprinted in Görlach fc.a).

109 ---. 1989a. "Word-formation and the ENL:ESL:EFL distinction". *EWW* 10:279-313. (Reprinted in Görlach fc.a).

110 ---. 1989b. "Varieties of English and ELT". *Spelt Newsletter* 4(2):3-6.

111 ---. 1990a. *Studies in the History of the English Language*. Heidelberg: Winter.

112 ---. 1990b. "Heteronymy in International English". *EWW* 11:239-74. (Reprinted in Görlach fc.a).

113 ---. 1991a. *Englishes. Studies in Varieties of English 1984-1988*. (VEAW, G11). Amsterdam: Benjamins. (Rev. in *EWW* 13:119-21).

114 ---. 1991b. "The dictionary of transplanted varieties of languages". Art. 198 in F.H. Hausmann, Oskar Reichmann, Herbert Ernst Wiegand & Ladislav Zgusta, eds. *Wörterbücher*. Vol. 2. Berlin: Mouton de Gruyter, 1475-99. (Reprinted in Görlach fc.a).

115 ---. fc.a. *More Englishes. New Studies in Varieties of English.* (VEAW, G14). Amsterdam: Benjamins.

116 ---. fc.b. "Innovation in New Englishes". In Görlach fc.a.

117 ---. fc.c. "Text types and Indian English". In Görlach fc.a.

118 --- & Konrad Schröder. 1985. "'Good usage' in an EFL context". In Greenbaum, 227-32.

119 Gold, David L. 1986. "Two desiderata for lexicography: allolingual and allotopolectal collaborators and the philological review: with examples from Canadian, Bahamian, and South African English". *Dictionaries* 8:112-45.

120 Gramley, Stephan & Kurt-Michael Pätzold. 1992. *A Survey of Modern English*. London & New York: Routledge. (Rev. in *EWW* 14:159-61). (German version: *Das moderne Englisch*. Paderborn: Schöningh, 1985).

121 Graustein, Gottfried & Wolfgang Thiele, eds. 1989. *Englische Textlinguistik und Varietätenforschung*. (Linguistische Arbeitsberichte 69: Sektion Theoretische und angewandte Sprachwissenschaft). Leipzig: Karl-Marx-Universität.

122 Greenbaum, Sidney, ed. 1985. *The English Language Today*. Oxford: Pergamon. (Rev. in *EWW* 6:297-9).

123 ---. 1990a. "Standard English and the International Corpus of English". *WE* 9:79-83.

124 ---. 1990b. "Whose English?". In Ricks & Michaels, 15-23.

125 ---. 1991a. "ICE: the International Corpus of English". *ET* 27:3-7.

126 ---. 1991b. "The development of the International Corpus of English". In Aijmer & Altenberg, 83-91.

127 Hall, Joan, *et al.*, eds. 1992. *Old English and New. Studies in Language and Linguistics in Honor of Frederick G. Cassidy*. New York & London: Garland.

128 Hammarström, Göran. 1992. "On sociolect". In [IV]Dutton, *et al.*, 149-56.

129 Hancock, Ian F., ed. 1985. *Diversity and Development in English-Related Creoles*. Ann Arbor: Karoma. (Rev. in *EWW* 6:323-8).

130 ---. 1986. "The domestic hypothesis, diffusion and componentiality. An account of Atlantic Anglophone creole origins". In Muysken & Smith, 71-102.

131 ---. 1987a. "A preliminary classification of the anglophone Atlantic creoles, with syntactic data from thirty-three representative dialects". In Gilbert, 264-333.

132 ---. 1987b. "History of research on pidgins and creoles". *Sociolinguistics: An International Handbook of the Science of Language and Society*. Vol. 1. Berlin: Mouton de Gruyter, 459-69.

133 Hansen, Klaus, ed. 1987. *Studien zur Sprachvariation (unter besonderer Berücksichtigung des Englischen)*. Berlin: Humboldt-Universität. (Rev. in *EWW* 9:129-30).

134 ---, ed. 1991a. *Studien zur Sprachvariation im Englischen und zur Textlinguistik* (unter besonderer Berücksichtigung der Lexik). Berlin: Humboldt-Universität.

135 ---. 1991b. "Zur nationalen Differenzierung des Englischen im Bereich der Lexik". In Hansen, 7-59.

136 Harris, John. 1986. "Expanding the superstrate: habitual aspect markers in Atlantic Englishes". *EWW* 7:171-99.

137 Heller, Monica, ed. 1988. *Code Switching: Anthropological and Sociological Perspectives*. Berlin: Mouton de Gruyter.

138 Herrick, Earl M. 1984. *Sociolinguistic Variation: A Formal Model.* University, Ala.: University of Alabama Press.

139 Hewitt, Roger. 1986. *White Talk Black Talk: Inter-racial Friendship and Communication Amongst Adolescents*. Cambridge: UP.

140 Hirschmüller, Helmut. 1989. "The use of complex prepositions in Indian English as compared with British and American English". In Graustein & Thiele, 52-8.

141 Holm, John. 1983. "On the relationship of Gullah and Bahamian". *AS* 58:308-18.

142 ---. 1984. "Variability of the copula in Black English and its creole kin". *AS* 59:291-309.

143 ---. 1986. "Substrate diffusion". In Muysken & Smith, 259-78.

144 ---. 1987. "African substratal influence on the Atlantic creoles". In P. Maurer & Thomas Stolz, eds. *Varia Creolica*. Bochum: Brockmeyer, 11-26.

145 ---. 1988/89. *Pidgins and Creoles*. Vol. I: *Theory and Structure*. Vol. II: *Reference Survey*. Cambridge: UP. (Rev. in *EWW* 11:129-35).

146 ---. 1989. "Creolistics and lexicography". In Ahrens, 236-45.

147 ---. 1990. "Features in the noun phrase common to the Atlantic creoles". *Linguistics* 28:867-81.

148 ---. 1991a. "The Atlantic creoles and the language of the ex-slave narratives". In Bailey, *et al.*, 231-48.

149 ---. 1991b. "Phonological features common to some West African and Atlantic creole languages". In Salikoko Mufwene, ed. *Africanisms in Afro-American Language Varieties*. Athens, Ga.: University of Georgia Press, 533-51.

150 Holtus, Günter & Edgar Radtke, eds. 1986. *Sprachlicher Substandard.* (Konzepte, 36). Tübingen: Niemeyer. (Rev. in *EWW* 8:147-9).

151 Homel, Peter, Michael Paliji & Doris Aaronson, eds. 1987. *Childhood Bilingualism: Aspects of Linguistic, Cognitive, and Social Development.* Hillsdale, N.J.: Erlbaum.

152 Hübler, Axel. 1985. *Einander verstehen. Englisch im Kontext internationaler Kommunikation*. (TBL, 251). Tübingen: Narr. (Rev. in *EWW* 7:330-3).

153 Hüllen, Werner & R. Schulze, eds. 1988. *Understanding the Lexicon: Meaning, Sense and World Knowledge in Lexical Semantics*. (Linguistische Arbeiten, 210). Tübingen: Niemeyer.

154 Hull, Alexander. 1993. "The transmission of creole languages". In Byrne & Holm, 391-7.

155 Hyldgaard-Jensen, Karl & Arne Zettersten, eds. 1988. *Symposium on Lexicography III: Proceedings of the Fourth International Symposium on Lexicography April 20-22, 1988 at the University of Copenhagen.* (Lexicographica, Series maior, 26). Tübingen: Niemeyer.

156 Ilson, Robert. 1985a. "Diversity in unity: British and American English". *ET* 4:7-11.

157 ---. 1985b. "Usage problems in British and American English". In Greenbaum, 166-82.

158 ---. 1990. "British and American English: ex uno plura?". In Ricks & Michaels, 33-41.

159 Jernudd, Björn H. 1987. "World languages in radio broadcasting and as official languages". In Laycock & Winter, 297-308.

160 Johnson, Robert Keith. 1990. "International English: towards an acceptable, teachable target variety". *WE* 9:301-15.

161 Johnston, Paul A., Jr. 1985. "Linguistic atlases and sociolinguistics". In [II]Kirk, *et al.*, 81-93.

162 Joseph, John E. 1989. "Four models of linguistic change". In Walsh, 147-57.

163 Kachru, Braj B. 1982. "The bilingual's linguistic repertoire". In Beverley Hartford, *et al.*, eds. *Issues in International Bilingual Education: The Role of the Vernacular*. New York: Plenum Publ., 25-52. (Reprinted in [IV]Kachru 1986:57-80).

164 ---. 1986. "The power and politics of English". *WE* 5:121-40.

165 ---. 1990. "World Englishes and applied linguistics". *WE* 9:3-20.

166 ---, ed. 1992a. *The Other Tongue. English Across Cultures*. 2nd ed. Urbana: University of Illinois Press. (Rev. in *EWW* 13:325-7).

167 ---. 1992b. "Teaching world Englishes". In Kachru, 355-65.

168 Kachru, Yamuna. 1992. "Culture, style, and discourse: expanding noetics of English". In B. Kachru, 340-52.

169 Kallen, Jeffrey L. 1991. "Intra-language transfer and the plural subject concord in Irish and Appalachian English". *Teanga* 11:20-34.

170 Kastovsky, Dieter & Alexander Szwedek, eds. 1986. *Linguistics Across Historical and Geographical Boundaries. In Honour of Jacek Fisiak.* 2 vols. (Trends in Linguistics, Studies and Monographs, 32). Berlin: Mouton de Gruyter. (Rev. in *EWW* 7:333-5).

171 Kirwin, William & Robert C. Hollet. 1986. "The West Country and Newfoundland: some SED evidence". *JEngL* 19:222-39.

172 Koopman, Willem, Frederike Van Der Leek, Olga Fischer & Roger Eaton, eds. 1987. *Explanation and Linguistic Change*. (Current Issues in Linguistic Theory, 45). Amsterdam: Benjamins.

173 Kramarae, Cheris, Murriel Schulz & William O'Barr, eds. 1984. *Language and Power*. Beverly Hills: Sage.

174 Kretzschmar, William A., Jr., Edgar W. Schneider & Ellen Johnson, eds. 1990. *Computer Methods in Dialectology*. (Special Issue of *JEngL* 22:1 (1989)). Athens, Ga.

175 Laforge, Lorne & Grant D. McConnell, eds. 1990. *Language Spread and Social Change. Dynamics and Measurement*. Sainte-Foy: Les Presses de l'Université Laval. (Rev. in *EWW* 13:143-5).

176 Lass, Roger. 1987. *The Shape of English. Structure and History*. London: Dent. (Rev. in *EWW* 9:332-3).

177 Laycock, Donald C. & Peter Mühlhäusler. 1990. "Language engineering: special languages". In Collinge, 843-75.

178 --- & Werner Winter, eds. 1987. *A World of Language: Papers Presented to Professor S.A. Wurm on his 65th Birthday*. (PacL C-100). Canberra: ANU.

179 Leisi, Ernst. [7]1985. *Das heutige Englisch*. Heidelberg: Winter.

180 Leitner, Gerhard. 1992a. "English as a pluricentric language". In Michael G. Clyne, ed. *Pluricentric Languages*. Berlin: Mouton de Gruyter, 179-237.

181 ---, ed. 1992b. *New Directions in English Language Corpora. Methodology, Results, Software Developments*. Berlin & New York: Mouton de Gruyter.

182 ---. 1992c. "International Corpus of English: Corpus design - problems and suggested solutions". In Leitner, 33-64.

183 Levitt, Jesse, Leonard R.N. Ashley & Kenneth H. Rogers, eds. 1987. *Geolinguistic Perspectives: Proceedings of the International Conference Celebrating the Twentieth Anniversary of the American Society of Geolinguistics, 1985*. Lanham, Md.: UP of America.

184 Lipski, John M. 1986. "English-Spanish contact in the United States and Central America: sociolinguistic mirror images?". In [IV]Görlach & Holm, 191-208.

185 Lörscher, Wolfgang & Rainer Schulze, eds. 1987. *Perspectives on Language in Performance: Studies in Linguistics, Literary Criticism, and Language Teaching and Learning: To Honour Werner Hüllen on the Occasion of his Sixtieth Birthday*. 2 vols. (TBL, 317). Tübingen: Narr.

186 Lovelace, Martin J. 1989. "Douglas Northover: "The language of Old Burton, Burton Bradstock, Dorset", with notes of parallels to Newfoundland usage by Martin J. Lovelace". *L&L* 8(2):3-31.

187 Lowenberg, Peter H., ed. 1988. *Language Spread and Language Policy: Issues, Implications and Case Studies*. (GURT '87). Washington, D.C.: Georgetown UP.

188 ---. 1992. "Testing English as a world language: issues in assessing nonnative proficiency". In Kachru, 108-21.

189 McArthur, Tom. 1992. *The Oxford Companion to the English Language*. Oxford: UP. (Rev. in *EWW* 14:149-51).

190 Macaulay, Ronald K.S. 1991. "'Coz it izny spelt when they say it': displaying dialect in writing". *AS* 66:280-91.

191 McCrum, Robert, William Cran & Robert McNeil. 1986. *The Story of English*. London: Faber & Faber. (Rev. in *EWW* 8:146-7). (New and revised ed. 1992; rev. in *EWW* 14:2).

192 Machan, Tim William & Charles T. Scott, eds. 1992. *English in Its Social Contexts. Essays in Historical Sociolinguistics*. New York & Oxford: Oxford UP. (Rev. in *EWW* 14:155-7).

193 Mackenzie, J. Lachlan & Richard Todd, eds. 1989. *In Other Words: Transcultural Studies in Philology, Translation and Lexicology Presented to Hans Heinrich Meier on the Occasion of his Sixty-fifth Birthday*. Dordrecht: Foris.

194 Marshall, David F., ed. 1991. *Language Planning. Focusschrift in Honor of Joshua A. Fishman*, Vol. III. Amsterdam: Benjamins. (Rev. in *EWW* 13:149-52).

195 Matsuda, Yutaka. 1990. "The American impact on British English". *Kwansei Gakuin University Annual Studies* 39:79-113.

195a Milliken, Margaret M. 1988. "Communication networks among dialects of American and Scottish English". *Texas Linguistic Forum* 30:240-9.

196 Milroy, James. 1992. *Linguistic Variation and Change*. On the historical sociolinguistics of English. (Language in Society, 19). Oxford: Blackwell. (Rev. in *EWW* 13:299-302).

197 --- & Lesley Milroy. 1985a. *Authority in Language: Investigating Language Prescription and Standardisation*. London: Routledge & Kegan Paul. (Rev. in *EWW* 7:151-2).

198 --- & ---. 1985b. "Linguistic change, social network, and speaker innovation". *JL* 21:339-84.

199 --- & ---. 1990. "Language in society: sociolinguistics". In Collinge, 485-517.

200 Milroy, Lesley. 1987. *Observing and Analysing Natural Language*. Oxford: Blackwell. (Rev. in *EWW* 9:119-21).

201 --- & James Milroy. 1992. "Social network and social class: toward an integrated sociolinguistic model". *LinS* 21:1-26.

202 Montgomery, Michael B. 1991b. "The roots of Appalachian English: Scotch-Irish or southern British?". In John Inscoe, ed. *Journal of the Appalachian Studies Association*. Johnson City, Tenn.: East Tennessee University Center for Appalachian Studies and Services, 177-91.

203 ---, ed. fc.a. *South Carolina, the Caribbean, and Africa: Linguistic and Cultural Perspectives*. Athens, Ga.: University of Georgia Press.

204 ---, ed. fc.b. *Studies in the Gulf States and Beyond: Honoring Lee Pederson and His Work*. Tuscaloosa, Ala.: University of Alabama Press.

205 --- & Cecil Ataide Melo. 1990. "The phonology of the lost cause: the English of the confederados in Brazil". *EWW* 11:195-216. [= 2374]

206 Mühlhäusler, Peter. 1986. *Pidgin and Creole Linguistics*. Oxford: Blackwell. (Rev. in *EWW* 8:322-5).

207 ---. 1992. "On redefining creolistics". In George Wolf, ed. *New Departures in Linguistics*. New York: Garland, 193-8.

208 Mufwene, Salikoko S. 1986. "Restrictive relativization in Gullah". *JPCL* 1:1-31.

209 ---. 1988. "English pidgins: form and function". *WE* 7:255-68.

210 ---, ed. 1993a. *Africanisms in Afro-American Language Varieties*. Athens, Ga. & London: University of Georgia Press.

211 ---. 1993b. "Are there possessive pronouns in Atlantic Creoles?". In Byrne & Holm, 133-43.

212 Muysken, Pieter & Norval Smith, eds. 1986. *Substrata versus Universals in Creole Genesis: Papers from the Amsterdam Creole Workshop, April 1985*. Amsterdam: Benjamins. (Rev. in *EWW* 8:337-9).

213 Napoli, D.J. & J.A. Kegl, eds. 1991. *Bridges between Psychology and Linguistics: A Swarthmore Festschrift for Lila Gleitman*. Hillsdale, N.J.: Erlbaum.

214 Newbrook, Mark. 1991. "Dialect and accent revisited". *Orbis* 34:116-28.

215 Newmeyer, Frederic, ed. 1988. *Linguistics: The Cambridge Survey*. Vol. IV: *Language: The Socio-Cultural Context*. Cambridge: UP.

216 Nichols, Patricia C. 1988. "English as a bridge between cultures: Scotland, Carolina, and California". *The CATESOL Journal* 1:5-16.

217 Nickel, Gerhard & James C. Stalker, eds. 1986. *Problems of Standardization and Linguistic Variation in Present-Day English*. (Studies in Descriptive Linguistics, 15). Heidelberg: Groos. (Rev. in *EWW* 9:330-2).

218 Nihalani, Paroo. 1992. "The International Computerized Corpus of English". In [IV]Pakir, 84-8.
219 Nixon, Graham. 1988. "The methods of urban linguistic surveys". In Nixon & Honey, 228-41.
220 --- & John Honey, eds. 1988. *An Historic Tongue. Studies in English Linguistics in Memory of Barbara Strang*. London: Routledge.
221 Ogura, Mieko. 1987. *Historical English Phonology. A Lexical Perspective.* Tokyo: Kenkyusha.
222 ---. 1990. *Dynamic Dialectology. A Study of Language in Time and Space.* Tokyo: Kenkyusha.
223 Paddock, Harold. 1986. "The actuation problem for gender change in Wessex versus Newfoundland". In A.M. Kinloch, *et al.*, eds., *Papers from the Tenth Annual Meeting of the Atlantic Provinces Linguistics Association.* Fredericton: University of New Brunswick, 130-40. (Reprinted in Fisiak 1988:377-95; revised version in Trudgill & Chambers 1991:29-46).
224 Påhlsson, Christer. 1984. "Stickers, shifters, and others: aspects of dialect space". In [II]Ringbom & Rissanen, 117-39.
225 ---. 1987. "On the concept of style in dialectology". In [II]Lindblad & Ljung, 281-90.
226 Paulston, Christina Bratt, ed. 1988. *International Handbook of Bilingualism and Bilingual Education.* New York: Greenwood Press.
227 Payne, Avis Kuwahara. 1982 (1985). "The unmarked plural noun: a 'Black English feature' found in rural England". *Orbis* 31:161-8.
228 Peters, Pam & Margery Fee. 1989. "New configurations: the balance of British and American English features in Australian and Canadian English". *AJL* 9:135-47.
229 Phillipson, Robert. 1992. *Linguistic Imperialism.* Oxford: UP.
230 Potts, Eli Daniel & Annette Potts. 1984. *Yanks Down Under 1941-45: The American Impact on Australia.* Melbourne: Oxford UP.
231 Preston, Dennis R. 1989. *Sociolinguistics and Second Language Acquisition.* Oxford: Blackwell. (Rev. in *EWW* 10:339-40).
232 Pütz, Martin & René Dirven, eds. 1989. *Wheels within Wheels. Papers of the Duisburg Symposium on Pidgin and Creole Languages.* Frankfurt/M.: Lang.
233 Quirk, Randolph. 1988. "The question of standards in the international use of English". In Lowenberg, 229-41.
234 ---. 1990. "Language varieties and standard languages". *ET* 21:3-10.
235 --- & Gabriele Stein. 1990. *English in Use.* Harlow: Longman.

236 --- & Henry G. Widdowson, eds. 1985. *English in the World: Teaching and Learning the Language and Literatures*. Cambridge: UP/The British Council. (Rev. in *EWW* 7:127-32).

237 ---, Sidney Greenbaum, Geoffrey Leech & Jan Svartvik. 1985. *A Comprehensive Grammar of the English Language*. London: Longman. (Rev. in *EWW* 8:123-8).

238 Ramsaran, Susan, ed. 1990. *Studies in the Pronunciation of English: A Commemorative Volume in Honour of A.C. Gimson*. London & New York: Routledge & Kegan Paul. (Rev. in *EWW* 11:296-300).

239 Rickford, John R. 1986. "Social contact and linguistic diffusion: Hiberno-English and New World Black English". *Language* 62:245-89.

240 ---. 1987. "The haves and the have nots: sociolinguistic surveys and the assessment of speaker competence". *LinS* 16:149-78.

241 ---, ed. 1988a. *Sociolinguistics and Pidgin-Creole Studies*. (*IJSL* 71). Berlin: Mouton de Gruyter. (Rev. in *EWW* 9:324-7).

242 ---. 1988b. "Connections between sociolinguistics and pidgin-creole studies". *IJSL* 71:51-8.

243 --- & Renée Blake. 1992. "Copula contraction and absence in Barbadian English, Samaná English and Vernacular Black English". In K. Hall, *et al.*, eds. *Proceedings of the 16th Annual Meeting of the Berkeley Linguistics Society*, 257-68.

244 Ricks, Christopher & Leonard Michaels, eds. 1990. *The State of the Language*. London: Faber & Faber, Berkeley: University of California Press. (Rev. in *EWW* 11:307-8).

245 Rissanen, Matti, Ossi Ihalainen, Terttu Nevalainen & Irma Taavitsainen, eds. 1992. *History of Englishes. New Methods and Interpretations in Historical Linguistics*. (Topics in English Linguistics, 10). Berlin & New York: Mouton de Gruyter. (Rev. in *EWW* 14:164-6).

246 Ritchie, William C. 1986. "Second language acquisition research and the study of non-native varieties of English: some issues in common". *WE* 5:15-30.

247 Roberts, Celia, Evelyn Davies & Tom Jupp. 1992. *Language and Discrimination. A Study of Communication in Multi-ethnic Workplaces*. London: Longman.

248 Romaine, Suzanne. 1985. "Relative clauses in child language, pidgins and creoles". In [IV]Romaine, *et al.*, 1-23.

249 ---. 1988a. *Pidgin & Creole Languages*. London: Longman. (Rev. in *EWW* 11:169-71).

250 ---. 1988b. "Contributions from pidgin and creole studies to a sociolinguistic theory of language change". *IJSL* 71:59-66.
251 Rubal-Lopez, Alma & Joshua A. Fishman. 1990."English as a world language revisited". In Laforge & McConnell, 97-102.
252 Sankoff, David, ed. 1986. *Diversity and Diachrony*. (Current Issues in Linguistic Theory, 53). Amsterdam: Benjamins.
253 Sayder, Stefan. 1989. "The subjunctive in Indian, British and American English. A corpus-based study". In Graustein & Thiele, 58-66.
254 Schneider, Edgar W. 1984. "Methodologische Probleme der Dialektometrie". In Goebl, 314-35.
255 ---. 1989. "Creolistics and historical linguistics". In Ahrens, 246-64.
256 --- & Wolfgang Viereck. 1984. "The use of the computer in American, Canadian and British English dialectology and sociolinguistics". In Goebl, 15-60.
257 Schouten, M.E.H. & P.Th. van Reenen, eds. 1989. *New Methods in Dialectology. Proceedings of a Workshop Held at the Free University, Amsterdam, December 7-10, 1987*. (Publications in Language Sciences, 33). Dordrecht & Providence, R.I.: Foris.
258 Sebba, Mark. 1987. *The Syntax of Serial Verbs: An Investigation into Serialisation in Sranan and Other Languages*. Amsterdam: Benjamins.
259 Shilling, Alison Watt. 1984. *Black English as a Creole: Some Bahamian Evidence*. St. Augustine, Trinidad: School of Education, University of West Indies.
260 Shorrocks, Graham. 1985. "Further thoughts on the Labovian interview". *L&L* 4:46-56.
261 ---. 1991. "*Away to go* in the Southwest of England and in Newfoundland, and the question of Celtic analogues". *CJL* 36:137-46.
262 Singler, John Victor. 1988. "The homogeneity of the substrate as a factor in pidgin/creole genesis". *Language* 64:27-51.
263 ---, ed. 1990a. *Pidgin and Creole Tense-Mood-Aspect Systems*. Amsterdam: Benjamins.
264 ---. 1990b. "On the use of sociohistorical criteria in the comparison of creoles". *Linguistics* 28:645-59.
265 ---. 1991a. "Liberian Settler English and the ex-slave recordings: a comparative study". In Bailey, *et al.*, 249-74.
266 ---. 1991b. "Copula variation in Liberian Settler English and American Black English". In Edwards & Winford, 129-64.
267 ---. 1992. "Nativization and pidgin/creole genesis: a reply to Bickerton". *JPCL* 7:319-33.

268 Smith, Larry E., ed. 1987. *Discourse Across Cultures. Strategies in World Englishes*. New York: Prentice Hall. (Rev. in *EWW* 9:329-30).

269 ---. 1992. "Spread of English and issues of intelligibility". In Kachru, 75-90.

270 --- & Cecil L. Nelson. 1985. "International intelligibility of English: directions and resources". *WE* 4:333-42.

271 --- & S.N. Sridhar, eds. 1992. *The Extended Family: English in Global Bilingualism (Studies in Honor of Braj B. Kachru)*. Special issue of *World Englishes*, Vol. 11:2/3.

272 Spolsky, Bernard, ed. 1986. *Language and Education in Multilingual Settings*. Clevedon: Multilingual Matters.

273 Sridhar, Kamal K. 1986. "Cognitive educational psychology and second language acquisition strategies". In *Perspectives on English Language Teaching*. (Reprinted in [IV]Sridhar 1989:66-74).

274 ---. 1987. "English for bilingualism and the creative potential: language as medium and symbol in the early novels of V.S. Naipaul". *Journal of Indian Writing* 15(1). (Reprinted in [IV]Sridhar 1989:136-46).

275 --- & S.N. Sridhar. 1980. "The syntax and psycholinguistics of bilingual code mixing". *Canadian Journal of Psychology* 34:409-16. (Reprinted in [IV]Sridhar 1989:75-87).

276 Stanley, Eric Gerald & D. Gray, eds. 1983. *Five Hundred Years of Words and Sounds: A Festschrift for Eric Dobson*. Totowa, N.J.: Brewer.

277 Stubbs, Michael. 1986. *Educational Linguistics*. Oxford: Blackwell. (Rev. in *EWW* 7:335-6).

278 Sutcliffe, David. 1984. "British Black English and West Indian Creoles". In [II]Trudgill, 219-37.

279 --- with John Figueroa. 1992. *System in Black Language*. (Multilingual Matters, 77). Clevedon: Multilingual Matters.

280 --- & Ansel Wong, eds. 1986. *The Language of the Black Experience. Cultural Expression through Word and Sound in the Caribbean and Black Britain*. Oxford: Blackwell. (Rev. in *EWW* 8:149-51).

281 Taylor, Brian. 1989. "American, British and other foreign influences on Australian English since World War II". In [IV]Collins & Blair, 225-54.

282 Tagliamonte, Sali Anna. 1991. "A matter of time: Past temporal reference verbal structures in Samaná English and the Ex-Slave Recordings". Ph.D., University of Ottawa. DAI 53:3 (1992), 795-A. (Summary in *EWW* 14:2).

283 Thomas, Alan R., ed. 1988. *Methods in Dialectology. Proceedings of the Sixth International Conference Held at the University College of North*

Wales, 3rd-7th August 1987. Clevedon: Multilingual Matters. (Rev. in *EWW* 10:155-8).
284 Thomason, Sarah G. & Terrence Kaufman. 1988. *Language Contact, Creolization, and Genetic Linguistics*. Berkeley: University of California Press. (Rev. in *EWW* 10:334-7).
285 Thumboo, Edwin. 1985. "English literature in a global context". In Quirk & Widdowson, 52-60.
286 Todd, Loreto. 1984. *Modern Englishes: Pidgins and Creoles*. Oxford: Blackwell. (Rev. in *EWW* 6:316-9).
287 --- & Ian Hancock. 1986. *International English Usage. A Comprehensive Survey of Written and Spoken English World-Wide*. London: Croom Helm.
288 Tottie, Gunnel. 1985. "The negation of epistemic necessity in present-day British and American English". *EWW* 6:87-116.
289 Troy, Jakelin. 1992. "'Der mary this is fine cuntry is there is in the wourld': Irish-English and Irish in late eighteenth and nineteenth century Australia". In [IV]Dutton, *et al.*, 459-77.
290 Truchot, Claude. 1990. *L'anglais dans le monde contemporain*. (Collection l'ordre des mots). Paris: Le Robert. (Rev. in *EWW* 12:315-6).
291 Trudgill, Peter. 1986. *Dialects in Contact*. Oxford: Blackwell. (Rev. in *EWW* 8:128-31).
292 --- & Jack K. Chambers, eds. 1991a. *Dialects of English. Studies in Grammatical Variation*. London & New York: Longman. (Rev. in *EWW* 12:325-7).
293 --- & ---. 1991b. "Introduction: English dialect grammar". In Trudgill & Chambers, 1-3.
294 --- & ---. 1991c. "Pronouns and pronominal systems in English". In Trudgill & Chambers, 7-10.
295 --- & ---. 1991d. "Verb systems in English dialects". In Trudgill & Chambers, 49-53.
296 --- & ---. 1991e. "Aspect in English dialects". In Trudgill & Chambers, 145-7.
297 --- & Jean Hannah. 1982. *International English*. London: Arnold. (Rev. in *EWW* 5:127-9). (2nd ed. 1985).
298 Van Leuvenstijn, J. & J. Berns, eds. 1992. *Dialect and Standard Language in the English, Dutch, German and Norwegian Language Areas*. Amsterdam: North-Holland. (Rev. in *EWW* 14:157-9).

299 Viereck, Wolfgang. 1984. "Der Einsatz des Computers in der amerikanisch-englischen und britisch-englischen Dialektologie und Soziolinguistik". *ZDL* 51:6-30/238.

300 ---. 1985. "On the interrelationship of British and American English: morphological evidence". In [II]Viereck, 247-300.

301 ---. 1986. "On colonial American English: a research proposal". In Winfried Herget & Karl Ortseifen, eds. *The Transit of Civilization from Europe to America*. Tübingen: Narr, 75-85.

302 ---. 1988. "The computerisation and quantification of linguistic data: dialectometrical methods". In Thomas, 524-50.

303 ---. 1992a. "On some hidden factors influencing the elicitation of data in dialectology". In Blank, II:25-32.

303a ---. 1992b. "British English dialectology and the computer". *Acta del XII Congreso Nacional de la Asociación Española de Estudios Anglo-Norteamericanos. Alicante, 19-22 de Diciembre de 1988*. Granada, 111-22.

304 ---, ed. 1993a. *Plenary Lectures/Computational Data Processing/Dialect Structure and Classification*. Proceedings of the International Congress of Dialectologists, Bamberg, 29.7. - 4.8.1990, Vol. 1. (*ZDL* Beihefte, 74). Stuttgart: Steiner. (Rev. in *EWW* 14:2).

305 ---, ed. 1993b. *Historical Dialectology and Linguistic Change. Linguistic Atlases and Dictionaries*. Proceedings of the International Congress of Dialectologists, Bamberg, 29.7. - 4.8. 1990, Vol. 2. (*ZDL* Beihefte, 75). Stuttgart: Steiner.

306 ---, ed. fc. *Proceedings of the International Congress of Dialectologists, Bamberg, 29.7. - 4.8.1990*. Vols. 3-4. Stuttgart: Steiner.

307 ---, Edgar Schneider & Manfred Görlach, comps. 1984. *A Bibliography of Writings on Varieties of English, 1965-1983*. (VEAW G3). Amsterdam: Benjamins. (Rev. in *EWW* 7:132-5).

308 --- & Wolf-Dietrich Bald, eds. 1986. *English in Contact with Other Languages*. Budapest: Akadémiai Kiadó. (Rev. in *EWW* 8:327-8).

309 Wakelin, Martyn F. 1986. "English on the Mayflower". *ET* 8:30-3.

310 ---. 1988. *The Archeology of English*. London: Batsford.

311 Walsh, Thomas J., ed. 1989. *Synchronic and Diachronic Approaches to Linguistic Variation and Change*. (GURT '88). Washington, D.C.: Georgetown UP.

312 Walters, Keith. 1988. "Dialectology". In Newmeyer, 119-39.

313 Wardhaugh, Ronald. 1986. *An Introduction to Sociolinguistics*. Oxford: Blackwell. (2nd ed. 1992). (Rev. in *EWW* 14:2).

314 ---. 1987. *Languages in Competition*. Oxford: Blackwell. (Rev. in *EWW* 9:132-4).

315 Warkentyne, H.J., ed. 1985. *Methods. Méthodes. V. Papers from the Fifth International Conference on Methods in Dialectology*. Victoria, B.C.: University of Victoria, Department of Linguistics. (Rev. in *EWW* 8:151-4).

316 Weise, Günter, ed. 1990. *Studien zur Sprachdifferenzierung. Roland Arnold zum 60. Geburtstag*. Greifswald: Ernst-Moritz-Arndt-Universität. (Rev. in *EWW* 12:144-7).

317 Wells, John C. 1990. *Longman Pronunciation Dictionary*. London: Longman. (Rev. in *EWW* 12:149-51).

318 Williams, Colin H., ed. 1988. *Language in Geographic Context*. Clevedon: Multilingual Matters. (Rev. in *EWW* 11:137-8).

319 ---., ed. 1991a. *Linguistic Minorities, Society and Territory*. Clevedon: Multilingual Matters. (Rev. in *EWW* 14:161-3).

320 ---. 1991b. "Linguistic minorities: West European and Canadian perspectives". In Williams, 1-43.

321 Williams, Jeffrey P. 1986. "Hiberno-English and white West Indian English - the historical link". In "Harris, *et al*., 83-94.

322 Williams, Jessica. 1986. "Production principles in non-native institutionalized varieties of English". Ph.D., University of Pennsylvania. (Summary in *EWW* 8:295-6).

323 ---. 1987. "Non-native institutionalized varieties of English". *EWW* 8:161-99.

324 ---. 1989. "Language acquisition, language contact and nativized varieties of English". *RELC Journal* 20:39-67.

325 Williams, R.T. 1989. "The (mis)identification of regional and national accents of English: paradigmatic, cognitive and social aspects". In García & Otheguy, 55-82.

326 Winford, Donald. 1988. "The creole continuum and the notion of the community as locus of language". *IJSL* 71:91-105.

327 ---. 1990. "Copula variability, accountability, and the concept of 'polylectal' grammars". *JPCL* 5:223-52.

328 ---. 1992. "Another look at the copula in Black English and Caribbean creoles". *AS* 67:21-60.

329 Wolfson, Nessa & Joan Manes, eds. 1985. *Language of Inequality*. (Contributions to the Sociology of Language, 36). Berlin: Mouton de Gruyter.

330 Wurm, Stephen A., ed. 1976. *Language, Culture, Society and the Modern World*. 2 vols. (PacL C-40). Canberra: ANU. (Rev. in *EWW* 5:104-6).

331 --- & Shirô Hattori, eds. 1982. *Language Atlas of the Pacific, Part One*. Canberra: The Australian Academy of the Humanities. (Rev. in *EWW* 5:107-8).

Part II: Writings on varieties of English spoken in England, Wales, Scotland and Ireland

BEAT GLAUSER

This bibliography continues where Wolfgang Viereck left off ten years ago. Its aim is the same, i.e. "as complete a listing as possible of contributions on regional, social and occupational varieties of English, on English varieties spoken by minorities in Britain and on attitudes towards these varieties" (Viereck 1984:6). The very few earlier items not listed in his bibliography are included here, entries that were incomplete there have been added as well. In spite of access to, and use of, computer databases, the difficulties encountered while compiling were basically the same in nature as those described by my predecessor. In number, they have increased: I have been able to 'lay hands' on fewer items than I would have liked to inspect personally, and the frequent references to 'mere' bibliographies, references and lists of publications received leave a feeling of uncertainty behind. In this situation, the criticism by Manfred Görlach, Edgar Schneider, Hans Käsmann, Walter Sauer and Jenny Cheshire, who commented on preliminary versions, was extremely helpful and is gratefully acknowledged. Keith Brown and Willy Elmer deserve thanks for clarifying points of detail. Finally, Anja Kellermann, unobtrusive, but quietly efficient, merits special mention. It goes without saying that any errors those helpers did not detect are of my own making.

For relevant collections of papers or contrastive studies on varieties of English spoken in England, Wales, Scotland and Ireland outside this section see in particular entries 237-8, 279-80 and 292.

332 Abercrombie, David. 1992. "RP today: its position and prospects". In *Blank, II:6-10.

333 Adams, G. Brendan. 1985. "Linguistic cross-links in phonology and grammar". In Ó Baoill, 27-35.

334 ---. 1986. *The English Dialects of Ulster: An Anthology of Articles on Ulster Speech*, eds. Michael V. Barry & Phillip M. Tilling. Holiwood: Ulster Folk and Transport Museum. (Rev. in *EWW* 7:342-3).

335 ---, Michael V. Barry & Phillip M. Tilling. 1985. "The Tape-recorded Survey of Hiberno-English Speech: a reappraisal of the techniques of traditional dialect geography". In Kirk, *et al.*, 67-80.

336 Agutter, Alexandra. 1988a. "The dangers of dialect parochialism: the Scottish vowel length rule". In *Fisiak, 1-22.

337 ---. 1988b. "The not-so-Scottish vowel length rule". In John Anderson & Norman Macleod, eds. *Edinburgh Studies in the English Language: Dedicated to Hermann Pálsson*. (ESEL, 1). Edinburgh: Donald, 120-32.

338 Aitken, Adam Jack. 1983. "The language of older Scots poetry". In McClure, 18-49.

339 ---. 1984a. "Scots and English in Scotland". In Trudgill, 517-32.

340 ---. 1984b. "Scottish accents and dialects". In Trudgill, 94-114.

341 ---. 1987a. "The period dictionaries". In *Burchfield, 94-116.

342 ---. 1987b. "The extinction of Scotland in popular dictionaries of English". In *Bailey, 99-120.

343 ---. 1988. "The lexicography of Scots: the current position". In *Hyldgaard-Jensen & Zettersten, 323-33.

344 ---. 1989. "The lexicography of Scots two hundred years since: Ruddiman and his successors". In *Mackenzie & Todd, 235-45.

344a ---. 1990. "The lexicography of Scots". In Franz Josef Hausmann, *et al.* *Wörterbücher, Dictionaries, Dictionnaires*. Vol. 2. Berlin & New York: De Gruyter, 1983-7.

345 ---. 1992. "Progress in the study of modern Scots since 1948". MS.

346 Algeo, John. 1988. "The tag question in British English: it's different, i'n'it?". *EWW* 9:171-91.

347 ---. 1989. "A dictionary of Briticisms". *EWW* 10:123-34.

348 Alinei, Mario, *et al.* 1983-90. *Atlas Linguarum Europae (ALE): Cartes et commentaires*. Vol. I. Fascicules 1 - 4. Assen: Van Gorcum.

349 Alladina, Safder. 1986. "Black people's languages in Britain: a historical and contemporary perspective". *JMMD* 7:349-59.

350 --- & Viv K. Edwards. 1991. *Multilingualism in the British Isles I: The Older Mother Tongues and Europe*. London: Longman.

351 Allan, Scott. 1985. "A note on AYE distribution". *JL* 21:191-4.

352 Anderl, Mary Anne. 1984. "The Great Vowel Shift in the light of English dialects". Ph.D., Princeton University. DAI 44:12 (1984), 3673-A. (Summary in *EWW* 5:239-40).

353 Anderson, Peter M. 1987. *A Structural Atlas of the English Dialects*. London: Croom Helm. (Rev. in *EWW* 9:313-8).

354 Arnold, Roland. 1986. "Zum britischen Nonstandard English und seiner funktionalen Variation". *ZAA* 34:250-6.

355 Ashley, Leonard R.N. 1985. "The geolinguistics of place in society: geographic and class influences on British speech". *Geolinguistics* 11:13-38.

356 Bailey, Guy & Garry Ross. 1988. "The shape of the superstrate: morphosyntactic features of Ship English". *EWW* 9:193-212.

357 Bailey, Richard W. 1987. "Teaching in the vernacular: Scotland, schools, and linguistic diversity". In Macafee & Macleod, 131-42.

358 Baird, Alexander. 1984. "Death of a dialect: historical implications of sound change in a Devon family". In Norman F. Blake & Charles Jones, eds. 1984. *English Historical Linguistics: Studies in Development*. (CECTAL Conference Paper Series, 3). Sheffield: University of Sheffield, 160-72.

359 Baker, Colin. 1985. *Aspects of Bilingualism in Wales*. Clevedon: Multilingual Matters, 19. (Rev. in *EWW* 7:341).

360 Ball, Martin J. 1984. "The centring diphthongs in Southern English: a sound change in progress". *JIPA* 14:38-44.

361 Bannerman, John. 1990. "The Scots language and the kin-based society". In Thomson, 1-19.

362 Barnes, Michael P. 1991. "Reflections on the structure and the demise of Orkney and Shetland Norn". In Ureland & Broderick, 429-60.

363 Barry, Michael V. 1984. "Manx English". In Trudgill, 167-77.

364 Beal, Joan C. 1985. "Lengthening of *a* in Tyneside English". In *Eaton, *et al.*, 31-44.

365 ---. 1989. "The grammar of Tyneside and Northumbrian English". In Milroy & Milroy.

366 Beck, Sigrid. 1990. "Zum Dialekt von Norfolk". In *Weise, 18-27.

367 Bellin, Wynford. 1984. "Welsh and English in Wales". In Trudgill, 449-79.

368 Bertz, Siegfried. 1987. "Variation in Dublin English". *Teanga* 7:35-53.

369 Bliss, Alan J. 1984. "English in the south of Ireland". In Trudgill, 135-51.

370 Bremann, Rolf. 1984. *Soziolinguistische Untersuchungen zum Englisch von Cornwall.* (BBES, 14). Frankfurt/M.: Lang. (Rev. in *EWW* 5:290-2).

371 Britain, David J. 1991. "Dialect and space. A geolinguistic study of speech variables in the Fens". Ph.D., University of Essex. (Summary in *EWW* 12:282-4).

372 Britton, Derek. 1992. "Secondary contraction and deletion of negative enclitics in English dialects". *ZDL* 59:38-49.

373 Brown, E. Keith. 1991. "Double modals in Hawick Scots". In *Trudgill & Chambers, 74-103.

374 Buckow, Michael. 1990. "Zur deutschen Wiedergabe englischer Nonstandardismen mit besonderen Effekten". In *Weise, 56-63.

375 Carr, Philip. 1991. "Weakening on Tyneside: postlexical neutralisation". In Ingrid Tieken-Boon van Ostade & John Frankis, eds. *Language Usage and Description: Studies Presented to N.E. Osselton on the Occasion of his Retirement*. Amsterdam: Rodopi, 69-74.

375a ---. 1992. "Strict cyclicity, structure preservation and the Scottish vowel-length rule". *JL* 28:91-114.

375b Carstensen, Broder & Herbert Grabes, eds. 1988. *Anglistentag 1985. Paderborn: Vorträge*. Gießen: Hoffmann.

376 Cheshire, Jenny L. 1984. "Indigenous nonstandard English varieties and education". In Trudgill, 546-58.

377 ---. 1985. "English *never* and the problem of where grammars stop". *Polyglot* 6:fiche 1.

378 ---. 1989a. "Great Britain". In *Ammon & Cheshire, 42-53. (Reprinted in *Travaux Neuchâtelois de Linguistique* 15 (1990):99-111).

379 ---. 1989b. "Social background to variation in British English syntax". In Milroy & Milroy.

380 ---. 1991. "Variation in the use of *ain't* in an urban British English dialect". In *Trudgill & Chambers, 54-73. (Reprinted from *LinS* 10:365-81).

381 ---. 1992. "'As the ancient author would have wrote': past tense verb forms in nonstandard English". In *Blank, II:11-24.

382 --- & Viv K. Edwards. 1991. "School children as sociolinguistic researchers". *Linguistics and Education* 3:225-50.

383 --- & Peter Trudgill. 1989. "Dialect and education in the United Kingdom". In Cheshire, *et al.*, eds., 94-109.

384 ---, H. Münstermann & B. Weltens, eds. 1989. *Dialect and Education: Some European Perspectives*. Clevedon: Multilingual Matters. (Rev. in *EWW* 11:143-5).

385 ---, Viv Edwards & Pamela Whittle. 1989. "Urban British dialect grammar: the question of dialect levelling". *EWW* 10:185-225.

385a Chevillet, François. 1991. "A Cockney, Cockney et demi: étude phonologique de l'accent de Londres". *Idéologies dans le monde anglo-saxon* 4:59-73. Grenoble: CREA (Université Stendhal).

385b ---. 1992a. "Dialectology and the *CLAE1*". *TYDS* 91/17.

385c ---. 1992b. "A la recherche d'une identité dialectale à travers les différents atlas linguistiques". *Idéologies dans le monde anglo-saxon* 5:79-106. Grenoble: CREA (Université Stendhal).

386 Christophersen, Paul. 1987. "In defence of RP". *ET* 11:17-9.

387 Collins, Beverley & Inger M. Mees. 1990. "The phonetics of Cardiff English". In Coupland & Thomas, 87-108.

388 Connolly, John H. 1990. "Port Talbot English". In Coupland & Thomas, 121-9.

389 Corrigan, Karen P. 1990. "Northern Hiberno-English: the state of the art". In Dolan, 91-119.

390 Couillaud, Xavier. 1985. *The Other Languages of England. Linguistic Minorities Project*. (Language, Education and Society). London: Routledge & Kegan Paul. (Rev. in *EWW* 7:155-6).

391 Coupland, Nikolas. 1981. "The social differentiation of functional language use: A sociolinguistic investigation of travel agency talk". Ph.D., University College, Cardiff (Wales). DAI 50:11 (1990), 3575-A. (Summary in *EWW* 12:285-6).

392 ---. 1984. "Accommodation at work: some phonological data and their implications". *IJSL* 46:49-70.

393 ---. 1985a. "'Hark, hark, the lark': social motivations for phonological style shifting". *L&C* 5:153-71.

394 ---. 1985b. "Sociolinguistic aspects of place-names: ethnic affiliation and the pronunciation of Welsh in the Welsh capital". In Viereck, 29-43.

395 ---. 1988. *Dialect in Use: Sociolinguistic Variation in Cardiff English*. Cardiff: University of Wales Press. (Rev. in *EWW* 12:305-9).

396 ---. 1990. "'Standard Welsh English': a variable semiotic". In Coupland & Thomas, 232-57.

397 ---, in association with Alan R. Thomas, eds. 1990a. *English in Wales: Diversity, Conflict and Change*. Clevedon: Multilingual Matters. (Rev. in *EWW* 11:126-8).

398 --- & Alan R. Thomas. 1990b. "Introduction: social and linguistic perspectives on English in Wales". In Coupland & Thomas, 1-16.

399 Cram, D. 1986. "Patterns of English-Gaelic and Gaelic-English code-switching". *ScoL* 5:126-30.

400 Crowley, Anthony Edward. 1989. "Standard English: the history of the term and concept in the nineteenth century and early twentieth centuries". Ph.D., DAI 49:8 (1989), 2198-A.

401 Crowther, James. 1987. "Joseph Crowther and Todmordian speech of a century ago". *TYDS* 86/17:9-18.

402 ---. 1987-89. "A Walsden word list of 1930, part I-III (based on the generation of my grandmother 1850-1935)". *TYDS* 87/17:42-51; 88/17:39-47; 89/17:34-43.

403 Dabydeen, David. 1990. "On not being Milton: Nigger Talk in England today". In *Ricks & Michaels, 3-14.

404 Davies, Alan. 1985. "Standard and dialect English: the unacknowledged idealisation of sociolinguistics". *JMMD* 6:183-92.

405 Devitt, Amy J. 1989. *Standardizing Written English: Diffusion in the Case of Scotland 1520-1659*. Cambridge: UP. (Rev. in *EWW* 11:300-4).

406 Diensberg, Bernhard. 1987. "A phonological and semantic description of animal sounds as found in modern English dialects". *SAP* 20:19-32.

407 Dietz, Klaus. 1986. "Modern English CRUIVE 'wicker salmon-trap'". In *Kastovsky & Szwedek, 277-91.

408 ---. 1989a. "Die historische Schichtung phonologischer Isoglossen in den englischen Dialekten: I. Altenglische Isoglossen". *Anglia* 107:295-329.

409 ---. 1989b. "Die historische Schichtung phonologischer Isoglossen in den englischen Dialekten: II. Mittelenglische Isoglossen". In Fischer, 133-75.

410 Dolan, T.P., ed. 1990. *The English of the Irish. (Special Issue, Irish University Review* 20:1). (Rev. in *EWW* 11:321-2).

411 Donaldson, William. 1989. *The Language of the People. Scots Prose from the Victorian Revival*. Aberdeen: UP. (Rev. in *EWW* 11:317-9).

412 Douglas-Cowie, Ellen. 1984. "The sociolinguistic situation in Northern Ireland". In Trudgill, 533-45.

413 Downes, John. 1986. *A Dictionary of Devon Dialect*. Padstow: Tobb.

414 Edwards, J. 1985. *Talk Tidy: The Art of Speaking Wenglish.* Cowbridge: Brown and Sons.
415 ---. 1986. *More Talk Tidy*. Cowbridge: Brown and Sons.
416 Edwards, John R. 1984. "Irish and English in Ireland". In Trudgill, 480-98.
417 ---. 1986. "Did English murder Irish?". *ET* 6 (2):7-10.
418 --- & Maryanne Jacobsen. 1987. "Standard and regional standard speech: distinctions and similarities". *LinS* 16:369-80.
419 Edwards, Vivian K. 1984. "British Black English and education". In Trudgill, 559-72.
420 ---. 1986. *Language in a Black Community*. Clevedon: Multilingual Matters, 24. (Rev. in *EWW* 7:339-40).
421 ---. 1988. "The speech of British Black women in Dudley, West Midlands". In *Coates & Cameron, 33-50.
422 ---. 1989a. "The grammar of Southern English". In Milroy & Milroy.
423 ---. 1989b. "Patois and the politics of protest: Black English in British classrooms". In *García & Otheguy, 359-72.
424 --- & Jenny L. Cheshire 1989. "The Survey of British Dialect Grammar". In Cheshire, *et al.*, eds., 200-15.
425 --- & Bert Weltens 1985. "Research on non-standard dialects of British English: progress and prospects". In Viereck, 97-139.
426 ---, Peter Trudgill & B. Weltens. 1984. *The Grammar of English Dialect: A Survey of Research.* London: Economic and Social Research Council. (Rev. in *EWW* 5:308).
427 Elert, Claes-Christian, Iréne Johansson & Eva Strangert, eds. 1984. *Nordic Prosody III: Papers from a Symposium.* (Umeå Studies in the Humanities, 59). Umeå University: Acta Universitatis Umensis. (Distr. Stockholm: Almqvist & Wiksell).
428 Ellis, Stanley. 1981. "Weak syllables in dialectal usage". *LSE*, N.S. 12: 291-3 plus 5 maps.
429 ---. 1989. "The joys of dialect detection". In Fischer, 223-30.
430 ---. 1992. "40 years on: is dialect dead?". *TYDS* 92/18:6-16.
431 Elmer, Willy. 1988. "An integrated view of linguistic variation in English". In Carstensen & Grabes, 346-59.
431a ---. 1989. "A questionnaire for the terminology of coalmining". In Fischer, 245-52.
432 El-Shakfeh, Fawzi. 1988. "The phonematics, phonotactics and paraphonotactics of Southern Standard British English". Ph.D., University of St. Andrews. DAI 49:2 (1988), 244-A.

433 Faiss, Klaus 1989. "Nicht-standardsprachliche und dialektale Erscheinungsformen der englischen Syntax unter Einbeziehung der Sprachgeschichte". In *Holtus & Radtke, 14-40.
434 Fenton, Alexander. 1987. "A North-East farmer's working vocabulary". In Macafee & Macleod, 153-65.
435 ---. 1989. "The working vocabulary of a farm in Northeast Scotland in the mid-twentieth century". In *Mackenzie & Todd, 315-25.
436 Filppula, Markku. 1985. "Observations on thematic interference between Irish and English". In Ó Baoill, 53-62.
437 ---. 1986a. "The equative sentence in Hiberno-English: another area of interference from Irish?". In Harris, *et al.*, 111-20.
438 ---. 1986b. *Some Aspects of Hiberno-English in a Functional Sentence Perspective*. Joensuu, Finland: University of Joensuu Publications in the Humanities.
438a ---. 1990. "Substratum, superstratum, and universals in the genesis of Hiberno-English". In Dolan, 41-54.
439 ---. 1991a. "Urban and rural varieties of Hiberno-English". In *Cheshire, 51-60.
440 ---. 1991b. "Subordinating *and* in Hiberno-English syntax: Irish or English origin?". In Ureland & Broderick, 617-31.
441 ---. 1991c. "The relevance of linguistic constraints on inter-language transfer: evidence from Irish English". *Teanga* 11:9-19.
442 Finlay, Catherine. 1987. "Grammatical variation in the speech of Belfast school children". Ph.D., University of Ulster. DAI 50:12 (1990), 3934-A. (Summary in *EWW* 12:287-8).
443 --- & M.F. McTear. 1985. "Syntactic variation in the speech of Belfast schoolchildren". In Harris, *et al.*, 175-86.
444 Fischer, Andreas, ed. 1989. *The History and the Dialects of English: Festschrift for Eduard Kolb*. Heidelberg: Winter.
445 --- & Daniel Ammann. 1991. *An Index to Dialect Maps of Great Britain*. (VEAW, G10). Amsterdam: Benjamins. (Rev. in *EWW* 13:121-4).
446 Fisiak, Jacek. 1985. "The voicing of initial fricatives in Middle English". In Viereck, 5-28.
447 Forster, Klaus. 1987. "Studien zur Syntax der nordenglischen Mundarten". Habilitationsschrift, Erlangen. (Summary in *EWW* 10:315-6).
448 Francis, William Nelson. 1985. "Amn't I, or the hole in the pattern". In Viereck, 141-52.

449 Frazer, Timothy C. 1987. "Attitudes towards regional pronunciation". *JEngL* 20:89-100.

450 French, J. Peter. 1988. "Word final /r/ in a Northern English accent: an interactional account of variable production". In Peter Auer & Aldo Di Luzio, eds. *Variation and Convergence: Studies in Social Dialectology*. Berlin: Mouton de Gruyter, 125-33.

451 ---, with Stephen Miller, Veronica Cade & Charles Hunt 1986. "Documenting language change in East Yorkshire". *TYDS* 86/16:29-36.

451a Funk, Wolf-Peter. 1987 (1990). "Applying 'multidimensional scaling' to linguistic variation: accents of Standard English". In *Bahner, *et al.*, 1496-9.

452 Gachelin, Jean-Marc. 1984. "William Barnes, linguiste et poète (1801-1886)". Ph.D., University of Haute-Normandie, Rouen.

453 ---. 1988. "William Barnes and the Dorset Dialect". In J. Stevens Cox & G. Stevens Cox, eds. *The Thomas Hardy Year Book* 15. Guernsey: Toucan.

454 ---. 1991a. "Transitivity and intransitivity in the dialects of Southwest England". In *Trudgill & Chambers, 218-28.

455 ---. 1991b. "Gender and deixis in southwestern dialects". *NM* 92:83-93.

456 Gerard, David. 1982. "A glossary of Nottinghamshire dialect and mining terms". In Keith Sagar, ed. *A D.H. Lawrence Handbook*. Manchester: UP, 165-76.

457 Giles, Howard. 1990. "Social meanings of Welsh English". In Coupland & Thomas, 258-82.

458 --- & Caroline Sassoon. 1983. "The effects of speaker's accent, social class background and message style on British listeners' social judgements". *L&C* 3:305-13.

458a ---, *et al.* 1990. "The social meaning of RP: an intergenerational perspective". In *Ramsaran, 191-211.

459 Gimson, Arthur C. 1984. "The RP accent". In Trudgill, 45-54.

460 Glauser, Beat 1984. *A Phonology of Present-day Speech in Grassington (North Yorkshire)*. (The Cooper Monographs, 32). Bern: Francke. (Rev. in *EWW* 7:135-7).

461 ---. 1985. "*Boys* and *girls*, *sons* and *daughters*. The evidence of the Survey of English Dialects (SED)". *EWW* 6:37-57.

462 ---. 1988. "Aitken's context in Northumberland, Cumberland and Durham: a computer-assisted analysis of material from the Survey of English Dialects (SED)". In *Thomas, 611-24.

463 ---. 1989. "*This*, *that* and tothers". In Fischer, 253-77.
464 ---. 1991. "Transition areas versus focal areas in English dialectology". *EWW* 12:1-24.
465 Görlach, Manfred, ed. 1985a. *Focus on: Scotland*. (VEAW, G5). Amsterdam: Benjamins. (Rev. in *EWW* 7:137-40).
466 ---. 1985b. "Scots and Low German: the social history of two minority languages". In Görlach, 19-36. (Reprinted in *Görlach 1991:144-62).
467 ---. 1987. "Lexical loss and survival: the case of English and Scots". *ScoL* 6:1-20. (Reprinted in *Görlach 1991:123-43).
468 ---. 1990. "'Haw, the wickit things weans dae!' Max and Moritz in Scots". *ScoL* 9:34-51.
469 ---. fc. "Irish English and Irish culture in dictionaries of English". In *Görlach fc.a.
470 Graham, Irving. 1983. "Medical terms in dialect". *Lakeland Dialect Society Journal* 44:18-21.
471 Grant, William & David D. Murison, eds. 1986. *The Compact Scottish National Dictionary, Containing all the Scottish Words Known to Be in Use or to Have Been in Use since c. 1700*. 2 vols. Aberdeen: UP. (Rev. in *EWW* 10:164-6).
472 Greenbaum, Sidney. 1986. "Spelling variants in British English". *JEngL* 19:258-68.
473 Gregg, Robert J. 1985. *The Scotch-Irish Dialect Boundaries in the Province of Ulster*. Ottawa: Canadian Federation for the Humanities. (Rev. in *EWW* 7:342).
474 Grey, Clive G. 1992. "Irish English: perceptions and reality, issues and materials". In *Blank, II:76-93.
475 Grillo, R.D. 1989. *Dominant Languages: Language and Hierarchy in Britain and France*. Cambridge: UP.
476 Gruenais, Max-Peter. 1989. "Irish-English: no model; a case". *LPLP* 10:272-81.
477 Gugerell-Scharsach, Heide. 1992. *The West Midlands as a Dialect Area. A Phonological, Lexical, and Morphological Investigation Based on the 'Survey of English Dialects'*. München: Avi-Druck.
478 Guy, Gregory R. 1988. "Language and social class". In *Newmeyer, 37-63.
479 Hansen, Klaus. 1986. "Arten und Ursachen der Sprachvariation: am Beispiel des Englischen". *ZAA* 34:311-24.
480 ---. 1990. "Besonderheiten des Southern Hiberno-English". In *Weise, 42-6.

481 Harris, John. 1983. "The Hiberno-English 'I've it eaten' construction: what is it and where does it come from?". *Teanga* 3:30-43.

482 ---. 1984a. "English in the north of Ireland". In Trudgill, 115-34.

483 ---. 1984b. "Syntactic variation and dialect divergence". *JL* 20:303-27.

484 ---. 1985a. "The lexicon in phonological variation". In Harris, *et al.*, 187-208.

485 ---. 1985b. *Phonological Variation and Change: Studies in Hiberno-English*. Cambridge: UP. (Rev. in *EWW* 7:316-7).

486 ---. 1987. "Conservatism vs. substratal transfer in Irish English". In N. Boretzky, *et al. Beiträge zum 3. Essener Kolloquium über Sprachwandel und seine bestimmenden Faktoren*. Bochum: Brockmeyer, 143-62. (Revised in *Trudgill & Chambers 1991:191-212).

487 ---. 1991. "Ireland". In *Cheshire, 37-50.

488 ---, David Little & David Singleton, eds. 1986. *Perspectives on the English Language in Ireland: Proceedings of the First Symposium on Hiberno-English, Dublin, September 1985*. Dublin: Trinity College, Centre for Language and Communication. (Rev. in *EWW* 7:345-6).

489 Harris, Martin. 1991. "Demonstrative adjectives and pronouns in a Devonshire dialect". In *Trudgill & Chambers, 20-8. (Reprinted from *TPS* (1968) 1969:1-11).

490 Henry, P.L. 1985. "Linguistic atlases and vocabulary: the Linguistic Survey of Anglo-Irish". In Kirk, *et al.*, 157-71.

491 Hickey, Raymond. 1982. "Syntactic ambiguity in Hiberno-English". *SAP* 15:39-45.

492 ---. 1984a. "Towards a contrastive syntax of Irish and English". In *Fisiak, 187-204.

493 ---. 1984b. "Syllable onsets in Irish English". *Word* 35:67-74.

494 ---. 1984c. "Coronal segments in Irish English". *JL* 20:233-51.

495 ---. 1985a. "Kontinuität und Innovation im Vokalsystem des irischen Englisch". *ZDL* 52:324-40.

496 ---. 1985b. "Contact, conservativism, convergence. A phonological typology of Southern Irish English". Habilitationsschrift, University of Bonn. (Summary in *EWW* 7:280-2).

497 ---. 1985c. "Length and frontness among low vowels in Irish English". *SL* 39:143-56.

498 ---. 1986. "Possible phonological parallels between Irish and Irish English". *EWW* 7:1-21.

498a ---. 1990. "Suprasegmental transfer: on prosodic traces of Irish in Irish English". In Jacek Fisiak, ed. *Further Insights into Contrastive Analysis*. (Linguistic and Literary Studies in Eastern Europe, 30). Amsterdam: Benjamins, 219-29.

499 Hinz, Joachim. 1990. "Die Einstellung der farbigen Bevölkerung von Leicester zu ihrer Sprache: Eine empirische Untersuchung". Staatsexamensarbeit, Heidelberg.

500 Hogg, Richard M. 1988. "*Snuck*: the development of irregular preterite forms". In *Nixon & Honey, 31-40.

501 Honey, John. 1985. "Aspect and hyperlect: the redefinition of English RP". *ES* 66:241-57.

502 ---. 1988. "'Talking proper': schooling and the establishment of English 'Received Pronunciation'". In *Nixon & Honey, 209-27.

503 ---. 1989a. "Acrolect and hyperlect: education and class as foci of linguistic identity". In *Ammon, 580-91.

504 ---. 1989b. *Does Accent Matter? The Pygmalion Factor*. London: Faber & Faber. (Rev. in *EWW* 11:151-3).

505 Houston, Ann C. 1985. "Continuity and change in English morphology: the variable (ING)". Ph.D. thesis, University of Pennsylvania.

506 ---. 1991. "A grammatical continuum for (*ing*)". In *Trudgill & Chambers, 241-57.

507 Hudspeth, Bill. 1988. "The dialect of Bolton in 1824". *JLDS* 37:9-12.

508 Hughes, G.A. & Peter Trudgill. 1987. *English Accents and Dialects: An Introduction to Social and Regional Varieties of English*. London: Arnold. (2nd ed.).

509 Ihalainen, Ossi. 1985a. "Synchronic variation and linguistic change: evidence from British English dialects". In *Eaton, *et al.*, 61-72.

510 ---. 1985b. "*He took the bottle and put 'n in his pocket*: the object pronoun *it* in present-day Somerset". In Viereck, 153-61.

511 ---. 1986. "An inquiry into the nature of mixed grammars: two cases of grammatical variation in dialectal British English". In *Kastovsky & Szwedek, 371-9.

512 ---. 1987. "Towards a grammar of the Somerset dialect: a case study of the language of J.M.". In Kahlas-Tarkka, 71-86.

513 ---. 1988a. "Creating linguistic databases from machine-readable dialect texts". In *Thomas, 569-84.

514 ---. 1988b. "Working with dialectal material stored in a dBase file". In Merja Kytö, *et al.*, eds. *Corpus Linguistics: Hard and Soft. Proceed-*

ings of the Eighth International Conference on English Language Research on Computerized Corpora. Amsterdam: Rodopi, 137-44.

515 ---. 1990a. "A source of data for the study of English dialectal syntax: the Helsinki corpus". In Jan Aarts & Willem Meys, eds. *Theory and Practice in Corpus Linguistics*. (Language and Computers: Studies in Practical Linguistics, 4). Amsterdam: Rodopi, 83-103.

516 ---. 1990b. "Methodological preliminaries to the study of linguistic change in dialectal English: evaluating the grammars of Barnes and Elworthy as sources of linguistic evidence". In *Adamson, *et al.*, 189-203.

517 ---. 1991a. "A point of verb syntax in South-western British English: an analysis of a dialect continuum". In *Aijmer & Altenberg, 290-302.

518 ---. 1991b. "On grammatical diffusion in Somerset folk speech". In *Trudgill & Chambers, 104-19.

519 ---. 1991c. *A Point of Verb Syntax in South-western British English: An Analysis of a Dialect Continuum*. London: Longman.

520 ---. 1991d. "Periphrastic *do* in affirmative sentences in the dialect of East Somerset". In *Trudgill & Chambers, 148-60. (Revised from *NM* 77 (1976):608-22).

521 ---. fc. "The dialects of England since 1776". In *Burchfield.

522 Ingham, Patricia. 1983. "Thomas Hardy and the Dorset dialect". In *Stanley & Gray, 84-91.

523 Jacobson, Sven, ed. 1986. *Papers from the Third Scandinavian Symposium on Syntactic Variation, Stockholm, May 11-12, 1985*. (Stockholm Studies in English, 65). Stockholm: Almqvist & Wiksell.

524 Johnston, Paul A., Jr. 1983. "Variation in the Standard Scottish English in Morningside". *EWW* 4:133-85.

525 ---. 1985. "The rise and fall of the Morningside/Kelvinside accent". In Görlach, 37-56.

526 Jones, Anne Pierce. 1989. "Language awareness in British schools". In Cheshire, *et al.*, eds., 269-81.

527 Jones, Bernard. 1992. "William Barnes and the south west dialect of English". In *Rissanen, *et al.*, 556-65.

528 Jones, Bob Morris. 1990a. "Constraints on Welsh English tags: some evidence from children's language". *EWW* 11:173-93.

529 ---. 1990b. "Welsh influence on children's English". In Coupland & Thomas, 195-231.

530 Jones, Malcolm & Patrick Dillon. 1987. *Dialect in Wiltshire*. Trowbridge: Wiltshire County Council, Library and Museum Service.

531 Jones, Val. 1985. "Tyneside syntax: a presentation of some data from the Tyneside Linguistic Survey". In Viereck, 163-77.

532 Jucker, Andreas J. 1992. *Social Stylistics. Syntactic Variation in British Newspapers*. (Topics in English Linguistics, 6). Berlin: Mouton de Gruyter. (Rev. in *EWW* 13:320-2).

533 Kahlas-Tarkka, Leena, ed. 1987. *Neophilologica Fennica: Société Néo-philologique 100 ans/Neuphilologischer Verein 100 Jahre/Modern Language Society 100 years*. (Mémoires de la Société Néophilologique de Helsinki, 45). Helsinki: Société Néophilologique.

534 Kallen, Jeffrey L. 1985a. "Bilingualism and the genesis of Hiberno-English syntax". *Teanga* 5:98-113.

535 ---. 1985b. "The study of Hiberno-English". In Ó Baoill, 1-15.

536 ---. 1985c. "A global view of the English language in Ireland". In Ó Baoill, 63-78.

537 ---. 1986a. "Linguistic fundamentals for Hiberno-English syntax". Ph.D., Trinity College Dublin. (Summary in *EWW* 9:300-1).

538 ---. 1986b. "The co-occurrence of *do* and *be* in Hiberno-English". In Harris, *et al.*, 133-47.

539 ---. 1988. "The English language in Ireland". *IJSL* 70:127-42.

540 ---. 1989. "Tense and aspect categories in Irish English". *EWW* 10:1-39.

541 ---. 1990. "The Hiberno-English perfect: grammaticalisation revisited". In Dolan, 120-36.

542 ---. 1991. "Sociolinguistic variation and methodology: *after* as a Dublin variable". In *Cheshire, 61-74.

543 ---. fc. "English in Ireland". In *Burchfield.

544 Kay, Billy. 1986. *Scots - The Mither Tongue*. Edinburgh: Mainstream. (Rev. in *EWW* 9:339-42). (2nd ed. 1993).

545 Kekäläinen, Kirsti. 1985. "Relative clauses in the dialect of Suffolk". *NM* 86:353-7.

546 Kellett, Arnold. 1991. *Basic Broad Yorkshire*. Otley: Smith Settle.

547 Kenj, Ute. 1990. "Zur Variation im Stadtdialekt von London, dem Cockney". In *Weise, 64-70.

547a Kerins, John. 1988. "An analysis of the non-standard realisation of the definite article by four generations of speakers in Lancashire". *L&L* 7:77-89.

548 Kerswill, Paul E. 1984. "Social and linguistic aspects of Durham (e:)". *JIPA* 14:13-34.

549 ---. 1987. "Levels of linguistic variation in Durham". *JL* 23:25-49.

550 Killian, Patricia Anne. 1986a. "English in Ireland: an attitudinal study". In Harris, *et al.*, 271-82.

551 ---. 1986b. "English in Ireland: an attitudinal study". Ph.D., University of Texas at Austin. DAI 46:10 (1986), 3018-A. (Summary in *EWW* 8:288-9).

552 Kingsmore, Rona K. 1983. "Coleraine speech - phonology and socio-linguistics". Ph.D., University of Ulster, Northern Ireland. DAI 51:11 (1991), 3725-A. (Summary in *EWW* 12:292-3).

553 Kirk, John M. 1985. "Linguistic atlases and grammar: the investigation and description of regional variation in English syntax". In Kirk, *et al.*, 130-56.

554 ---. 1986. "Aspects of the grammar in a corpus of dramatic texts in Scots". Ph.D., University of Sheffield. (Summary in *EWW* 9:301-2).

555 ---. 1987a. "The heteronomy of Scots with Standard English". In Macafee & Macleod, 166-81.

555a ---. 1987b. "Auxiliary verbs, frequencies, and the identity of Scots". *JMMD* 8:159-71.

555b ---. 1987c. "Tag questions, pragmatics, and the expression of solidarity in dramatic texts". *Belfast Working Papers in Language and Literature* 9:228-72.

556 ---. 1988. "The dialectology of Scots: the use of dramatic texts". In *Thomas, 492-509.

557 ---. 1991. "Language contact and Scots". In Ureland & Broderick, 535-57.

558 ---. 1992. "The Northern Ireland transcribed corpus of speech". In *Leitner, 65-74.

559 --- & William A. Kretzschmar, Jr. 1992. "Interactive linguistic mapping of dialect features". *Literary and Linguistic Computing* 7:168-75. [= 1279]

560 ---, Stewart Sanderson & John D.A. Widdowson, eds. 1985. *Studies in Linguistic Geography. The Dialects of English in Britain and Ireland.* London: Croom Helm. (Rev. in *EWW* 8:131-5).

560a Kirsten, Hans. 1989. "Hiberno-Englisch und Britisches Englisch". *Linguistische Arbeitsberichte* 69:37-42.

561 Klemola, Juhani. 1993. "Dialect areas in the south-west of England: an exercise in cluster analysis". In *Viereck fc., Vol. 3.

562 Knight, Lorna. 1992. "Glasgow slang". In *Blank, II:69-75.

563 Kocmanova, Jessie. 1987. "Lallans today: the evolution of modern Scots (Lowlands) prose". *Sbornik Praci Filosoficke Fakulty Brnenske University*, K 9 (BSE 17):141-7.

564 Kontic, René. 1990. *Dialects in East-Anglia and the South-east of England.* Basel: Econom.

565 Krause, Christine. 1989. "A computerized analysis of the stressed vowel systems of Lowick/Northumberland". M.A., Heidelberg.

566 Kreidler, Charles W. 1989. *The Pronunciation of English: A Coursebook in Phonology*. Oxford: Blackwell.

567 Labov, William. 1992. "Evidence for regular sound change in English dialect geography". In *Rissanen, *et al.*, 42-71.

568 Laing, Margaret, ed. 1989. *Middle English Dialectology. Essays on Some Principles and Problems by Angus McIntosh, M.L. Samuels and Margaret Laing*. Aberdeen: UP.

569 Lamb, Gregor. 1988. *Orkney Wordbook. A Dictionary of the Dialect of Orkney*. Birsay, Orkney: Byrgisey. (Rev. in *EWW* 11:320-1).

570 Lass, Roger. 1986. "'Irish influence': reflections on 'standard' English and its opposites, and the identification of calques". *SAP* 18:81-7.

570a ---. 1990. "Early mainland residues in Southern Hiberno-English". In Dolan, 137-48.

571 Lavers, Jack. 1988. *A Dictionary of the Isle of Wight Dialect.* Stanbridge, Wimborne, Dorset: Dovecote Press.

572 Lazar-Meyn, Heidi Ann. 1991. "The colour systems of the modern Celtic languages: effects of language contact". In Ureland & Broderick, 227-42.

573 Letley, Emma. 1988. *From Galt to Douglas Brown. Nineteenth-Century Fiction and Scots Language*. Edinburgh: Scottish Academic Press. (Rev. in *EWW* 10:141-5).

574 Lewis, J. Windsor. 1990. "Syntax and lexis in Glamorgan English". In Coupland & Thomas, 109-20.

575 Lindblad, Ishrat & Magnus Ljung, eds. 1987. *Proceedings from the Third Nordic Conference for English Studies, Hässelby, Sept. 25-27, 1986. Vol.I.* (Stockholm Studies in English, 73). Stockholm: Almqvist & Wiksell.

576 Lindsay, Cora F. 1993. "Welsh and English in the city of Bangor: a study in functional differentiation". *LinS* 22:1-17.

577 Local, John K. 1986. "Some rhythm, resonance and quality variations in urban Tyneside speech". *YPL* 12:127-34.

577a ---. 1990. "Some rhythm, resonance and quality variations in urban Tyneside speech". In *Ramsaran, 286-92.

578 Lodge, Keith. 1983. "The acquisition of phonology: a Stockport sample". *Lingua* 61:335-51.

579 Macafee, Caroline. 1983. *Glasgow*. (VEAW, T2). Amsterdam: Benjamins. (Rev. in *EWW* 5:265-70).

580 ---. 1985. "Nationalism and the Scots Renaissance now". In Görlach, 7-17. (Reprinted with minor changes from *EWW* 2 (1981):29-38).

581 ---. 1987. "Language and modern life: notes from Glasgow". In Macafee & Macleod, 182-94.

582 ---. 1988. "Some studies in the Glasgow vernacular". Ph.D., Glasgow, to appear in Cooper Monographs.

582a ---. 1989. "Qualitative insights into working-class language attitudes". *YPL* 13:191-202.

583 ---. 1992. "Acumsinery: Is it too late to collect traditional dialect?". *Folk Life* 30:71-7.

584 ---. 1993a. "The Ulster Dictionary project". *Belfast Working Papers in Language and Linguistics*.

584a ---. 1993b. "A *Concise Ulster Dictionary* - and beyond?". *EWW* 14:2.

585 ---, ed. fc. *A Concise Ulster Dictionary*.

586 --- & Iseabail Macleod, eds. 1987. *The Nuttis Shell: Essays on the Scots Language Presented to A.J. Aitken*. Aberdeen: UP. (Rev. in *EWW* 9:121-3).

586a McArthur, Tom. 1992. "The Scots - bilingual or just confused?". *WE* 11 (2/3):101-10.

587 Macaulay, Ronald K.S. 1984. "Chattering, nattering and blethering: informal interviews as speech events". In *Enninger & Haynes, 51-64.

588 ---. 1985a. "The narrative skills of a Scottish coal miner". In Görlach, 101-24.

589 ---. 1985b. "Linguistic maps: visual aid or abstract art?". In Kirk, *et al.*, 172-86.

590 ---. 1987. "The social significance of Scottish dialect humour". *IJSL* 65:53-63.

591 ---. 1988a. "A microsociolinguistic study of the dialect of Ayr". In *Thomas, 456-63.

591a ---. 1988b. "RP R.I.P.". *AppL* 9:115-24.

591b ---. 1988c. "Urbanity in urban dialect: the poetry of Tom Leonard". *Studies in Scottish Literature* 23:150-63.

592 ---. 1989. "'He was some man him': emphatic pronouns in Scottish English". In *Walsh, 179-87.

593 ---. 1991. *Locating Dialect in Discourse: The Language of Honest Men and Bonnie Lasses in Ayr*. (Oxford Studies in Sociolinguistics). New York & Oxford: Oxford UP.

594 Mace, Renate. 1987. *Funktionen des Dialektes im regionalen Roman von Gaskell bis Lawrence*. (ScriptOralia, 3). Tübingen: Narr.

595 McClure, J. Derrick, ed. 1983. *Scotland and the Lowland Tongue. Studies in the Language and Literature of Lowland Scotland in Honour of David D. Murison*. Aberdeen: UP.

596 ---. 1984. "Lowland Scots: an ambivalent national tongue". *Multilingua* 3:143-51.

597 ---. 1985. "The debate on Scots orthography". In Görlach, 203-9.

598 ---. 1986. "What Scots owes to Gaelic". *ScoL* 5:85-98.

599 ---. 1987. "'Lallans' and 'Doric' in north-eastern Scottish poetry". *EWW* 8:215-34.

600 ---. 1988. *Why Scots Matters*. (Saltire Pamphlets, New Series, 10). Edinburgh: Saltire Society. (Rev. in *EWW* 10:170-3).

601 ---. 1993. "Varieties of Scots in recent and contemporary narrative prose". *EWW* 14:1-22.

602 ---. fc. "English in Scotland". In *Burchfield.

603 McConnell, Seamus. 1989. *Talk of the Town. A Derry Phrase Book*. Londonderry: Guildhall Press.

604 McDavid, Raven I., Jr. 1985. "The sound system of a West Midland dialect: Kniveton, Derbyshire". In Viereck, 45-77.

604a McDiarmid, Matthew P., Thomas Crawford & J. Derrick McClure. 1986. "The Scots-English round-table discussion 'Scots: its development and present condition - potential modes of its future' - three Scots contributions". In Dietrich Strauss & Horst W. Drescher, eds. *Scottish Language and Literature, Medieval and Renaissance: Fourth International Conference 1984 - Proceedings*. (Scottish Studies, 4). Frankfurt/M: Lang, 93-9.

605 McIntyre, Rae, ed. 1990. *Some Handlin'. The Dialect Heritage of North Ulster*. Limavady: North-West Books.

606 Mackinnon, Kenneth M. 1984a. "Power at the periphery: the language dimension and the case of Gaelic Scotland". *JMMD* 5:491-510.

607 ---. 1984b. "Scottish Gaelic and English in the Highlands". In Trudgill, 499-516.

608 ---. 1991. "Language-maintenance and viability in contemporary Gaelic communities: Skye and the Western Isles today". In Ureland & Broderick, 495-533.

609 Macleod, Iseabail. 1987a. "Eighteenth-century Scots food terminology". In Macafee & Macleod, 219-26.

610 ---. 1987b. "Scots dictionaries in the late 1980s". *ScoL* 6:45-8.

611 ---, ed. 1990. *The Scots Thesaurus*. Aberdeen: UP. (Rev: in *EWW* 12:128-30).

612 ---. 1993. "Research in progress: Some problems of Scottish lexicography". *EWW* 14:115-28.

613 ---, Ruth Martin & Pauline Cairns, eds. 1988. *The Pocket Scots Dictionary*. Aberdeen: UP. (Rev. in *EWW* 10:166-8).

614 McMahon, April M.S. 1991. "Lexical phonology and sound change: the case of the Scottish vowel length rule". *JL* 27:29-53.

615 Martin, Sydney. 1989. "Dialect words of boyhood". *TYDS* 88/17:37-8.

616 ---. 1990. "More dialect words". *TYDS* 89/17:28-31.

617 Martin-Jones, Marilyn. 1984. "The newer minorities: literacy and educational issues". In Trudgill, 425-48.

618 Mather, James Y. & Hans-Henning Speitel, eds. 1986. *The Linguistic Atlas of Scotland: Scots Section. Volume 3. Phonology*. London: Croom Helm. (Rev. in *EWW* 7:287-310).

619 Mees, Inger M. 1983. "The speech of Cardiff schoolchildren: a real time study". Ph.D., Leiden. (Summary in *EWW* 6:289-90).

620 ---. 1987. "Glottal stop as a prestigious feature in Cardiff English". *EWW* 8:25-39.

621 ---. 1990. "Patterns of sociophonetic variation in the speech of Cardiff schoolchildren". In Coupland & Thomas, 167-94.

622 Melchers, Gunnel. 1984. "Is the structure of the syllable in Shetland dialect 'Scandinavian'?". In Elert, *et al.*, 179-86.

623 ---. 1985. "'Knappin,' 'Proper English,' 'Modified Scottish': some language attitudes in the Shetland Isles". In Görlach, 87-100.

624 ---. 1986. "Narrowing and extension of meaning in the Scandinavian-based vocabulary of Shetland dialect". *ScoL* 5:110-9.

625 ---. 1987a. "On the Low German and Dutch element in Shetland dialect". In Ureland, 295-316.

626 ---. 1987b. "Is du heard about yun afore?: on the use of be as a perfective auxiliary in Shetland dialect". *Studier i Modern Språkvetenskap* 8:56-60.

627 ---. 1987c. "This-that-yon - a three-term deictic system?". In Lindblad & Ljung, 221-8.

628 ---. 1991. "Norn-Scots: a complicated language contact situation in Shetland". In Ureland & Broderick, 461-77.

629 ---. 1992. "'Du's no heard da last o' dis' - on the use of *be* as a perfective auxiliary in Shetland dialect". In *Rissanen, *et al.*, 602-10.

629a Meurman-Solin, Anneli. 1993. *Variation and Change in Early Scottish Prose*. Studies based on the Helsinki Corpus of Older Scots. (Annales Academiae Scientiarum Fennicae Dissertationes Humanorum Litterarum, 65). Helsinki: Suomalainen Tiedeakatemia.

630 Millar, Sharon. 1987. "The question of ethno-linguistic differences in Northern Ireland". *EWW* 8:201-13.

631 Miller, James. 1989. "The grammar of Scottish English". In Milroy & Milroy.

632 Milliken, Margaret E. 1988. "Phonological divergence and intelligibility: a case study of English and Scots". Ph.D., Cornell University. DAI 49:10 (1989). (Summary in *EWW* 11:284-5).

633 Milroy, James. 1991. "The interpretation of social constraints on variation in Belfast English". In Cheshire, 75-85.

634 --- & Lesley Milroy, eds. 1989. *Regional Variation in British English Syntax*. London: Economic Research Council. (Rev. in *EWW* 10:341-2).

635 Milroy, Lesley. 1984. "Urban dialects in the British Isles". In Trudgill, 199-218.

636 --- & Wei Li. 1991. "A social network perspective on code-switching and language choice: the example of the Tyneside community". (Papers for the Symposium on code-switching in bilingual studies: theory, significance and perspectives). Strasbourg: European Science Foundation.

637 ---, --- & S. Moffatt. 1991. "Discourse patterns and fieldwork strategies in urban settings". *JMMD* 12:287-300.

638 Milton, Colin. 1992. "Language, class and education in twentieth-century Scottish writing". *EWW* 13:219-51.

638a Mobärg, Mats. 1989. *English 'Standard' Pronunciations: A Study of Attitudes*. (Gothenburg Studies in English, 62). Göteborg: Acta Universitatis Gothoburgensis.

638b Moessner, Lilo. 1988. "Is the subject-verb concord in Scots a number concord?". In Richard Matthews & Joachim Schmole-Rostosky, eds.

Papers on Lanugage and Mediaeval Studies Presented to Alfred Schopf. Frankfurt/M.: Lang, 177-91.

638c Montgomery, Michael B. fc. "The lexicography of Hiberno-English". *Irish Studies Working Papers*.

639 Muldowney, J.E. 1991. "The Stillingfleet glossary: an early word list". *TYDS* 91/17:19-34.

640 Murdoch, Brian. 1983. "Some observations on London (Cockney) rhyming slang". *Revista Canaria de Estudios Ingleses* 7:21-38.

641 Murison, David D. 1981. *Scots Saws: From the Folk-Wisdom of Scotland*. Edinburgh: The Mercat Press.

642 ---. 1987. "Scottish lexicography". In Macafee & Macleod, 17-24.

643 Myachinskaya, Elvira. 1993. "Some aspects of phonological interpretation of vocalic variability in English dialects". In *Viereck fc., Vol. 3.

644 Newbrook, Mark. 1986. *Sociolinguistic Reflexes of Dialect Interference in West Wirral*. (BBES, 18). Frankfurt/M.: Lang. (Rev. in *EWW* 8:304-7).

645 ---. 1985-87 (1991). "Dialect and accent revisited". *Orbis* 34:116-28.

646 Nicolaisen, W.F.H. 1983. "An onomastic vernacular in Scottish literature". In McClure, 209-18.

647 North, David J. 1983. *Studies in Anglo-Cornish Phonology*. Redruth, Cornwall: Institute of Cornish Studies.

648 ---. 1984. "The development of Middle English *ā*, *ai* and *ī* in Surrey, Kent and Sussex". *LSE* 15:146-64.

649 ---. 1985. "Spatial aspects of linguistic change in Surrey, Kent and Sussex". In Viereck, 79-96.

650 ---. 1988. "Towards a framework for the analysis of English in Cornwall". *LSE* 19:203-30.

650a Ó Baoill, Colm. 1991. "Borrowing between Scots and Gaelic". *ScoL* 10:9-17.

651 Ó Baoill, Dónall P., ed. 1985. *Papers on Irish English*. Dublin: Irish Association for Applied Linguistics. (Rev. in *EWW* 7:344).

651a ---. 1990. "Language contact in Ireland: the Irish phonological substratum in Irish-English". In *Edmondson, *et al.*, 147-72.

652 ---. 1991. "Contact phenomena in the phonology of Irish and English in Ireland". In Ureland & Broderick, 581-95.

652a Ó Muirithe, Diarmaid. 1990. "A modern glossary of the dialect of Forth and Bargy". In Dolan, 149-62.

653 Ó Sé, Diarmuid. 1985. "Word-stress in Hiberno-English". In Harris, *et al.*, 97-107.

654 ---. 1991. "Prosodic change in Manx and lexical diffusion". In Ureland & Broderick, 157-80.

655 Odlin, Terence. 1991a. "Syntactic variation in Hiberno-English". In Ureland & Broderick, 597-615.

656 ---. 1991b. "Irish English idioms and language transfer". *EWW* 12:175-93.

657 Ojanen, Anna-Liisa. 1985. "Use and non-use of prepositions in spatial expressions in the dialect of Cambridgeshire". In Viereck, 179-212.

658 Parker, Michael. 1984. "Boating language - a new discovery in English language". *TYDS* 84/15:22-30.

659 Parry, David. 1985a. "English dialects in Gwent". *Planet: The Welsh Internationalist* 53:82-90.

660 ---. 1985b. "On producing a linguistic atlas: the survey of Anglo-Welsh dialects". In Kirk, *et al.*, 51-66.

661 ---. 1990a. "The conservative dialects of North Carmarthenshire". In Coupland & Thomas, 142-50.

662 ---. 1990b. "The conservative English dialects of South Pembrokeshire". In Coupland & Thomas, 151-61.

663 Paulin, Tom. 1987. "Vernaculars: a personal essay". *LSE* 18:125-33.

664 Payne, A.K. 1985. "The unmarked plural noun: a 'Black English feature' found in rural England". *Orbis* 31:161-8.

665 Peitsara, Kirsti. 1985. "On the uses of the variants for *and*". *NM* 86:539-43.

666 ---. 1987. "On the uses of *this/these here* in the dialect of Suffolk". In Kahlas-Tarkka, 351-61.

667 ---. 1988. "On existential sentences in the dialect of Suffolk". *NM* 89:72-99.

668 Penhallurick, Robert J. 1985. "Fieldwork for the Survey of Anglo-Welsh Dialects: North Wales 1980-81". In Viereck, 223-33.

669 ---. 1991. *The Anglo-Welsh Dialects of North Wales*. (BBES, 27). Frankfurt/M.: Lang. (Rev. in *EWW* 13:161-3).

669a ---. 1993. "Welsh English: A national language?". *Dialectologia et Geolinguistica* 1:28-46.

670 Petyt, K. Malcolm. 1985. *'Dialect' and 'Accent' in Industrial West Yorkshire*. (VEAW, G6). Amsterdam: Benjamins. (Rev. in *EWW* 8:135-9).

671 ---. 1992. "The influence of the standard variety on northern forms of British English". In *Van Leuvenstijn & Berns, 106-18.

671a Pilch, Herbert. 1990. "Hiberno-English: empirical model of a phonemic substratum". *Celtica* 21:576-87.

672 Pistor, Jutta. 1991. "Das Verb *to be* in den englischen Dialekten". Magisterarbeit, Heidelberg.

673 Pitts, Ann H. 1985a. "Differing prestige values for the (ky) variable in Lurgan". In Harris, *et al.*, 209-21.

674 ---. 1985b. "Urban influence on phonological variation in a Northern Irish speech community". *EWW* 6:59-85.

675 Pointon, Graham. 1988. "The BBC and English pronunciation". *ET* 15: 8-12.

676 Pollner, Clausdirk. 1985a. "Old words in a young town". *ScoL* 4:5-15.

677 ---. 1985b. "Linguistic fieldwork in a Scottish New Town". In Görlach, 57-68.

678 ---. 1985c. *English in Livingston: ausgewählte sprachliche Erscheinungen in einer schottischen New Town.* (BBES, 16). Frankfurt/M.: Lang. (Rev. in *EWW* 6:313-6).

678a ---. 1988. "My children don't speak the way I do" - adolescent and adult speakers in Livingston, Scotland". In Carstensen & Grabes, 389-403.

678b ---. 1990/91. "From riches to rags, from rags to riches? The case of Scots and English in Scotland". *Anglistik und Englischunterricht* 38/39:51-69.

679 Poussa, Patricia. 1986. "Historical implications of the distribution of the zero-pronoun relative clause in modern English dialects: looking backwards towards OE from Map S5 of *The Linguistic Atlas of England*". In Jacobson, 99-117.

680 ---. 1988. "The relative *what*: two kinds of evidence". In *Fisiak, 443-74.

681 ---. 1990. "A contact-universals origin for periphrastic *do* with special consideration of Old English-Celtic contact". In *Adamson, *et al.*, 407-34.

682 ---. 1991. "Origins of the non-standard relativizers *what* and *as* in English". In Ureland & Broderick, 295-315.

683 Price, Glanville. 1984. *The Languages of Britain*. London: Arnold. (Rev. in *EWW* 5:283-90).

684 Pride, Glen L. 1987. "Scottish building terms". *ScoL* 6:30-44.

685 Pryce, W.T.R. 1990. "Language shift in Gwent, c. 1770-1981". In Coupland & Thomas, 48-83.

686 Püttmann, Christina. 1991. "Lexikalische Untersuchung des Dialekts in East Anglia". Magisterarbeit, Heidelberg.

687 Ramisch, Heinrich. 1989. *The Variation of English in Guernsey, Channel Islands*. (BBES, 24). Frankfurt/M.: Lang. (Rev. in *EWW* 11:157-8).

688 Reid, Euan. 1984. "The newer minorities: spoken languages and varieties". In Trudgill, 408-24.

689 Reitz, Ulla-Carina. 1992. *Dialekt bei D.H. Lawrence*. (Neue Studien zur Anglistik und Amerikanistik, 56). Frankfurt/M.: Lang. (Rev. in *EWW* 14:2).

690 Riach, W.A.D. 1985. *Galloway Dialect*. St. John's, Newfoundland: Memorial University. (Reprinted privately).

691 ---. 1988. *A Galloway Glossary*. (Association for Scottish Literary Studies, Occasional Papers, 7). Aberdeen.

692 Ringbom, Hakån & Matti Rissanen, eds. 1984. *Proceedings from the Second Nordic Conference for English Studies*. Åbo: Åbo Akademi.

693 Robertson, T.A. & John J. Graham. 1991. *Grammar and Usage of the Shetland Dialect*. Lerwick: Shetland Times. (Rev. in *EWW* 13:165).

694 Robinson, Mairi, ed. 1985. *A Concise Scots Dictionary*. Aberdeen: UP. (Rev. in *EWW* 7:157-9).

695 ---. 1987. "The Concise Scots Dictionary as a tool for linguistic research". In Macafee & Macleod, 59-72.

696 Romaine, Suzanne. 1985. "The problem of short /a/ in Scotland". *EWW* 6:165-97.

697 ---. 1986. "Syntactic variation and the acquisition of strategies of relativization in the language of Edinburgh schoolchildren". In Jacobson, 19-33.

698 Rydland, Kurt. 1992a. "The Orton Corpus: a collection of dialect material from the north-east of England". *Anglia* 110:1-35.

699 ---. 1992b. "[ea]-type diphthongs in northern English traditional dialects". *ES* 73:152-79.

700 Rynell, Alarik. 1985. "On the confusion between Lay and Lie". *Moderna Språk* 79:21-6.

701 Sabban, Annette. 1985. "On the variability of Hebridean English syntax: the verbal group". In Görlach, 125-44.

702 Sampson, Rodney. 1985. "The 'goat split': a phonological puzzle in one variety of English". *Anglia* 103:282-96.

703 Samuels, Michael L. 1985. "The great Scandinavian belt". In *Eaton, *et al.*, 269-81. (Reprinted in Laing 1989:106-15).

704 Sanderson, Stewart F. & John D.A. Widdowson. 1985. "Linguistic geography in England: progress and prospects". In Kirk, *et al.*, 34-50.

705 Sandred, Karl Inge. 1983. *Good or Bad Scots? Attitudes to Optional Lexical and Grammatical Usages in Edinburgh*. (Studia Anglistica Upsaliensia, 48). Stockholm: Almqvist & Wiksell. (Rev. in *EWW* 5:270-3).

706 ---. 1985. "Overt and covert prestige: evaluative boundaries in the speech community". In Görlach, 69-86.

707 ---. 1987. "Measurement by the hand in Lowland Scots: a study of four Scandinavian loanwords". In Macafee & Macleod, 227-35.

708 ---. 1991. "The study of Scandinavian in England: a survey of Swedish contributions including ongoing research in East Anglia". In Ureland & Broderick, 317-36.

708a Sasaki, Hideki. 1992. "The *Linguistic Atlas of England* (*LAE*): History, fieldwork, and evaluation". *Kenkyu Kijo* [The Faculty Journal of Komazawa Women's Junior College] 25:79-113.

708b ---. 1993. "What dialects underlie the standard pronunciation of present British English?". *Kenkyu Kijo* 26:89-117.

709 Schmidt, Christa M. 1991. *Das Englisch des Darren Valley (Südost-Wales). Eine phonologische Untersuchung unter Berücksichtigung des kymrischen Substrats*. Freiburg i. Br.: Privatdruck.

710 Schneider, Edgar W. 1988. "Informants' response ratings in the Survey of English Dialects". In *Thomas, 396-405.

711 Schnitt, Claudia. 1988. "Der Dialekt in Lincolnshire: eine lexikalische Untersuchung". Magisterarbeit, Heidelberg.

712 Schur, Norman W. 1987. *British English, A to Zed*. New York: Facts on File.

713 Sebba, Mark & Shirley Tate. 1986. "*You know what I mean?* Agreement marking British Black English". *JPrag* 10:163-72.

714 Sellers, Cedric. 1984. "Talking of keels". *TYDS* 84/15:8-20.

715 Shevchenko, T.I. 1984. "An analysis of regional variation in English intonation". In Van den Broecke & Cohen, 580-2.

716 Shire, Helena M. 1990. "The languages of Scotland in poems by Oliver Fraser". In Thomson, 53-6.

717 Shorrocks, Graham. 1984. "The syntax of the dependent pronoun in the dialect of Farnworth and district (Greater Manchester County, formerly Lancashire)". *TYDS* 84/15:40-50.

718 ---. 1985a. "Aspects of affirmation and negation in the dialect of Farnworth and district (Greater Manchester County, formerly Lancashire)". *JLDS* 34:20-9.

719 ---. 1985b. "Ein phonemischer und phonetischer Schlüssel zur Orthographie des Dialektschriftstellers James Taylor Staton (1817-1875) aus Lancashire". *ZDL* 52:306-23.

720 ---. 1985-87 (1991). "The definite article in the dialect of Farnworth and District (Greater Manchester County, formerly Lancashire)". *Orbis* 34:173-86.

721 ---. 1988a. "Glottalization and gemination in an English urban dialect". *CJL* 33:59-64.

722 ---. 1988b. "A phonemic and phonetic key to the orthography of the Lancashire dialect author James Taylor Staton (1817-1875)". *L&L* 7:91-108.

723 ---. 1990a. "Infinitive phrases in the urban dialects of the Bolton and Wigan areas (Greater Manchester County, formerly Lancashire)". *ZDL* 57:28-41.

724 ---. 1990b. "A translation of Joseph Wright's 'Englische Mundarten'". *TYDS* 89/17:10-19.

725 ---. 1990c. "Of *gardens* and *gerdins*: mid-central vowels before /r/ in the North of England". *JLDS* 39:24-8.

726 ---. 1990d. "Linguistic geography and dialect syntax". *JLDS* 39:35-40.

727 ---. 1990e. "Linguistic Survey of Scotland". *JLDS* 39:41-50.

728 ---. 1991. "A.J. Ellis as dialectologist: a reassessment". *Historiographia Linguistica* 18:321-34.

729 ---. 1992. "Response. Case assignment in simple and coordinate constructions in present-day English". *AS* 67:432-44.

730 Shuken, Cynthia R. 1984. "Highland and Island English". In Trudgill, 152-66.

731 ---. 1985a. "Vowel systems in Hebridean English". *ScoL* 5:131-9.

732 ---. 1985b. "Variation in Hebridean English". In Görlach, 145-58.

732a Spray, Martin. 1987. "An example of survival in Sheffield speech". *L&L* 6:65-90.

733 Staczek, John J. 1988. "Variation in the plural reflexive in spoken English". In *Thomas, 674-83.

734 Stenson, Nancy. 1991. "Code-switching vs. borrowing in Modern Irish". In Ureland & Broderick, 559-79.

735 Stevenson, James A.C. & Iseabail Macleod. 1989. *Scoor-oot: A Dictionary of Scots Words and Phrases in Current Use*. London: Athlone Press. (Rev. in *EWW* 12:125-7).

736 Stewart, Alasdair M. 1992. "'Scotland the what'". In *Blank, II:62-8.

737 Sullivan, Anthea E. 1992. *Sound Change in Progress: A Study of Phonological Change and Lexical Diffusion, with Reference to Glottalization and r-loss in the Speech of some Exeter Schoolchildren*. (Exeter Linguistic Studies, 17). Exeter: UP.

738 SURVEY OF ENGLISH DIALECTS. 1989. *Tape Recordings from Northumberland, Tyne & Wear and Co. Durham (SED Localities 1.1-9, 3.1-2).* (New edition by The North Western Sound Archive, Clitheroe. Tapes (NS1-7 & NT1-4, 6-7)). Leeds: University.
739 Swinney, Janet. 1989. "The invisible Scot". *ET* 5:3-8.
740 Tecław, Malgorzata. 1990. "The development of ME ó from open syllable lengthening in the West Midlands". In *Adamson, *et al.*, 459-70.
741 Tench, Paul. 1990. "The pronunciation of English in Abercrave". In Coupland & Thomas, 130-41.
742 Thomas, Alan R. 1984. "Welsh English". In Trudgill, 178-84.
743 ---. fc. "English in Wales". In *Burchfield.
744 Thomas, Beth. 1982. "Fieldwork problems in a Welsh Valley community". *Cardiff Working Papers in Welsh Linguistics* 2:53-72.
745 ---. 1987. "Accounting for language shift in a South Wales mining community". *Cardiff Working Papers in Welsh Linguistics* 5:55-100.
746 ---. 1988. "Differences of sex and sects: linguistic variation and social networks in a Welsh mining village". In *Coates & Cameron, 51-60.
747 Thomas, Charles. 1987. "Dialect studies, V: S.E.D. II.3.5. 'Turn left!' (to horses)". *Cornish Studies* 15:15-18.
748 Thomson, Derick S., ed. 1990. *Gaelic and Scots in Harmony: Proceedings of the Second International Conference on the Languages of Scotland (University of Glasgow, 1988).* Glasgow: University of Glasgow, Dept. of Celtic.
749 Thomson, Robert L. 1991. "Foreign elements in the Manx vocabulary". In Ureland & Broderick, 127-40.
750 Tilling, Philip M. 1985. "A tape-recorded survey of Hiberno-English in its context". In O Baoill, 16-26.
751 Todd, Loreto. 1984. "By their tongue divided: towards an analysis of speech communities in Northern Ireland". *EWW* 5:159-80.
751a ---. 1989. "Cultures in conflict: varieties of English in Northern Ireland". In *García & Otheguy, 335-55.
752 ---. 1990. *Words Apart: A Dictionary of Northern Ireland English.* Gerrards Cross: Smythe. (Rev. in *EWW* 12:155-7).
753 Trudgill, Peter, ed. 1984a. *Language in the British Isles.* Cambridge: UP. (Rev. in *EWW* 5:283-90).
754 ---. 1984b. "Standard English in England". In Trudgill, 32-44.
755 ---. 1988a. "Norwich revisited: recent linguistic changes in an English urban dialect". *EWW* 9:33-49.

756 ---. 1988b. "On the role of dialect contact and interdialect in linguistic change". In *Fisiak, 547-63.

757 ---. 1990. *The Dialects of England*. Oxford: Blackwell. (Rev. in *EWW* 11:316-7).

758 Tulloch, Graham. 1988a. "The language of two Scots versions of the New Testament". In T.L. Burton & Jill Burton, eds. *Lexicographical and Linguistic Studies: Essays in Honour of G.W. Turner*. Cambridge: Boydell & Brewer, 91-102.

758a ---. 1988b. *Scots: An Introduction*. Adelaide: English Discipline, Flinders University.

758b ---. 1989. *A History of the Scots Bible with Selected Texts*. Aberdeen: UP.

759 Upton, Clive. 1993. "Design for the *Dictionary of the Survey of English Dialects*". In *Viereck 1993b:519-28.

760 ---, Stewart Sanderson & John D.A. Widdowson. 1987. *Word Maps: A Dialect Atlas of England*. London: Croom Helm. (Rev. in *EWW* 9:313-8).

761 ---, John D.A. Widdowson & David Parry. 1993. *Survey of English Dialects: The Dictionary and Grammar*. London: Routledge.

762 Ureland, P. Sture, ed. 1987. *Sprachkontakt in der Hanse: Aspekte des Sprachausgleichs im Ostsee- und Nordseeraum: Akten des 7. internationalen Symposiums über Sprachkontakt in Europa, Lübeck 1986*. (Linguistische Arbeiten, 191). Tübingen: Niemeyer.

763 ---. 1990. "Multilingualism, diglossia, and research methods: Focus on the Alps and Ireland". In *Edmondson, *et al.*, 587-617.

764 ---. 1991. "Bilingualism and writing in the Irish Gaeltacht and the Grisons (Switzerland) with special reference to Irish and English". In Ureland & Broderick, 633-94.

765 --- & George Broderick, eds. 1991. *Language Contact in the British Isles: Proceedings of the Eighth International Symposium on Language Contact in Europe, Douglas, Isle of Man, 1988*. (Linguistische Arbeiten, 238). Tübingen: Niemeyer. (Rev. in *EWW* 12:319-22).

766 Van Buuren, Luke. 1988. "Margaret Thatcher's pronunciation: an exercise in eartraining". *JIPA* 18:26-38.

767 Van den Broecke, M.P.R. & A. Cohen, eds. 1984. *Proceedings of the Tenth International Congress of Phonetic Sciences*. Dordrecht: Foris.

768 Van den Eynden, Nadine. 1986. "Grammatical variation in the Dorset dialect: linguistic stagnation exemplified?". In *Papers Presented at the*

1986 Meeting of the Belgian Association of Anglicists in Higher Education (BAAHE). Liège: University, English Department.

769 ---. 1989. "The Dorset dialect: well-explored territory". *The Dorset Year Book 1989*:90-94.

770 ---. 1991. "Aspects of non-standard relativization. A study of relative clauses in the Dorset dialect, in the vein of traditional dialectology, with some socio-linguistic refinements". Ph.D., University of Leuven.

771 ---. 1992. "Relativization in the Dorset dialect". In *Rissanen, *et al.*, 532-55.

772 ---. 1993. *Syntactic Variation and Unconscious Linguistic Change*. A study of adjectival relative clauses in the dialect of Dorset. (BBES, 33). Frankfurt/M.: Lang.

773 ---. fc. "Linguistic variation and unconscious change". In K. Davidse & B. Rudzka-Ostijn, eds. *Festschrift in Honour of Prof. Emma Vorlat*.

774 Van Ryckeghem, Brigitte. 1986. "A Hiberno-English glossary collected and edited from printed sources published in the twentieth century". Ph.D., University College Dublin.

775 Venz, Silke. 1988. "Zur Darstellung des Dialektes von Derbyshire im Roman 'Lady Chatterley's Lover' von D.H. Lawrence, unter besonderer Berücksichtigung der Sprachverwendung des Wildhüters Oliver Mellors". Ph.D., Ernst-Moritz-Arndt-Universität, Greifswald. (Summary in *EWW* 11:288-9).

776 ---. 1990. "Zum Stand der Erforschung der englischen Dialekte". In *Weise, 82-8.

777 Viereck, Wolfgang. 1984. "A bibliography of writings on varieties of English spoken in England, Wales, Scotland and Ireland and on attitudes towards them (1965 - mid-1983)". In *Viereck, Schneider & Görlach, 5-87.

778 ---, ed. 1985a. *Focus on: England and Wales*. (VEAW, G4). Amsterdam: Benjamins. (Rev. in *EWW* 7:311-5).

779 ---. 1985b. "Language variation and the school". In Wolfgang Bandhauer & Robert Tanzmeister, eds. *Romanistik Integrativ. Festschrift für Wolfgang Pollak*. (Wiener Romanistische Arbeiten, 13). Wien: Braumüller, 621-8.

780 ---. 1985c. "Linguistic atlases and dialectometry: the Survey of English Dialects". In Kirk, *et al.*, 94-112.

781 ---. 1985d. "The data of the Survey of English Dialects computerised: key and conventions". In Viereck, 235-46.

782 ---. 1986a. "Zur Erforschung des *Substandard English*". In *Holtus & Radtke, 219-29.

783 ---. 1986b. "Dialectal speech areas in England: Orton's lexical evidence". In *Kastovsky & Szwedek, 725-40.

783a ---. 1986c. "Dialectal speech areas in England: Orton's phonetic and grammatical evidence". *JEngL* 19:240-57.

784 ---. 1987. "Lowman's southern English dialect data and dialectometry". *EWW* 8:11-23.

785 ---. 1988a. "The Channel Islands: an anglicist's no man's land". In Josef Klegraf & Dietrich Nehls, eds. 1988. *Essays on the English Language and Applied Linguistics on the Occasion of Gerhard Nickel's 60th Birthday*. Heidelberg: Groos, 468-78.

786 ---. 1988b. "The data of the 'Survey of English Dialects' computerized - problems and applications". In Merja Kytö, *et al.*, eds. *Corpus Linguistics: Hard and Soft. Proceedings of the Eighth International Conference on English Language Research on Computerized Corpora.* Amsterdam: Rodopi, 267-78.

787 ---. 1988c. "A dictionary of English dialects - the data of the Survey of English dialects dictionarized". In *Hyldgaard-Jensen & Zettersten, 101-13.

788 ---, in collaboration with Heinrich Ramisch and Harald Händler, Petra Hoffmann, Wolfgang Putschke (computational production). 1991. *A Computer Developed Linguistic Atlas of England, I.* Tübingen: Niemeyer. (Rev. in *EWW* 13:302-6).

788a ---. 1992a. "The Computer Developed Linguistic Atlas of England (CLAE): a preview on Volume 2". *Nikon hagen kenkyukai* [Dialectological Circle of Japan] 55:55-114. [in Japanese and English]

788b ---. 1992b. "Prince Louis-Lucien Bonaparte and English dialectology". *Nazioarteko Dialectologia Biltzarra. Agiriak/ (...) /Proceedings of the International Congress on Dialectology. Bilbo, 21. - 25. X. 1991.* Bilbo, 17-30.

788c ---. fc. "Realisations of the definite article in dialectal English and how and when they originated". In Jacek Fisiak, ed. *Medieval Dialectology.* Berlin: Mouton de Gruyter.

789 Voß, Ute. 1988. "Zur Darstellung des Cockney in William Somerset Maughams *Liza of Lambeth* (1897)". Ph.D., Ernst-Moritz-Arndt-Universität, Greifswald. (Summary in *EWW* 11:289-90).

790 Wakelin, Martyn F. 1983. "The stability of English dialect boundaries". *EWW* 4:1-15.
791 ---. 1984a. "Rural dialects in England". In Trudgill, 70-93.
792 ---. 1984b. "Cornish English". In Trudgill, 195-8.
793 ---. 1985. "The 'Exmoor Courtship' and 'Exmoor Scolding': an evaluation of two eighteenth-century dialect texts". In *Kastovsky & Szwedek, 741-51.
794 ---. 1986. *The Southwest of England*. (VEAW, T5). Amsterdam: Benjamins. (Rev. in *EWW* 8:301-4).
795 ---. 1987. "The treatment of dialect in English dictionaries". In *Burchfield, 156-77.
796 ---. 1991. "The Cornishness of Cornwall's English". In Ureland & Broderick, 199-225.
797 ---. 1992. "'Mummerset': the delineation of a popular genre". In *Blank, II:49-61.
798 Wall, Richard. 1986. *An Anglo-Irish Dialect Glossary for Joyce's Works*. Gerrards Cross: Smythe.
799 ---. 1990. "Dialect in Irish literature: the hermetic core". In Dolan, 8-18.
800 Warrack, Alexander, ed. 1989. *Scots Dialect Dictionary*. New Orchard Editions. [reprint of 1911]
801 Wells, John C. 1984. "English accents in England". In Trudgill, 55-69.
802 ---. 1990. "Accents of English in Wales: a postscript". In Coupland & Thomas, 162-4.
803 Widdowson, John D.A. 1988. "Provenance and persistence of standard and literary forms in English regional dialects". In Eric Gerald Stanley & T.F. Hoad, eds. 1988. *Words: For Robert Burchfield's Sixty-Fifth Birthday*. Cambridge: Brewer, 185-96.
804 Williams, Ann. 1989. "Dialect in school work". In Cheshire, *et al.*, eds., 182-99.
805 Williams, Colin H. 1980. "Language contact and language change in Wales: a study in historical geolinguistics". *The Welsh History Review* 10:207-38.
806 ---. 1987. "The land in linguistic consciousness: evidence from the British Isles". *Sociolinguistica* 1:13-29.
807 ---. 1990. "The anglicisation of Wales". In Coupland & Thomas, 19-47.
808 Wright, Peter. 1987. "Lancashire dialect: a step to international understanding?". *JLDS* 36:6-11.
809 ---. 1988. "Curious south-western fishing language". *JLDS* 37:13-7.

810 ---. 1989a. "The dialect of English secondary schoolchildren". In Fischer, 231-44.
811 ---. [3]1989b. *Cumbrian Chat: How It Is Spoke*. Clapham: Dalesman.
812 ---. 1992. "Humour in dialect speech". In *Blank, II:33-49.

Part III: Writings on varieties of American and Canadian English

EDGAR W. SCHNEIDER

This bibliography supplements and updates my earlier contribution to Viereck, Schneider & Görlach (1984). Obviously, this relationship explains the starting point of the period of coverage; more precisely, it means that the present bibliography excludes titles which are in the 1984 bibliography and, conversely, lists a few publications of the early 1980s not referred to there. The search for the present bibliography was terminated in April 1993.

In order to maintain compatibility and the complementary function of the present work, the principles of inclusion and exclusion have largely remained the same. The basic idea is to cover writings in the fields of American dialectology and sociolinguistics, including mainly data-oriented descriptive works, but also contributions to the history, the theory and methodology of both fields, especially if they contain a substantial amount of AmE data for illustration. Publications on AmE as such have been collected only if they relate to distinctively American linguistic features, but not if statements on (general) English grammar just happen to have been illustrated with AmE material. Writings on bilingualism, language contact and language interference are included unless they concentrate mainly upon the non-English language involved. Publications on literary dialect, on bilingual education and the language education of minority children, on modern and historical lexicography and on slang and argot as well as reprints of books have been included selectively. The bibliography does not list reviews (except substantial review articles and, due to the publication context of this volume, reviews in *EWW*); reprints of articles; unpublished manuscripts (except some items known to be in print at the time of compilation) and papers read at conferences; onomastic studies; discussions of language policy (such as the "English Only" movement); and writings in non-scholarly publications, such as newspapers.

I am grateful to Melanie Schäfer and Claudia Blank, who assisted me in compiling this bibliography. A preliminary version was sent out to the subscribers of the electronic mail list of the American Dialect Society (ADS-L) in late November 1992. I would like to say thanks to those colleagues who responded and sent me hints, additions and corrections, as well as to others who contributed to this listing, including J.K. Chambers, Lawrence Davis, Timothy Frazer, Beat Glauser, Manfred Görlach, Ellen Johnson, Miklos Kontra, William Kretzschmar, Michael Montgomery, Salikoko S. Mufwene, and Robert Wachal.

For relevant collections of papers or contrastive studies on varieties of American and Canadian English outside this section see in particular entries 11, 20, 85-6, and 203-4.

813 Abney, Lisa. 1989. "Preterites in early Southern White English". *SECOLR* 13:180-93.

814 Adams, Karen L. 1990. "Ethnic and linguistic minorities in the Southwest: an overview". In Adams & Brink, 183-97.

815 --- & Daniel T. Brink, eds. 1990. *Perspectives on Official English: The Campaign for English as the Official Language of the USA*. Berlin: Mouton de Gruyter. (Rev. in *EWW* 12:327-8).

816 Adger, Carolyn Temple. 1986. "When difference does not conflict: successful arguments between black and Vietnamese classmates". *Text* 6:223-37.

817 Aguirre, Adalberto, Jr. 1985. "An experimental study of code alternation". *IJSL* 53:59-82.

818 ---, ed. 1985. "Language in the Chicano speech community". *IJSL* 53:5-128.

819 Alexander, Clara Franklin. 1985. "Black English dialect and the classroom teacher". In Brooks, *et al.*, 20-9.

820 Alford, Randall & Judith B. Strother. 1990. "Attitudes of native and nonnative speakers toward selected regional accents of U.S. English". *TESOLQ* 24:479-95.

821 Algeo, John. 1984. "Usage". In *Needed Research in American English (1983)*, 36-53.

822 ---, ed. fc. *English in North America*. Vol. VI. *Cambridge History of the English Language*. Cambridge: UP.

823 Allen, Harold B. 1985a. "Sex-linked variation in the responses of dialect informants. Part 1: lexicon". *JEngL* 18:97-123.

824 ---. 1985b. "Sex-linked variation in the responses of dialect informants. Part 2: pronunciation". *JEngL* 19:4-24.

825 ---. 1985c. "Sex-linked variation in the responses of dialect informants. Part 3: grammar". *JEngL* 19:149-76.

826 ---. 1985d. "Attitudes of the National Council of Teachers of English". In *Greenbaum, 139-46.

827 ---. 1987. "*LAUM* and the ABC's of *DARE*". *AS* 62:81-3.

828 ---. 1989a. "Canadian raising in the upper Midwest". *AS* 64:74-5.

829 ---. 1989b. "New or old-fashioned? Informant awareness of chronological status". *AS* 64:3-11.

830 Allen, Irving Louis. 1987. "The contempt for provincial life in historical American slang". In *Levitt, *et al.*, 231-58.

831 ---. 1993. *The City in Slang: New York Life and Popular Speech*. New York: Oxford UP.

832 Alvarez, Celia. 1989. "Code-switching in narrative performance: a Puerto Rican speech community in New York". In *García & Otheguy, 373-86.

833 Amastae, John. 1984. "The Pan-American project". In Ornstein-Galicia, 135-42.

834 ---. 1990. "Official English and the learning of English". In Adams & Brink, 199-208.

835 Anderson, Carolyn, Mariene G. Fine & Fern L. Johnson. 1983. "Black talk on television: a constructivist approach to viewers' perceptions of BEV in *Roots II*". *JMMD* 4:181-95.

836 Anokye, Akua Duku. 1991. "Linguistic form and social function: A discourse analysis of rhetorical and narrative structure in oral and written African-American folk narrative texts". Ph.D., City University of New York. DAI 52:5 (1991), 1729-A. (Summary in *EWW* 13:276).

837 Antecki, Andrzej. 1986. "Spanish influence upon American English in the 19th century". *ZNOP, Filologia Angielska* 1:5-14.

838 Aponte, Irene A. 1986. "The relationship between linguistic diversity and language performance". Ph.D., Yeshiva University. DAI 46:11 (1985), 3301-A.

839 Armour, Malcolm. 1983. "The social stratification of (e) in Midlothian Texas". In *Edmondson, 2-21.

839a Arter-Lamprecht, Lotti. 1992. *Deutsch-englischer Sprachkontakt*. Die Mehrsprachigkeit einer Old Order Amish Gemeinde in Ohio aus soziolinguistischer und interferenzlinguistischer Sicht. (*SAA*, 117). Tübingen: Francke.

840 Arthurs, James. 1988. "Terminology vs. jargon: Canadian hockey talk". In *Thomas, 155-63.

841 Asante, Molefi Kete. 1985. "The African essence in African-American language". In Molefi Kete Asante & Kariamu Welsh Asante, eds. *African Culture: The Rhythms of Unity*. Westport, Conn.: Greenwood, 233-52.

842 ---. 1990. "African elements in African-American English". In Joseph E. Holloway, ed. *Africanisms in American Culture*. Bloomington: Indiana UP, 19-33.

843 Ash, Sharon & John Myhill. 1986. "Linguistic correlates of inter-ethnic contact". In *Sankoff, 33-44.

844 August, Diane & Eugene E. Garcia. 1988. *Language Minority Education in the United States: Research, Policy, and Practice*. Springfield, Ill.: Thomas.
845 Avis, Walter S. 1983. "Canadian English in its North American context". *CJL* 28:3-15.
846 ---. 1986. "The contemporary context of Canadian English". In *Allen & Linn, 212-16.
847 Babitch, Rose Mary. 1988. "Diachronic interlinguistic contact as reflected in the typological structure of today's Acadian fishermen's terminology". In *Thomas, 121-37.
848 Bailey, Guy. 1989a. "Sociolinguistic constraints on language change and the evolution of *are* in early modern black English". *TSL* 31:158-71.
849 ---. 1989b. "Black Speech". In Wilson & Ferris, 194-5.
850 ---. 1989c. "Conch". In Wilson & Ferris, 786.
851 ---. 1989d. "Linguistic Atlas of the Gulf States project". In Wilson & Ferris, 788.
852 ---. 1991. "Directions of change in Texas English". *Journal of American Culture* 14:125-34.
853 ---. 1992. "The second round of dialectology". In *Hall, *et al.*, 415-40.
854 ---. 1993. "A perspective on African-American English". In Preston, 287-318.
855 --- & Marvin Bassett. 1986. "Invariant *be* in the lower South". In Montgomery & Bailey, 158-79.
856 --- & Cynthia Bernstein. 1989. "Methodology for a phonological survey of Texas". In *Kretzschmar, *et al.*, 6-16.
857 --- & ---. 1990. "The idea of black English". *SECOLR* 14:1-24.
858 --- & Margie Dyer. 1992. "An approach to sampling in dialectology". *AS* 67:3-20.
859 --- & Natalie Maynor. 1985a. "The present tense of *be* in Southern black folk speech". *AS* 60:195-213.
860 --- & ---. 1985b. "The present tense of *be* in white folk speech of the southern United States". *EWW* 6:199-216.
861 --- & ---. 1987. "Decreolization?". *LinS* 16:449-73.
862 --- & ---. 1989. "The divergence controversy". *AS* 64:12-39.
863 --- & Garry Ross. 1992. "The evolution of a vernacular". In *Rissanen, *et al.*, 519-31.
864 --- & Clyde Smith. 1992. "Southern English in Brazil, no?". *SECOLR* 16:71-89.

865 ---, Tom Wikle & Lori Sand. 1991a. "The focus of linguistic innovation in Texas". *EWW* 12:195-214.

866 ---, ---, Jan Tillery & Lori Sand. 1991b. "The apparent time construct". *LVC* 3:241-64.

867 ---, ---, --- & ---. fc. "Methodology for a Survey of Oklahoma Dialects". In *Proceedings of the Mid-America Linguistic Conference.*

868 Bailey, Larry Jerome. 1988. "Dialectal characteristics and congruence between measures of Southern black fifth-grade school children". Ph.D., Florida State University. DAI 50:8 (1990), 3430-1B.

869 Bailey, Richard W. 1983. "Education and the law: the *King* case in Ann Arbor". In Chambers, 1-28.

870 ---. 1991a. "Dialects of Canadian English". *ET* 27:20-5.

871 Baird, Keith E. & Mary A. Twining. fc. "Names and naming in the Sea Islands". In *Montgomery fc.a.

872 Baird, Scott. 1985. "English dialects in San Antonio". *Names* 33:232-42.

873 Baker, Charlotte Pierce. 1985. "Acquisition of /t,d/ deletion in vernacular Black English: a study of head start preschoolers". Ph.D., Temple University. DAI 46:8 (1986), 2280-A. (Summary in *EWW* 7:269-70).

874 Barker, Marie E. 1988. "Nonstandard dialects in bilingual education: the read-aloud strategy in children literature". In Bixler-Márquez & Ornstein-Galicia, 101-8.

875 Bartelt, H. Guillermo. 1983. "Mode and aspect transfer in Navajo and Western Apache English narrative technique". *IRAL* 21:105-24.

876 ---. 1986a. "Language contact in Arizona: the case of Apachean English". *Anthropos* 81:692-5.

877 ---. 1986b. "Nonanterior tense in American Indian English". *AS* 61:327-9.

878 ---. 1986c. "Tense/aspect variation in American Indian English". *Nordic Journal of Linguistics* 9:47-53.

879 ---. 1987. "Mode and aspect transfer in Navajo and western Apache English narrative technique". In Dietrich Nehls, ed. *Interlanguage Studies*. Heidelberg: Groos, 115-34.

880 ---. 1988. "Cognitive processes in Apachean English". *PSCL* 24:183-98.

881 ---. 1991a. "American Indian English: a phylogenetic dilemma". In *Byrne & Huebner, 29-39.

882 ---. 1991b. "The early spread of English among American Indians". *Anthropos* 86:187-92.

883 ---. 1993. "Urban American Indian intertribal discourse". *EWW* 14:57-70.

884 Bartholomew, Charles. 1988. "The effect of dialect differences on the scoring of ambiguous WISC-R responses: an evaluation of scoring bias". Ph.D., University of Southern Mississippi. DAI 49:4 (1989), 1428-B.

885 Bassett, Marvin Winslett. 1983. "Social differences in the grammar of Lower Alabama". Ph.D., Emory University.

886 Bates-Mims, Merelyn B. 1986. "Chez les noirs: a comparative historical analysis of pidgin and creole languages". Ph.D., University of Cincinnati. DAI 47:6 (1987), 2142-A.

887 Battistella, Edwin L. 1987. "Marked and unmarked pronouns in English". *SECOLR* 11:66-77.

888 ---. 1991. "The treatment of negation in double modal constructions". *Linguistic Analysis* 21:49-65.

889 Baugh, John. 1983a. *Black Street Speech: Its History, Structure and Survival*. Austin: University of Texas Press.

890 ---. 1983b. "A survey of Afro-American English". *Annual Review of Anthropology* 12:335-54.

891 ---. 1983c. "Language variation in American English vernaculars". In Chambers, 71-80.

892 ---. 1984a. "Chicano English: the anguish of definition". In Ornstein-Galicia, 3-13.

893 ---. 1984b. "*Steady*: progressive aspect in black vernacular English". *AS* 59:3-12.

894 ---. 1986. "Bilingualism and bidialectalism among American minorities". In *Nickel & Stalker, 84-94.

895 ---. 1988a. "Beyond linguistic divergence in black American English: competing norms of linguistic prestige and variation". In *Thomas, 175-86.

896 ---. 1988b. "Language and race: some implications for linguistic science". In *Newmeyer, 64-74.

897 ---. 1990. "Survey of the suffix /-s/ analyses in Black English". In *Edmondson, *et al.*, 297-307.

898 ---. 1991. "The politicization of changing terms of self-reference among American slave descendants". *AS* 66:133-46.

899 ---. 1992. "Adapting dialectology: the conduct of community language studies". In Miklós Kontra & Tamás Váradi, eds. *Studies in Spoken Languages: English, German, Finno-Ugric*. Budapest: Linguistics Institute, Hungarian Academy of Sciences, 15-39.

900 ---. 1993. "Adapting dialectology: the conduct of community language studies". In Preston, 167-92.

901 Baumann, Richard. 1984. "The making and breaking of context in West Texas oral anecdotes". *GURT*:160-74.

902 Bayerl, F. & M. Williams, eds. 1985. *The Canadian Style: A Guide to Writing and Editing*. Toronto: Dundurn Press. (The Secretary of State, Translation Bureau).

903 Beaty, Stuart. 1985. "Post-secondary bilingual education in British Columbia: to be or not to be". *CMLR* 41:816-8.

904 Benes, Peter & Jane Montague Benes, eds. 1985. *American Speech: 1600 to the Present*. Boston, Mass.: Boston UP.

905 Bentley, Robert H. 1987. "Social dialects: educational implications of the study of black English". In Philip C. Boardman, ed. *The Legacy of Language: a Tribute to Charlton Laird*. Reno: University of Nevada Press, 69-80.

906 Bergin, Kendall Russell. 1988. "The development of rating scales for black English grammar, pronunciation, rhythm/intonation, and overall black English usage". Ph.D., University of Tennessee. DAI 50:2 (1989), 429-A.

907 Bernstein, Cynthia. 1988. "A variant of the 'invariant' *be*". *AS* 63:119-24.

908 Billiard, Charles E. 1986. "Correlates among social dialects, language development, and reading achievement of urban children". In Montgomery & Bailey, 365-72.

909 Birns, William. 1986. "Dialect in the Catskills: a study in language and culture". Ph. D., Indiana University of Pennsylvania. DAI 47:6 (1986), 2142-A. (Summary in *EWW* 8:279-80).

910 Bister, Helga & Roland Willemyns. 1990. "Meertaligheid in de Verenigde Staten van Amerika". *De Vlaamse Gids* 74:32-8.

911 Bixler-Márquez, Dennis J. & Jacob Ornstein-Galicia, eds. 1988. *Chicano Speech in the Bilingual Classroom*. New York: Lang.

912 Blanton, Linda. 1989. "Mountain language". In Wilson & Ferris, 777-8.

913 Blanton, Mackie J.V. 1989. "New Orleans English". In Wilson & Ferris, 780-1.

914 Bluestein, Gene. 1989. *Anglistic/Yiddish: Yiddish in American Life and Literature*. Athens, Ga.: University of Georgia Press.

915 Boertien, Harmon S. 1986. "Constituent structure of double modals". In Montgomery & Bailey, 294-318.

916 Bountress, Nicholas G. 1983. "Effect of segregated and integrated educational settings upon selected dialectal features". *Perceptual and Motor Skills* 57:71-8.

917 Bourhis, Richard Y. 1984a. *Conflict and Language Planning in Québec*. Clevedon: Multilingual Matters.

918 ---. 1984b. "Cross-cultural communication in Montreal: two field studies since Bill 101". *IJSL* 46:33-47.

919 Braden, Waldo W. 1989. "Black language [in the South]". In Wilson & Ferris, 767-8.

920 Brewer, Jeutonne P. 1986. "Durative marker or hypercorrection? The case of *-s* in the WPA ex-slave narratives". In Montgomery & Bailey, 131-48.

921 ---. 1991. "Songs, sermons, and life stories: the legacy of the ex-slave narratives". In *Bailey, *et al.*, 155-71.

922 Briggs, Charles. 1993. "The patterning of variation in performance". In Preston, 379-432.

923 Brooke, Maxey. 1986. "Varieties of American English". *WWays* 19:125-6.

924 ---. 1988. "Texican". *Verbatim* 15:13.

925 Brooks, Charlotte, *et al.*, eds. 1985. *Tapping Potential: English and Language Arts for the Black Learner*. Urbana, Ill.: Black Caucus of National Council of Teachers of English.

926 Brooks, Cleanth. 1985. *The Language of the American South*. Athens: University of Georgia Press. (Rev. in *EWW* 7:159-61).

927 Brosig, Elly. 1989. "Soziolinguistische Untersuchungen über die Prozesse des Lexiswandels im amerikanischen Armeeslang". [Sociolinguistic dynamics of lexical change in US army slang]. Ph.D., University of Stuttgart. (Summary in *EWW* 11:279-81).

928 Brown, Vivian Ruby. 1990. "Phonetic constraints on the merger of /ɪ/ and /ɛ/ before nasals in North Carolina and Tennessee". *SECOLR* 14:87-100.

929 ---. 1991a. "The social and linguistic history of a merger: /I/ and /E/ before nasals in Southern American English". Ph.D., Texas A&M University. DAI 52:2 (1991), 524-A. (Summary in *EWW* 14:2).

930 ---. 1991b. "Evolution of the merger of /ɪ/ and /ɛ/ before nasals in Tennessee". *AS* 66:303-15.

931 Bruce, Harry. "Language of the U.S. military". *etc.* 44:295-6.

932 Buckingham, Andrew. 1983. "The stratification of the sociolinguistic variable (e) in the speech of residents of Midlothian, Texas". In *Edmondson, 22-36.

933 Burnaby, Barbara. 1988. "Language in native education in Canada". In *Paulston, 141-61.

934 Burton, Lydia. 1982. "In search of a Canadian style". *Scholarly Publishing* 13:347-54.

935 Butters, Ronald R. 1984. "When is English 'Black English Vernacular'?". *JEngL* 17:29-36.

936 ---. 1987a. "More on singular *y'all*". *AS* 62:191-2.

937 ---. 1987b. "Linguistic convergence in a North Carolina community". In *Denning, 52-60.

938 ---. 1987c. "Verbal *-s* as past-time indication in various narratives". In Linda L. McIntyre, ed. *Proceedings of the Annual Linguistics Colloquium, University of North Carolina at Chapel Hill*. Chapel Hill: UNC Linguistics Circle, 9-18.

939 ---. 1988. "The historical present as evidence of black/white convergence/divergence". In *Thomas, 637-49.

940 ---. 1989. *The Death of Black English: Divergence and Convergence in Black and White Vernaculars*. (BBES, 25). Frankfurt/M.: Lang. (Rev. in *EWW* 14:134-8).

941 ---. 1991. "Multiple modals in United States Black English: Synchronic and diachronic aspects". In *Edwards & Winford, 165-76.

942 --- & Ruth A. Nix. 1986. "The English of blacks in Wilmington, North Carolina". In Montgomery & Bailey, 254-63.

943 --- & Kristin Stettler. 1986. "Existential and causative *have ... to*". *AS* 61:184-90.

944 Caldas, Stephen J. & Suzanne Caron-Caldas. 1992. "Rearing bilingual children in a monolingual culture: a Louisiana experience". *AS* 67:290-6.

945 Callary, Edward. 1990. "The Northern-Midland boundary in Illinois: a retro-spective". *KanQ* 22:163-78.

946 Cameron, Deborah. 1992. "Naming of parts: gender, culture, and terms for the penis among American college students". *AS* 67:367-82.

947 Canetuson, Mary Alice. 1982. "A perceptual study of English teachers and language arts supervisors concerning the use of vernacular black English by students and teachers in the State of Texas". Ph.D., North Texas State University. DAI 43:7 (1983), 2338-9A.

948 Cantrell, Robert Jeffrey. 1991. "Dialect and spelling in Appalachian first-grade children". Ed.D., University of Virginia. DAI 53:1 (1992), 112-A. (Summary in *EWW* 13:278).
949 Caratini, Migdalia. 1984. "Social variation in present perfect and preterit use among selected adult English learners in Puerto Rico". Ph.D., New York University. DAI 46:1 (1985), 138-A. (Summary in *EWW* 7:273).
950 Cartwright, Don. 1987. "Accommodation among the anglophone minority in Quebec to official language policy: a shift in traditional patterns of language contact". *JMMD* 8:193-4.
951 ---. 1988. "Language policy and internal geopolitics: the Canadian situation". In *Williams, 238-66.
952 Carver, Craig M. 1986. "The influence of the Mississipi River on Northern dialect boundaries". *AS* 61:245-61.
953 ---. 1987. *American Regional Dialects: A Word Geography*. Ann Arbor, Mich.: University of Michigan Press. (Rev. in *EWW* 8:308-11).
954 ---. 1993. "Regional speech variation in Wisconsin". In Frazer, 199-214.
955 Cassidy, Frederic G. 1983. "Sources of the African element in Gullah". In Lawrence Carrington, ed. *Studies in Caribbean Language*. St. Augustine, Trinidad: Society for Caribbean Linguistics, 75-81.
956 ---. 1984. "Regional speech and localisms". In *Needed Research in American English (1983)*, 32-5.
957 ---, ed. 1985. *Dictionary of American Regional English*. Vol.1: *Introduction and A-C*. Cambridge, Mass., London: The Belknap Press of Harvard UP. (Rev. in *EWW* 7:317-21).
958 ---. 1987a. "DARE replies to Claiborne". *ET* 11:8.
959 ---. 1987b. "The *Dictionary of American Regional English* as a resource for language study". In *Burchfield, 117-35.
960 ---. 1987c. "The fallible computer and DARE". *ET* 9:27-30.
961 ---. 1988. "Focus of change in American folk speech". In *Thomas, 326-32.
962 ---. 1989. "Gullah". In Wilson & Ferris, 772-3.
963 ---. 1991. "The *for*-plus-adjective construction". *AS* 66:106-8.
964 ---. 1993. "Area lexicon: the making of DARE". In Preston, 93-106.
965 ---. fc. "Gullah and the Caribbean connection". In *Montgomery fc.a.
966 --- & Audrey M. Duckert. 1985. "The Hanley disks: presentation to the Library of Congress". *NADS* 17:10-12.
967 --- & Joan Houston Hall, eds. 1991. *Dictionary of American Regional English*. Vol.2: *D-H*. Cambridge, Mass., London: The Belknap Press of Harvard UP.

968 Castonguay, Charles. 1987. "The anglicization of Canada, 1971-1981". *LPLP* 11:22-34.
969 Cavender, Anthony. 1989. "Language and medicine in the Appalachian South project: a study in applied folklore". *Tennessee Folklore Society Bulletin* 54:11-13.
970 ---, ed. 1990. *A Folk Medical Lexicon of South Central Appalachia.* Johnson City, Tenn.: East Tennessee State University.
971 Chafe, Wallace L., John W. Du Bois & Sandra A. Thompson. 1991. "Towards a new corpus of spoken American English". In *Aijmer & Altenberg, 64-82.
972 Chambers, Jack K. 1985. "Group and individual participation in a sound-change in progress". In *Warkentyne, 119-36.
973 ---. 1986. "Three kinds of standard in Canadian English". In Lougheed, 1-15.
974 ---. 1987. "The complementizer *'cep 'fer*". *AS* 62:378-9.
975 ---. 1988. "Acquisition of phonological variants". In *Thomas, 650-65.
976 ---. 1989. "Canadian raising: blocking, fronting, etc". *AS* 64:75-88.
977 ---. 1990a. "Forensic dialectology and the Bear Island land claim". In R. Rieber & W. Stewart, eds., *The Language Scientist as Expert in the Legal Setting*. (Annals of the New York Academy of Sciences, 606), 19-31.
978 ---. 1990b. "The Canada-U.S. border as a vanishing isogloss: the evidence of *chesterfield*". *JEngL* 23. (fc., issue delayed)
979 ---. 1990c. "Canadian *hubba bubba*". *AS* 65:93.
980 ---. 1991. "Canada". In *Cheshire, 89-107.
981 ---. 1992. "Dialect acquisition". *Language* 68:673-705. [= 47]
982 ---. 1993a. "'Lawless and vulgar innovations': Victorian views of Canadian English". In Clarke, 1-26. (First printed in S. Ehrlich & S. Embleton, eds. 1982. *Toronto Working Papers in Linguistics* 2).
983 ---. 1993b. "Sociolinguistic dialectology". In Preston, 133-66.
984 ---. fc. "The acquisition of lexical and pronunciation variants". In *Viereck.
985 --- & Margaret F. Hardwick. 1985. "Dialect homogeneity and incipient variation: changes in progress in Toronto and Vancouver". In J. Harris & R. Hawkins, eds. *Sheffield Working Papers in Language and Linguistics, Vol. 2*. Sheffield: School of Modern Languages and Linguistics, University of Sheffield, 28-49.
986 --- & ---. 1986. "Comparative sociolinguistics of a sound change in Canadian English". *EWW* 7:23-46.

987 [entry deleted]

988 Chambers, John W., Jr., ed. 1983. *Black English: Educational Equity and the Law*. Ann Arbor, Mich.: Karoma. (Rev. in *EWW* 5:292-6).

989 Chamot, Anna U. 1988. "Bilingualism in education and bilingual education: the state of the art in the United States". In J. Gimbel, ed. *Papers from the Fifth Nordic Conference on Bilingualism*. Clevedon: Multilingual Matters, 11-35.

990 Chase, Dennis. 1988. "If someone asks, 'where y'at?' say 'N'awlins's a Connecticut Yankee in King Creole's court'". *Lamar Journal of the Humanities* 14:19-29.

991 Chaston, John Malcolm. 1987. "Aspect choice in preterit and imperfect usage in the speech of Mexican-American college students in Texas: a sociolinguistic approach". Ph.D., University of Texas at Austin.

992 Chávez, Regino & Ray A. Chesterfield. 1985. "Teacher language use in a bilingual preschool setting". *IJSL* 53:83-97.

993 Ching, Marvin K.L. 1987. "How fixed is *fixin' to*?". *AS* 62:332-45.

994 ---. 1988. "*Ma'am* and *Sir*: modes of mitigation and politeness in the Southern United States". In *Thomas, 20-45.

995 Christian, Donna. 1991. "The personal dative in Appalachian speech". In *Trudgill & Chambers, 11-19.

996 ---, Walt Wolfram & Nanjo Dube. 1988. *Variation and Change in Geographically Isolated Communities: Appalachian English and Ozark English*. (PADS, 74). Tuscaloosa, Ala.: University of Alabama Press. (Rev. in *EWW* 11:305-6).

997 Cichocki, Wladyslaw. 1986. "Linguistic applications of dual scaling in variation studies". Ph.D., University of Toronto.

998 ---. 1988. "Uses of dual scaling in social dialectology: multidimensional analysis of vowel variation". In *Thomas, 187-99.

999 Ciske, Mary Desjarlais. 1987. "An error analysis of standard English verb use by speakers of a nonstandard black dialect". Ph.D., George Mason University. DAI 48:10 (1988), 2615-A.

1000 Clark, Thomas L. 1983. "Linguistic atlases: archival data for language study in the Western United States". *JEngL* 16:3-17.

1001 ---. 1984, "Historical perspective". In *Needed Research in American English (1983)*, 1-3.

1002 Clarke, Sandra. 1980. "Sex as a sociolinguistic variable: the significance of sex in attitudinal stereotypes". In A.M. Kinloch & Anthony B. House, eds. *Papers from the Fourth Annual Meeting of the Atlantic*

Provinces Linguistic Association. Fredericton: University of New Brunswick, 60-76.

1003 ---. 1981. "Dialect stereotyping in rural Newfoundland". In T.K. Pratt, ed. *Papers from the Fifth Annual Meeting of the Atlantic Provinces Linguistic Association*. Charlottetown, P.E.I.: University of Prince Edward Island, 39-57.

1004 ---. 1982. "Sampling attitudes to dialect varieties in St. John's". In Paddock, 90-105.

1005 ---. 1984a. "The role of linguistic feature types in dialect stereotyping". In J. Barnstead, *et al.*, eds. *Papers from the Eighth Annual Meeting of the Atlantic Provinces Linguistic Association*. Halifax: Dalhousie UP, 19-32.

1006 ---. 1984b. "Differences in male and female language usage: the Newfoundland context". *Women and Language/Femmes et langage* 13:33-5.

1007 ---. 1985. "Sociolinguistic variation in a small urban context: the St. John's survey". In *Warkentyne, 143-54.

1008 ---. 1986. "Sociolinguistic patterning in a New-World dialect of Hiberno-English: the speech of St. John's, Newfoundland". In [II]Harris, 67-81.

1009 ---. 1987. "Dialect mixing and linguistic variation in a non-overtly stratified society". In *Denning, *et al.*, 74-85.

1010 ---. 1988. "Linguistic variation in the non-stratified context". In *Thomas, 684-99.

1011 ---. 1991a. "Phonological variation and recent language change in St. John's English". In *Cheshire, 108-22.

1012 ---. 1991b. "Dialect convergence in a non-overtly stratified society". In *Bahner, *et al.*, II:1335-9.

1013 ---, ed. 1993a. *Focus on Canada*. Amsterdam & Philadelphia: Benjamins.

1014 ---. 1993b. "The Americanization of Canadian pronunciation: a survey of palatal glide usage". In Clarke, 85-108.

1015 Cobarrubias, J. & J.-D. Gendron, eds. 1984. *Language Policy in Canada: Current Issues*. Quebec: Laval University.

1016 Cobden, M. 1986. "The standard in Canadian journalism". In Lougheed, 120-5.

1017 Coe, Elizabeth Beaubien. 1984. "Assessing Afro-American comprehension by student teachers whose mother tongue is mainstream English". Ed. D., University of Houston. DAI 46:4 (1985), 963-A. (Summary in *EWW* 7:274-5).

1018 Coe, Richard M. 1988. "Anglo-Canadian rhetoric and identity: a preface". *College English* 50:849-60.

1019 Colbourne, B. Wade. 1982. "A sociolinguistic study of Long Island, Notre Dame Bay, Newfoundland". *RLS* 10:20-1.

1020 Cole, Patricia Anne. 1986. "Learning disability in black second grade children: an investigation of selected morphological features". Ph.D., Howard University. DAI 48:8 (1987), 2289-B.

1021 Collins, Mary Evelyn & Lawrence R. Clayton. 1991. "Gone with the drawl: changing patterns in Texas folk speech". *Journal of American Culture* 14:135-7.

1022 Conklin, Nancy Faires & Margaret A. Lourie. 1983. *A Host of Tongues: Language Communities in the United States*. New York: Free Press. (Rev. in *EWW* 7:161-2).

1023 Cook, Albert B. 1990. "Kansas word geography: a summary of findings". *KanQ* 22:77-107.

1024 Coye, Dale. 1986. "The *sneakers/tennis shoes* boundary". *AS* 61:366-9.

1025 Craig, Beth. 1991. "American Indian English". *EWW* 12:25-61.

1026 Crespo Gonzalez, Elba Iris. 1989. "It loses something in the translation: the communication of emotion among Puerto Ricans living in the U.S". Ph.D., Adelphi University. DAI 50:11 (1990), 5376-B.

1027 Crystal, David. 1986. "The best tense we ever had". *ET* 6:28.

1028 Cukor-Avila, Patricia. 1989. "Determining change in progress vs. stable variation in two studies of Black English Vernacular". *SECOLR* 13:92-124.

1029 Cummins, Jim. 1984. "Linguistic minorities and multicultural policy in Canada". In Edwards, 81-105.

1030 Cunningham, Irma Aloyce Ewing. 1988. "Some innovative linguistic and procedural solutions, relative to Sea Island Creole, in general; some aspects of the Sea Island Creole verbal auxiliary in particular". In *Thomas, 46-54.

1031 ---. 1992. *A Syntactic Analysis of Sea Island Creole*. (PADS, 75). Tuscaloosa, London: University of Alabama Press.

1032 Currie, Haver. 1989. "Salient developments in sociolinguistics in the United States". *Sociolinguistics* 18:65-74.

1033 Dalby, Jonathan Maker. 1984. "Phonetic structure of fast speech in American English". Ph.D., Indiana University. DAI 46 (1985), 138A.

1034 Dale, Ian. 1989. "Correlational study with a large mainframe database". In *Kretzschmar, *et al.*, 76-82.

1035 Danesi, Marcel. 1987. "*Pubilect*: observations on North American teenager talk". *LACUS* 14:433-41.

1036 Davey, William. 1985. "The stressed vowel phonemes of a New Brunswick idiolect and central/prairie Canadian English". In Lilian Falk, K. Flikeid & M. Harry, eds. 1985, *Papers from the Ninth Annual Meeting of the Atlantic Provinces Linguistic Association, November 8-9, 1985*. Fredericton, New Brunswick: University of New Brunswick, 25-32.

1037 Davis, Boyd H. 1986. "The talking word map: eliciting Southern adolescent language". In Montgomery & Bailey, 359-64.

1038 Davis, Lawrence M. 1983. "The elicitation of contextual styles in English". *JEngL* 16:18-26.

1039 ---. 1985. "The problem of social class grouping in sociolinguistic research". *AS* 60:214-21.

1040 ---. 1986. "Sampling and statistical inference in dialectology". *JEngL* 19:42-8.

1041 ---. 1988. "The limits of chi-square". In *Thomas, 225-40.

1042 --- & Charles L. Houck. 1990. "Female regional speech and occupational classification: linguistic attitudes in Hoosierdom". *AS* 65:127-35.

1043 --- & ---. 1992a. "Is there a Midland dialect?--Again". *AS* 67:61-70.

1044 --- & ---. 1992b. "Can she be prestigious and nice at the same time? Perceptions of female speech in Hoosierdom". *AS* 67:115-22.

1045 ---, --- & Brian B. Kelly. 1989. "Easily manipulatable databases for linguistic atlases: using Intergraph". In *Kretzschmar, *et al.*, 30-9.

1046 Davison, John. 1987. "On saying /aw/ in Victoria". *Toronto Working Papers in Linguistics* 7:109-22.

1047 DeBlassie, Richard R. & Juan N. Franco. 1983. "Psychological and educational assessment of bilingual children". In Donald R. Omark & Joan Good Erickson, eds. *The Bilingual Exceptional Child.* San Diego: College-Hill, 55-68.

1048 DeBose, Charles & Nicholas Faraclas. 1993. "An Africanist approach to the linguistic study of Black English: getting to the roots of the tense-aspect-modality systems in Afro-American". In *Mufwene, 364-87.

1049 Denning, Keith. 1989. "Convergence with divergence: a sound change in Vernacular Black English". *LVC* 1:145-67.

1050 Deser, Toni. 1990. "Dialect transmission and variation: an acoustic analysis of vowels in six urban Detroit families". Ph.D., Boston University. DAI 50:12 (1990), 3933-A.

1051 Devereux, Robert. 1983. "Southern Amerind lexical contributions". *Verbatim* 9:1-3.

1052 de Vries, John. 1991. "The spatial organisation of language in Canada, 1981". In Williams, 247-68.

1053 de Wolf, Gaelan Dodds. 1983. "A comparison of phonetically-ordered phonological variables in two major Canadian urban surveys". *IPAJ* 13:90-6.

1054 ---. 1985. "Methods in statistical analyses of compatible data from two major Canadian urban sociolinguistic surveys". In *Warkentyne, 191-200.

1055 ---. 1986. "Word choice in two Canadian urban surveys". In B. Hesser, *et al.*, eds. *Working Papers of the Linguistics Circle of the University of Victoria* 5:45-50.

1056 ---. 1988a. "On phonological variability in Canadian English in Ottawa and Vancouver". *IPAJ* 18:110-24.

1057 ---. 1988b. "A study of selected social and regional factors in Canadian English: A comparison of phonological variables and grammatical items in Ottawa and Vancouver". Ph.D., University of Victoria. DAI 49:9 (1988), 2639-A. (Summary in *EWW* 9:295-7).

1058 ---. 1989. "Analytical methods in a Labovian framework: a mainframe comparison of Canadian urban sociodialect data". In *Kretzschmar, *et al.*, 119-28.

1059 ---. 1990a. "Patterns of usage in urban Canadian English". *EWW* 11:1-31.

1060 ---. 1990b. "Social and regional differences in grammatical usage in Canadian English: Ottawa and Vancouver". *AS* 65:3-32.

1061 ---. 1992. *Social and Regional Factors in Canadian English. A Study of Phonological Variables and Grammatical Items in Ottawa and Vancouver*. Toronto: Canadian Scholars' Press. (Rev. in *EWW* 14:2).

1062 ---. 1993. "Local patterns and markers of speech in Vancouver English". In Clarke, 269-94.

1062a ---, ed. fc.a. *The Survey of Vancouver English, 1976-1984: A Sociolinguistic Study of Urban Canadian English*. Kingston, Ont.: Strathy Language Unit, Queen's University.

1062b ---. fc.b. "Accent and prestige in Canadian English: The pronunciation of lexical items". In de Wolf fc.a.

1062c ---. fc.c. "Social and areal roles in speech". *Proceedings of the XV International Congress of Linguists*, Québec City, Canada, August 9-15, 1992.

1062d ---. fc.d. "Word choice: Lexical variation in Canadian surveys". *JEngL* 22:2.
1063 --- & Erika L. Hasebe-Ludt. 1988. "Canadian urban survey methodology: a summary of research techniques and results". In *Thomas, 55-66.
1064 --- & ---. 1991. "The relationship of speakers' language attitudes to intervocalic voicing in formal and informal speech". In *Bahner, *et al.*, 1562-7.
1065 --- & ---. 1993. "A Linguistic Atlas of British Columbia: a first for Canadian English". In *Viereck 1993b:302-42.
1066 Diamond, Stanley. 1990. "English - the official language of California". In Adams & Brink, 11-19.
1067 Dillard, Joey L. 1985. *Toward a Social History of American English.* With a chapter on Appalachian English by Linda L. Blanton. Berlin: Mouton de Gruyter. (Rev. in *EWW* 7:321-3).
1068 ---. 1988. "Slave language". In Randal M. Miller & John David Smith, eds. *Dictionary of Afro-American Slavery*. New York: Greenwood, 391-3.
1069 ---. 1992. *A History of American English.* London, New York: Longman. (Rev. in *EWW* 13:327-8).
1070 ---. 1993. "The value (linguistic and philological) of the WPA ex-slave narratives". In *Mufwene, 222-31.
1071 --- & Shirley A. Rivers. 1989. "Dialectology in our time?: the English of the Cajuns". In *García & Otheguy, 305-17.
1072 Di Paolo, Marianna. 1986. "A study of double modals in Texas English". Ph. D., University of Texas at Austin. DAI 47:6 (1986), 2143-A. (Summary in *EWW* 8:281-2).
1073 ---. 1989. "Double modals as single lexical items". *AS* 64:224.
1074 --- & Alice Faber. 1990. "Phonation differences and the phonetic content of the tense-lax contrast in Utah English". *LVC* 2:155-204.
1075 Donahue, Thomas S. 1984. "What the sociology of language has to say about American dialectology". *LACUS* 11:460-70.
1076 ---. 1985. "'U.S. English': its life and works". *IJSL* 56:99-112.
1077 ---. 1993. "On inland northern and the factors for dialect spread and shift". In Frazer, 49-59.
1078 Dorrill, George Townsend. 1986a. *Black and White Speech in the Southern United States: Evidence from the Middle and South Atlantic States*. (BBES, 19). Frankfurt/M.: Lang. (Rev. in *EWW* 8:140-3).

1079 ---. 1986b. "A comparison of stressed vowels of black and white speakers in the south". In Montgomery & Bailey, 149-57.

1080 ---. 1989. "Linguistic Atlas of the Middle and South Atlantic States". In Wilson & Ferris, 788-9.

1081 Douaud, Patrick C. 1985. "Multilingualism as a relaxed affair: the case of the Western Canadian halfbreeds". *Teanga* 5:1-9.

1082 Downes, William. 1984. *Language and Society*. London: Fontana.

1083 Dozier, Judy Burges. 1985. "Language change in Charleston: deletion and relexicalization". *SECOLR* 9:217-35.

1084 Drake, Glendon F. 1984. "Problems of language planning in the United States". In Edwards, 141-9.

1085 Draskoy, George F. 1985. *The Terminology of Early Newfoundland Loggers*. St. John's: Government of Newfoundland and Labrador, Dept. of Culture, Recreation and Youth.

1086 Duckert, Audrey R. 1986. "The speech of rural New England". In *Allen & Linn, 136-41.

1087 --- & John T. Lowney, Jr. 1986. "From the linguistic Atlas archives: the Hanley disks". *JEngL* 19:206-21.

1088 Dyste, Connie. 1989. "Proposition 63: the California English language amendment". *AppL* 10:313-30.

1089 Eble, Connie C. 1983. "Slang: derivation or norm". *LACUS* 10:409-16.

1090 ---. 1985. "American speech in *American Speech*". *ET* 4:16-9.

1091 ---. 1986. "The subversiveness of slang". *LACUS* 13:477-82.

1092 ---. 1987. "Slang as poetry". *LACUS* 14:442-5.

1093 ---. 1988. "The ephemerality of American college slang". *LACUS* 15:457-69.

1094 ---. 1989. "College slang in the conversational structure". *LACUS* 16:451-9.

1095 ---. 1990. "Forms of address in the speech of college students". *LACUS* 17:483-7.

1096 Ebsworth, Timothy John. 1992. "Cross-cultural expectations and interpretations of appropriateness: Comparing English usage by people encultured in Puerto Rico with that of people encultured in the New York metropolitan area". Ph.D., New York University. DAI 53:3 (1992), 789-A. (Summary in *EWW* 14:2).

1097 Eckert, Penelope. 1989. "The whole woman: sex and gender differences in variation". *LVC* 1:245-67.

1098 ---. 1991. "Social polarization and the choice of linguistic variants". In *Eckert, 213-32.
1099 Edwards, John. 1991. "Gaelic in Nova Scotia". In Williams, 269-97.
1100 --- & Maryanne Jacobson. 1987. "Standard and regional standard speech: distinctions and similarities". *LinS* 16:369-80.
1101 Edwards, Walter F. 1990. "Phonetic differentiation between black and white speech in East-Side Detroit". *Word* 41:203-18.
1102 ---. 1992. "Sociolinguistic behavior in a Detroit inner-city black neighborhood". *LinS* 21:93-115.
1103 Eisenstein, Miriam R. 1989. "Dialect variation and second-language intelligibility". In Miriam R. Eisenstein, ed. *The Dynamic Interlanguage. Empirical Studies in Second Language Variation.* New York: Plenum, 175-85.
1104 Eitner, Walter. 1991. "Affirmative 'any more' in present-day American English". In *Trudgill & Chambers, 267-72.
1105 Elgin, Suzette Haden & Rebecca Haden. 1991. *A Celebration of Ozark English.* Huntsville, Ark.: Ozark Center for Language Studies.
1106 Ellis, Michael. 1992a. "Dialects". In John E. Kleber, ed. *The Kentucky Encyclopedia.* Lexington: University Press of Kentucky, 265.
1107 ---. 1992b. "On the use of dialect as evidence: *Albion's Seed* in Appalachia". *Appalachian Journal* 19:278-97.
1108 Enninger, Werner. 1984. "Funktion, Struktur und Erwerb der Varietäten Pennsylvaniadeutsch, Amisch Hochdeutsch und Amerikanisches Englisch bei den Altamischen". In Els Oksaar, ed. *Spracherwerb, Sprachkontakt, Sprachkonflikt.* Berlin: Mouton de Gruyter, 220-42.
1109 ---, ed. 1986a. *Studies on the Language and the Verbal Behavior of the Pennsylvania Germans.* I. Stuttgart: Steiner.
1110 ---. 1986b. "The ethnolinguistic profile of the Old Order Amish in transit and transition". In Winfried Herget & Karl Ortseifen, eds. *The Transit of Civilization from Europe to America.* Tübingen: Niemeyer, 197-215.
1111 ---. 1987a. "Amish English: Dutchified?". In *Lörscher & Schulze, II:547-78.
1112 ---. 1987b. "Notes on the receding contact-influences of (Pennsylvania–) German on English". In Enninger & Stolz, 99-125.
1113 ---. 1987c. "On the organization of sign-processes in an Old Order Amish (OOA) school". *Research in Language and Social Interaction* 21:143-70.

1114 ---, *et al*. 1984. "The English of the Old Order Amish of Delaware: phonological, morpho-syntactical and lexical variation of English in the language contact situation of a trilingual speech community". *EWW* 5:1-24.

1115 Escott, Paul D. 1991. "Speaking of slavery: the historical value of the recordings with former slaves". In Bailey, *et al*., 123-32.

1116 Esling, John H. 1986. "Some analyses of vowels by social group in the survey of Vancouver English". *Working Papers of the Linguistic Circle of the University of Victoria* 5:21-32.

1117 ---. 1987. "Vowel shift and long term average spectra in the survey of Vancouver English". *Proceedings of the Eleventh International Congress of the Phonetic Sciences,* Vol. 5. Tallin: Academy of Sciences of the Estonian S.S.R., 243-6.

1118 ---. 1991. "Sociophonetic variation in Vancouver". In *Cheshire, 123-33.

1118a ---. fc. "Vowel systems and voice setting in the Survey of Vancouver English". In de Wolf fc.a.

1119 --- & Henry J. Warkentyne. 1993. "Retracting of /æ/ in Vancouver English". In Clarke, 229-46.

1120 Esman, Milton J. 1985. "The politics of official bilingualism in Canada". In William R. Beer & James E. Jacob, eds. *Language Policy and National Unity*. Totowa, N.J.: Rowman & Allanheld, 45-66.

1121 Etter-Lewis, Gwendolyn. 1985. "Sociolinguistic patterns of code switching in the language of preschool black children". Ph.D., University of Michigan. DAI 46:7 (1986), 1920-A. (Summary in *EWW* 7:276-7).

1122 Evans, William W. 1989. "Literary dialect [in the South]". In Wilson & Ferris, 775-7.

1123 Falk-Banó, Klára. 1988. "Characteristics of language shift in two American Hungarian bilingual communities". *PSCL* 24:161-70.

1124 Faries, Rachel B. & Donald M. Lance. 1993. "Regional variation in Missouri". In Frazer, 245-56.

1125 Fasold, Ralph W, *et al*. 1987. "Are black and white vernaculars diverging? Papers from the NWAVE XIV panel discussion". *AS* 62:62-80.

1126 Feagin, Crawford. 1986a. "More evidence for major vowel change in the South". In *Sankoff, 83-95.

1127 ---. 1986b. "Competing norms in the white speech of Anniston, Alabama". In Montgomery & Bailey, 216-34.

1128 ---. 1990a. "The dynamics of sound change in southern states English: from r-less to r-ful in three generations". In *Edmondson, *et al.*, 129-46.

1129 ---. 1990b. "Two vowel shifts in Southern States English: an acoustic study of change in progress". In Bahner, *et al.*, 1357-60.

1130 ---. 1991. "Preverbal *done* in Southern States English". In *Trudgill & Chambers, 161-90.

1130a Fee, Margery. 1988. "Post-Fowlerism: The problem of a usage guide for Canadians". In T.K. Pratt, ed. *Papers from the Twelfth Annual Meeting of the Atlantic Provinces Linguistic Association*. Charlottetown: University of Prince Edward Island, 22-30.

1131 Feng, Jian. 1987. "Remarks on modern American slang". *Waiguoyu* 5(51):43-7. [in Chinese]

1132 Fenno, Charles R. 1983. "Nineteenth-century Illinois dialect: Robert Casey". *AS* 58:244-54.

1133 Ferrara, Kathleen. 1986. "Morphological explanations of Chicano writing needs". *LACUS* 13:483-96.

1134 Finegan, Edward. 1985. "Unconscious attitudes towards linguistic variation". In *Greenbaum, 92-8.

1135 Fishman, Joshua A. 1984a. "Mother tongue claiming in the United States since 1960: trends and correlates related to the revival of ethnicity". *IJSL* 50:21-99.

1136 ---. 1984b. "Studies of language as an aspect of ethnicity and nationalism (a bibliographic introduction)". *Sociolinguistics* 14:1-6.

1137 Flanigan, Beverly Olson. 1985. "American Indian English and error analysis: the case of Lakota English". *EWW* 6:217-36.

1138 ---. 1987. "Language variation among native Americans: observations on Lakota English". *JEngL* 20:181-99.

1139 Flores-Caraballo, Eliut Daniel. 1991. "The politics of culture in Puerto Rican television: A macro/micro study of English vs. Spanish language television usage". Ph.D., University of Texas at Austin. DAI 52:7 (1992), 2309-A. (Summary in *EWW* 13:280-1).

1140 Forbes, Jack D., *et al.* 1984. "The use of the terms 'negro' and 'black' to include persons of native American ancestry in 'Anglo' North America". *Explorations in Ethnic Studies* 7:11-26.

1141 Ford, Cecilia E. 1984. "The influence of speech variety on teachers' evaluation of students with comparable academic ability". *TESOLQ* 18:25-40.

1142 Forgue, Guy Jean. 1983. "L'anglais américain". *RFEA* 8(18):395-461.
1143 Fourakis, Marios. 1990. "Tempo, stress, and vowel reduction in American English". *Journal of the Acoustical Society of America* 90 (4/1):1816-27.
1144 Francis, W. Nelson. 1993. "The historical and cultural interpretation of dialect". In Preston, 13-30.
1145 Frazer, Timothy C. 1983a. "Language variation in the military tract". *Western Illinois Regional Studies* 5:54-64.
1146 ---. 1983b. "Cultural assimilation in the post-frontier era: linguistic atlas evidence". *Midwestern Journal of Language and Folklore* 9:5-23.
1147 ---. 1983c. "Sound change and social structure in a rural community". *LinS* 12:313-28.
1148 ---. 1986. "Microdialectology: internal variation in a LANCS community". *AS* 61:307-17.
1149 ---. 1987a. "Attitudes towards regional pronunciation". *JEngL* 20:89-100.
1150 ---. 1987b. *Midland Illinois Dialect Patterns*. (PADS, 73). University, Ala: University of Alabama Press.
1151 ---. 1987c. "Breaking new ground in dialectology". *AS* 62:154-9.
1152 ---. 1988. "Commercial television as a source of language data". In *Thomas, 89-94.
1153 ---. 1990a. "'Midwestern English': facts and fictions". *KanQ* 22:5-14.
1154 ---. 1990b. "More on the semantics of a-prefixing". *AS* 65:89-93.
1155 ---, ed. 1993a. *'Heartland' English. Variation and Transition in the American Midwest*. Tuscaloosa, Ala.: University of Alabama Press.
1156 ---. 1993b. "Problems in Midwest English: Introduction and overview". In Frazer, 1-22.
1157 ---. 1993c. "The language of Yankee cultural imperialism: Pioneer ideology and 'General American'". In Frazer, 59-66.
1158 ---. fc.a. "Perception and gender in Virginia speech: The case of /aw/". *AS*.
1159 ---. fc.b. "On transition areas and the 'Midland' dialect: a reply to Davis and Houck". *AS*.
1160 Galang, Rosita. 1988. "The language situation of Filipino Americans". In McKay & Wong, 229-51.
1161 Galindo, Delma Letticia. 1987. "Linguistic influence and variation on the English of Chicano adolescents in Austin, Texas". Ph.D., University of Texas at Austin. DAI 48:10 (1988), 2616-A. (Summary in *EWW* 9:298).

1162 Galinsky, Hans. repr. 1985. *Das amerikanische Englisch: seine innere Entwicklung und internationale Ausstrahlung. Ein kritischer Forschungsbericht als Einführung in die Grundlegungsphase der sprachwissenschaftlichen Amerikanistik. (1919-1945).* Darmstadt: Wissenschaftliche Buchgesellschaft.

1163 Gallardo, Andres. 1984. *The Standardization of American English.* Concepción: University de Concepción.

1164 Garcia, Eugene E. 1984. "Early childhood bilingualism". In Garcia, *et al.*, 209-26.

1165 ---, Francisco A. Lomeli & Isidro D. Ortiz, eds. 1984. *Chicano Studies: a Multidisciplinary Approach*. New York: Teachers' College Press.

1166 Garcia, John A., Theresa Córdova & Juan R. Garcia, eds. 1984. *The Chicano Struggle: Analyses of Past and Present Efforts*. Binghamton, N.Y.: Bilingual Press.

1167 García, Maryellen. 1984. "Parameters of the East Los Angeles speech community". In Ornstein-Galicia, 85-98.

1168 García, Ofelia. 1983. "Sociolinguistics and language planning in bilingual education for Hispanics in the United States". *IJSL* 44:43-54.

1169 ---. 1984. "La problemática del idioma en el ensayo puertorriqueno: proyecciones de la sociolinguistica". *Circulo* 13:79-86.

1170 ---. 1985. "Bilingualism in the United States: present attitudes in the light of past policies". In *Greenbaum, 147-58.

1171 Garner, T. & D.L. Rubin. 1986. "Middle class blacks' perceptions of dialect and style shifting: the case of southern attorneys". *JLSP* 5:33-48.

1172 Garigue, Philippe. 1985. "Bilingual university education in Ontario". *CMLR* 41:941-6.

1173 Gee, James Paul. 1989. "Two styles of narrative construction and their linguistic and educational implications". *Discourse Processes* 12:287-307.

1174 Gilbert, Glenn G. 1986. "The English of the Brandywine population: a triracial isolate in southern Maryland". In Montgomery & Bailey, 102-10.

1175 ---. 1993. "Historical development of the creole origin hypothesis of Black English: the pivotal role of Melville J. Herskovits". In *Mufwene, 458-75.

1176 Gilyard, R. Keith. 1986. "Voicing myself: a study of sociolinguistic competence". Ph.D., New York University. DAI 46:12 (1986), 3636-A.

1177 Girard, Dennis & Donald Larmouth. 1988. "Log-linear statistical models: explaining the dynamics of dialect diffusion". In *Thomas, 251-77.
1178 --- & ---. 1993. "Some applications of mathematical and statistical models in dialect geography". In Preston, 107-32.
1179 Godinez, Manuel, Jr. 1984. "Chicano English phonology: norms vs. interference phenomena". In Ornstein-Galicia, 42-8.
1180 --- & Ian Maddieson. 1985. "Vowel differences between Chicano and general Californian English?". *IJSL* 53:43-58.
1181 Görlach, Manfred. 1987. "Die Stellung des kanadischen Englisch". *Zeitschrift der Gesellschaft für Kanada-Studien* 7:133-45.
1182 ---. 1991. "The identity of Canadian English". In *Görlach, 108-21.
1183 Gold, David L. 1984. "More on a Dutch-origin word in New York City English". *Leuvense Bijdragen* 73:171-5.
1184 ---. 1985. "Askenazic English *to sit shive*". *AS* 60:368-70.
1185 ---. 1986. "Still more on the origin of New York City English *Sliding Pon(d)*". *Leuvense Bijdragen* 75:335-57.
1186 Goldberg, John R. 1989. "/au/ - a variable of Kansas English". *Orbis* 33:187-94.
1187 Goldman, Lorraine. 1986. "Tex-Mex: Where Texas, Mexico, English & Spanish meet". *ET* 5:23-6.
1188 Goldstein, Lynn Meg. 1986. "Linguistic variation in English as a second language as a function of contact versus identification". Ph.D., Columbia University. DAI 47:3 (1986), 887-A. (Summary in *EWW* 8:283-4).
1189 ---. 1987. "Standard English: the only target for nonnative speakers of English?". *TESOLQ* 21:417-36.
1190 Gonzáles, Gustavo. 1984. "The range of Chicano English". In Ornstein-Galicia, 32-41.
1191 ---. 1988. "Chicano English". In Bixler-Márquez & Ornstein-Galicia, 71-82.
1192 Goodwin, Marjorie Harness. 1990. *He-Said-She-Said: Talk as Social Organization among Black Children*. Bloomington, Indianapolis: Indiana UP. (Rev. in *EWW* 12:332-3).
1193 Gozzi, Raymond D., Jr. 1987. "New words in American English: a study in language, technology and social reality". Ph.D., University of Massachusetts. DAI 49:3 (1988), 380-A.
1194 ---. 1990. *New Words and a Changing American Culture*. Columbia: University of South Carolina Press.

1195 Graff, David, William Labov & Wendell A. Harris. 1986. "Testing listeners' reactions to phonological markers of ethnic identity: a new method for sociolinguistic research". In *Sankoff, 45-58.

1196 Gregg, Robert J. 1983. "Local lexical items in the sociodialectical survey of Vancouver English". *CJL* 28:17-23.

1197 ---. 1984. *An Urban Dialect Survey of the English Spoken in Vancouver*. Final Report to the Social Sciences and Humanities Research Council of Canada, Ottawa. Univ. of British Columbia: Linguistics Department.

1198 ---. 1985. "The Vancouver survey: grammatical usage". In *Warkentyne, 179-84.

1199 ---. 1986. "The standard and where we stand now". In Lougheed, 157-68.

1200 ---. 1988. "The study of linguistic change in the Survey of Vancouver English". In *Thomas, 434-41.

1201 ---. 1991. "The survival of local lexical items as specific markers in Vancouver English". *Orbis* 34:231-41.

1202 ---. 1992. "The Survey of Vancouver English". *AS* 67:250-67.

1203 ---. 1993. "Canadian English lexicography". In Clarke, 27-44.

1203a ---. fc. "The Survey of Vancouver English: Planning, implementation and analysis". In de Wolf fc.a.

1204 ---, *et al.* 1985. "The Vancouver survey: analysis and measurement". In *Warkentyne, 179-200.

1205 Guy, Gregory R. 1991. "Explanation in variable phonology: An exponential model of morphological constraints". *LVC* 3:1-22

1206 ---. 1993. "The quantitative analysis of linguistic variation". In Preston, 223-50.

1207 Habick, Timothy. 1991. "Burnouts versus rednecks: effects of group membership on the phonemic system". In *Eckert, 185-212.

1208 ---. 1993. "Farmer City, Illinois: sound system shifting South". In Frazer, 97-124.

1209 Haden, Rebecca. 1993a. "Speaking Baptist". *Ozark English Quarterly* 1:3-4.

1210 ---. 1993b. "The Ozark which-that, which we now know what it means". *Ozark English Quarterly* 1:5-6.

1211 ---. 1993c. "Notes on the for-to complement in Ozark English". *Ozark English Quarterly* 1:7-8.

1212 ---. 1993d. "School talk and cool talk". *Ozark English Quarterly* 1:8.

1213 Hall, Joan. 1986. "Black speech: lexical evidence from DARE". In Montgomery & Bailey, 319-32.
1214 ---. 1988. "Caught in the web of change". In *Thomas, 557-68.
1215 Hancock, Ian. 1986a. "On the classification of Afro-Seminole". In Montgomery & Bailey, 85-101.
1216 ---. 1986b. "The cryptolectal speech of the American roads: traveler cant and American Angloromani". *AS* 61:206-20.
1217 Hansen, Renee Elise. 1984. "Categorization preference and lexical ambiguity among black second grade children". Ph.D., New York University.
1218 Harris, Barbara P. 1985. "The Vancouver Survey: self-image, perception of stereotypes and language variants". In *Warkentyne, 201-10.
1219 ---. 1989. "Metaphor as a productive process in the formation of nominal compounds: Canadian English". *Pacific Coast Philology* 24:62-71.
1220 Hartmann, James W. 1984. "Some possible trends in the pronunciation of young Americans (maybe)". *AS* 59:220-5.
1221 ---. 1985. "Guide to pronunciation". In Cassidy, 41-61.
1222 Hasebe-Ludt, Erika. 1985. "The Vancouver survey: analysis and measurement: methodology of spontaneous speech analysis". In *Warkentyne, 197-200.
1223 Haskins, Jim & Hugh F. Butts. 1987. "America's debt to the language of black Americans". In Errol Hill, ed. *The Theater of Black Americans: A Collection of Critical Essays*. New York: Applause, 79-88.
1224 Hastings, Pat. 1983. "Age stratification of (u) in Lillian, Texas". In *Edmondson, 37-57.
1225 Hatfield, Deborah Helen. 1986. "Tense marking in the spoken English of Vietnamese refugees". Ph.D., Georgetown University. DAI 47:12 (1987), 4377-A.
1226 Hausmann, Robert B. 1988. "Linguistics and dialectology: controlling strange data". In *Thomas, 285-305.
1227 Heap, Norman A. 1983. *A Word List from Bucks County, Pennsylvania, 1850-1876*. (PADS, 70). University, Ala: University of Alabama Press.
1228 Hecht, Michael. 1987. "Afro-American identity labels and communication effectiveness". *JLSP* 6:319-26.
1229 Heiser, Margaret. 1982 [1985]. "Verb forms of the Western Reserve Area in Northeastern Ontario". *Orbis* 31:72-86.

1230 Heller, Monica. 1985. "Ethnic relations and language use in Montréal". In *Wolfson & Manes, 75-90.
1231 Hendrickson, Robert. 1987. *American Talk: The Words and Ways of American Dialect*. New York: Penguin.
1232 Hensey, Fritz G. 1984. "Chicano English in literary and oral media". In Ornstein-Galicia, 176-205.
1233 Herndobler, Robin. 1993. "Sound change and gender in a working class community". In Frazer, 137-56.
1234 Herold, Ruth, 1990, "Mechanisms of merger: the implementation and distribution of the low merger in Eastern Pennsylvania". Ph.D., University of Pennsylvania. DAI 51:5 (1990), 1596-A.
1235 Hewson, John. 1983. "The speech of nations". *CJL* 28:33-46.
1236 Hinton, Leanne. 1987. "It's not just the valley girls: a study of Californian English". *Berkeley Linguistics Society* 13:117-28.
1237 Hirshberg, Jeffrey. 1984. "The mythical hedgehogs of North Carolina: a note on lexicographical method". *AS* 59:281-3.
1238 Hiscock, Philip. 1989. "Newfoundland folklore and language: a bibliography". *RLS* 12:2-56.
1239 Hollett, Robert C. 1982. "Linguistic research in Newfoundland". *RLS* 10:11-4.
1240 ---. 1987. "Linguistic research in Newfoundland". *RLS* 11:21-30.
1241 Holm, John, 1991. "The Atlantic creoles and the language of the ex-slave recordings". In *Bailey, *et al.*, 231-48.
1242 Holton, Sylvia Wallace. 1985. *Down Home and Uptown: The Representation of Black Speech in American Fiction*. Rutherford, N.J.: Fairleigh Dickinson UP.
1243 Hopkins, Tometro. 1992. "Issues in the study of Afro-creoles: Afro-Cuban and Gullah". Ph.D., Indiana University. DAI 53:6 (1992), 1889-A. (Summary in *EWW* 14:2).
1244 ---. fc. "Aspects of the use of the auxiliary də in Gullah". In *Montgomery fc.a.
1245 Hudson, Barbara Hill. 1982. "A descriptive study of male and female speech stereotypes on selected television shows with predominantly black characters". Ph.D., Howard University. DAI 44:10 (1984), 3049-A.
1246 Huffines, Marion Lois. 1984a. "Language contact across generations: the English of the Pennsylvania Germans". In Wolfgang W. Moelleken,

ed. *Dialectology, Linguistics, Literature: Festschrift for Carol E. Reed*. Göppingen: Kümmerle, 93-103.

1247 ---. 1984b. "Word gain and loss in the English of the Pennsylvania Germans". *Pennsylvania Folklife* 34:30-3.

1248 ---. 1984c. "The English of the Pennsylvania Germans: a reflection of the ethnic affiliation". *The German Quarterly* 57:173-82.

1249 ---. 1986. "Strategies of language maintenance and ethnic marking among the Pennsylvania Germans". *Language Sciences* 8:1-16.

1250 Hung, Henrietta. 1987. "Canadian raising à la Montréalaise". *Toronto Working Papers in Linguistics* 7:123-39.

1251 ---, John Davison & Jack K. Chambers. 1993. "Comparative sociolinguistics of (aw) fronting". In Clarke, 247-67.

1252 Huspek, Michael R. 1986. "Linguistic variation, context and meaning: a case of *ing/in'* variation in North American workers' speech". *LinS* 15:149-63.

1253 Ikemiya, Tsuneko. 1988. "Acoustic comparative study of contradictory /a:/ and /ae/ between Maine dialect and general American". In *Thomas, 306-25.

1254 Ingram, Charles Emerson. 1989. Attitudes of sixth-grade teachers toward standard and nonstandard dialects, bidialectalism, and sociolinguistics". Ph.D., Georgia State University. DAI 50:12 (1990), 3875-A. (Summary in *EWW* 12:291).

1255 Isajiw, Wsevolod W. 1990. "Ethnic identity retention in four ethnic groups: does it matter?". *Journal of Baltic Studies* 21:289-304.

1256 Jacobson, Phyllis L. 1984. "The social context of Franco-American schooling in New England". *The French Review* 57:641-56.

1257 Jacobson, Rodolfo. 1985. "Uncovering the covert bilingual: how to retrieve the hidden home language". In *Garcia & Padilla, 150-80.

1258 Jameson, W.C. 1991. "The language of the trail drivers: an examination of the origin and diffusion of an industry-oriented vocabulary". *Journal of American Culture* 14:117-20.

1259 Jay, Timothy. 1992. *Cursing in America: A Psychological Study of Dirty Language in the Courts, in the Movies, in the Schoolyards and on the Streets*. Amsterdam, Philadelphia: Benjamins.

1260 Johnson, Ellen. 1992. "Lexical change and variation in the southeastern United States in the twentieth century". Ph.D., University of Georgia.

1261 ---. fc. "The distribution of variants of /ai/ in the Middle and South Atlantic States". In *Viereck.

1262 Johnstone, Barbara. 1992. "Violence and civility in discourse: uses of mitigation by rural southern white men". *SECOLR* 16:1-19.

1263 Jolly, Grace, Lily Gaudreault, Francine Paradis & John Darbelnet. 1983. "La codification de l'anglais canadien". In *Bédard & Maurais, 731-62.

1264 Jones-Jackson, Patricia. 1983. "Contemporary Gullah speech: some persistent linguistic features". *Journal of Black Studies* 13:289-303.

1265 ---. 1984. "On decreolization and language death in Gullah". *LinS* 13:351-62.

1266 ---. 1986. "On the status of Gullah on the Sea Islands". In Montgomery & Bailey, 63-72.

1267 ---. 1987. *When Roots Die: Endangered Traditions on the Sea Islands.* Athens, London: The University of Georgia Press. (Rev. in *EWW* 9:343-5).

1268 Joyner, Charles. 1984. *Down by the Riverside: A South Carolina Slave Community.* Urbana, Chicago: University of Illinois Press.

1269 ---. 1986. "'If you ain't got education': slave language and slave thought in antebellum Charleston". In Michael O'Brian & David Moltke-Hansen; eds. *Intellectual Life in Antebellum Charleston.* Knoxville: University of Tennessee Press, 255-78.

1270 ---. 1989. "Creolization". In Wilson & Ferris, 147-9.

1271 Karhu, Carolyn G. 1988. "Tennessee prison talk". *AS* 63: 125-36.

1272 Kent-Paxton, Laura Belle. 1983. "A linguistic analysis of the diaries of M.E. Anderson-Kent, pioneer woman". Ph.D., East Texas State University. DAI 44:6 (1983), 1777-A.

1273 Kettemann, Bernhard. 1988. *Die Phonologie morphologischer Prozesse im amerikanischen Englisch.* Tübingen: Narr. (Rev. in *EWW* 10:328-34).

1274 Kilbury, James. 1983. "Talking about phonemics: centralized diphthongs in a Chicago-area idiolect". In Frederick B. Agard, *et al.*, eds. *Essays in Honor of Charles F. Hockett.* Leiden: Brill, 336-41.

1275 King, Ruth & Robert Ryan. 1988. "The construction of a rural sociolinguistic corpus: the Prince Edward Island study". In *Thomas, 95-108.

1276 Kingscott, Geoffrey. 1991. "The language professional's guide to ...: the Canadian language question". *Language International: The Magazine for the Language Professions* 3(3):23-26.

1277 Kinloch, A.M. 1985. "The English language in New Brunswick 1784-1984". In Reavley Gair, ed. *A Literary and Linguistic History of New*

Brunswick. Fredericton: Fiddlehead Poetry Books & Goose Lane Editions, 59-74.

1278 Kinloch, A.M. & Walter Avis. 1989. "Central Canadian English and Received Standard English: a comparison of pronunciation". In *García & Otheguy, 403-20.

1279 Kirk, John M. & William A. Kretzschmar, Jr. 1992. "Interactive linguistic mapping of dialect features". *Literary and Linguistic Computing* 7:168-75. [= 559]

1280 Kirwin, William J. 1982. "Bibliography of writings on Newfoundland English". *RLS* 10:25.

1281 ---. 1987. "Bibliography of writings on Newfoundland English". *RLS* 11:30.

1282 ---. 1988. "How the Newfoundland *Dictionary* is faring". *This Land* 3(3):38-9, 92, 94, 97.

1283 ---. 1991. "The rise and fall of dialect representation in Newfoundland writings". In Thomas & Widdowson, 227-44.

1284 ---. 1993. "The planting of Anglo-Irish in Newfoundland". In Clarke, 65-84.

1285 --- & G.M. Story. 1986. "The etymology of *High liner*: problems of inclusion in *The Dictionary of Newfoundland English*". *AS* 61:281-4.

1286 Knack, Rebecca. 1991. "Ethnic boundaries in linguistic variation". In *Eckert, 251-72.

1287 Kniesza, Veronika. 1984. "The origin and originality of American English dialects". In Tibor Frank, ed. *The Origin and Originality of American Culture*. Budapest: Akadémiai Kiadó, 691-9.

1288 Kochman, Thomas. 1986. "Strategic ambiguity in black speech genres: cross-cultural interference in participant-observation research". *Text* 6:153-70.

1289 Koerner, Konrad. 1988. "The sources of modern sociolinguistics". *LACUS* 15:343-53.

1290 ---. 1991. "Toward a history of modern sociolinguistics". *AS* 66:57-70.

1291 Koike, D.A. 1987. "Code switching in the bilingual Chicano narrative". *Hispania* 70:148-54.

1292 Kokolis, James F. 1986. "Revisiting Armstrong County, Pennsylvania, dialect through Kittaning High School Seniors". Ph.D., Indiana University of Pennsylvania. DAI 48:1 (1987), 118-A. (Summary in *EWW* 9:303).

1293 Kontra, Miklós. 1981. "Language usage: an interview with a Hungarian American". *Hungarian Studies Review* 8:99-118.

1294 ---. 1985. "Hungarian-American bilingualism: a bibliographic essay". *Hungarian Studies* 1:257-82.

1295 Kratz, H. 1983. "Sociolinguistic aspects of Fanny Trollope's picture of American English". *Orbis* 30:80-94.

1296 Kretzschmar, William A., Jr. 1984. "Computer needs". In *Needed Research in American English (1983)*, 71-6.

1297 ---. 1988. "Computers and the American Linguistic Atlas". In *Thomas, 200-24.

1298 ---. 1990. "Modern American dialect study". In G. Caie, *et al.*, eds. *Proceedings from the 4th Nordic Conference for English Studies.* Copenhagen: University of Copenhagen, Vol. 1:231-41.

1299 ---. 1991. "Whither dialectology I". *Quaderni di Semantica* 24:257-62.

1300 ---. 1992a. "Isoglosses and predictive modeling". *AS* 67:227-49.

1301 ---. 1992b. "Dialects: traditions in culture and innovation in analysis". In W.J. Davey & Bernard LeVert, eds. *Papers from the Fifteenth Annual Meeting of the Atlantic Provinces Linguistic Association.* Sydney, NS: UCCB, SSHRC, 38-63.

1302 ---. 1992c. "Interactive computer mapping for the Linguistic Atlas of the Middle and South Atlantic States (LAMSAS)". In *Hall, *et al.*, 400-14.

1303 ---. 1992d. "Where is dialectology going? II". *Quaderni di Semantica* 25:115-21.

1304 --- & Jay Lee. fc. "Linguistic studies with GIS". *International Journal of GIS.*

1305 --- & Edgar W. Schneider. fc. *Postmodern Dialectology: Computers, Statistics, and the Linguistic Atlas of the Middle and South Atlantic States (LAMSAS).*

1306 ---, Virginia G. McDavid, Theodore K. Lerud & Ellen Johnson, eds. 1993. *Handbook of the Linguistic Atlas of the Middle and South Atlantic States.* Chicago, London: University of Chicago Press.

1307 Krzyston, S.S., Nelleke Van-Deusen & Jerrie Scott. 1987. "Listener's response to regional and ethnic accents in broadcasting". *SECOLR* 11:115-34.

1308 Kuiper, Koenraad. 1992. "The oral tradition in auction speech". *AS* 67:279-89.

1309 --- & Frederick Tillis. 1985. "The chant of the tobacco auctioneer". *AS* 60:141-9.
1309a Kytö, Merja. 1991. *Variation and Diachrony, with Early American Englishin Focus.* (BBES, 28). Frankfurt/M.: Lang. (Rev. in *EWW* 13:124-9).
1310 Labov, Teresa. 1992. "Social and language boundaries among adolescents". *AS* 67:339-66.
1311 Labov, William. 1983. "Recognizing black English in the classroom". In Chambers, 29-55.
1312 ---. 1984. "Field methods of the project on linguistic change". In John Baugh & J. Sherzer, eds. *Language in Use: Readings in Sociolinguistics*. Englewood Cliffs, N.J.: Prentice-Hall, 26-66.
1313 ---. 1987. "The interpretation of zeroes". In Wolfgang U. Dressler, *et al.*, eds. *Phonologica 1984*. London: Cambridge UP, 135-56.
1314 ---. 1989. "The exact description of the speech community: short *a* in Philadelphia". In *Fasold & Schiffrin, 1-57.
1315 ---. 1990. "The intersection of sex and social class in the course of linguistic change". *LVC* 2:205-54.
1316 ---. 1991a. "The three dialects of English". In *Eckert, 1-44.
1317 ---. 1991b. "The boundaries of a grammar: inter-dialectal reactions to positive *any more*". In *Trudgill & Chambers, 273-88.
1318 --- & Wendell A. Harris. 1986. "De facto segregation of black and white vernaculars". In *Sankoff, 1-24.
1319 ---, Mark Karen & Corey Miller. 1991. "Near-mergers and the suspension of phonemic contrast". *LVC* 3:33-74.
1320 Labrie, Normand. 1987/88. "Canada". In *Ammon, *et al.*, 1307-13.
1321 Lance, Donald M. 1993. "Some dialect features in the speech of Missouri Germans". In Frazer, 187-98.
1322 Landry, Rodrigue & Real Allard. 1990. "Contact des langues et dévelopement bilingue: un modèle macroscopique". *CMLR* 46:527-53.
1323 Lardner, David F. 1991. "Dreams reflected: The Ann Arbor King School 'Black English' case". Ph.D., University of Michigan. DAI 52:7 (1992), 2444-A. (Summary in *EWW* 13:283-4).
1324 Larmouth, Donald W. 1990. "Belgian English in Wisconsin's Door Peninsula". *KanQ* 22:135-41.
1325 --- & Marjorie Remsing. 1993. "'Kentuck' English in Wisconsin's cutover region". In Frazer, 215-28.

1326 Lass, Roger & Jo-Anne W. Higgs, 1984. "Phonetics and language history: American /r/ as a candidate for an archaism". *Occasional Papers in Linguistics and Language Learning* 9:91-109.
1327 Lavely, Marcia Marvin. 1991. "A study of American literature which incorporates the use of the Gullah dialect". Ph.D., The University of Mississippi. DAI 53:5 (1992), 1501-A. (Summary in *EWW* 14:2).
1328 Lay, Clarry H. 1989. "Responses to French-Canadian accented English speech: the role of context". *JLSP* 8:321-5.
1329 Leap, William. 1992. "American Indian English". In John Reyhner, ed. *Teaching American Indian Students*. Norman, Okla.: University of Oklahoma Press, 143-53.
1330 Lederer, Richard M., Jr. 1985. *Colonial American English, A Glossary*. Essex, Conn.: Verbatim.
1331 Levine, Marc V. 1990. *The Reconquest of Montreal: Language Policy and Social Change in a Bilingual City*. Philadelphia: Temple UP.
1332 Lindsey, Geoff. 1990. "Quantity and quality in British and American vowel systems". In *Ramsaran, 106-18.
1333 Linn, Michael D. 1983. "Informant selection in dialectology". *AS* 58:225-43.
1334 ---. 1988. "The origin and development of the Iron Range dialect in northern Minnesota". *SAP* 21:75-87.
1335 ---. 1990. "The development of dialect patterns in the Upper Midwest". *KanQ* 22:15-28.
1336 ---. 1993. "Resources for research". In Preston, 433-52.
1337 --- & Ronald R. Regal. 1988. "Verb analysis of the Linguistic Atlas of the North Central States: a case study in preliminary analysis of a large data set". In *Thomas, 138-54.
1338 --- & ---. 1993. "Missing data and computer mapping". In *Viereck 1993a:253-67.
1339 Lipski, John M. 1993. "*Y'all* in American English: from black to white, from phrase to pronoun". *EWW* 14:23-56.
1340 Lissewski, Monika. 1991. *Early Black English in South Carolina: Variation und Kovariation morphologischer und syntaktischer Varianten*. Trier: Wissenschaftlicher Verlag Trier. (Rev. in *EWW* 13:306-14.)
1341 Little, Greta & Michael B. Montgomery, eds. fc. *Centennial Usage Studies*. (PADS, 78). Tuscaloosa, Ala.: University of Alabama Press.
1342 Logue, Cal M. 1989. "Oratory". In Wilson & Ferris, 781-2.

1343 Lougheed, W.C., ed. 1986. *In Search of the Standard in Canadian English*. Kingston, Ontario: Queen's University, Strathy Language Unit. (Rev. in *EWW* 9:319-21).

1344 ---. 1987. *Writings on Canadian English, 1976-1987: A Selective/Annotated Bibliography*. Kingston, Ontario: Queen's University, Strathy Language Unit. (Rev. in *EWW* 11:163).

1345 Lowy, Esther G., *et al.* 1983. "Ethnic activists view the ethnic revival and its language consequences: an interview study of three American ethnolinguistic minorities". *JMMD* 4:237-54.

1346 Lucas, Ceil. 1986. "I ain't got none/you don't have any: noticing and correcting variation in the classroom". In Montgomery & Bailey, 348-58.

1347 Luhman, Ried. 1990. "Appalachian English stereotypes: language attitudes in Kentucky". *LinS* 19:331-48.

1348 Luthin, Herbert W. 1987. "The story of California (ow): The coming-of-age of English in California". In *Denning, 312-24.

1349 Lux, Paul A. 1991. "Discourse styles of Anglo and Latin American college student writers". Ph.D., Arizona State University. DAI 52:6 (1991), 2128-A.

1350 McArthur, Tom. 1989. *The English Language as Used in Quebec: a Survey*. Kingston, Ontario: Queen's University, Strathy Language Unit. (Rev. in *EWW* 11:163.4).

1351 Macauly, Marcia I. 1990. *Processing Varieties in English: An Examination of Oral and Written Speech across Genres*. Vancouver: University of British Columbia Press.

1352 McDaniel, Susan Leas. 1989a. "Databases of the LAGS Automatic Atlas". In *Kretzschmar, *et al.*, 63-8.

1353 ---. 1989b. "Urban speech [in the South]". In Wilson & Ferris, 784-5.

1354 McDavid, Raven I., Jr. 1984a. "The failure of intuition". *SECOLR* 8:128-39.

1355 ---. 1984b. "Lessons learned in half a century: experience of a practicing dialectologist". In Ornstein-Galicia, 117-34.

1356 ---. 1984c. "Linguistic geography". In *Needed Research in American English (1983)*, 4-31.

1357 ---. 1985a. "American dialectology: a historical perspective". In *Warkentyne, 13-34.

1358 ---. 1985b. "Eliciting: direct, indirect, and oblique". *AS* 60:305-17.

1359 ---. 1985c. "A linguist to the lay audience". In *Greenbaum, 280-92.

1360 --- & Theodore Lerud. 1984. "German relics in the English of South Carolina". In Wolfgang Moelleken, ed. *Dialectology, Linguistics, Literature: Festschrift for Carol E. Reed.* Göppingen: Kümmerle, 133-49.

1361 --- & Virginia G. McDavid. 1985. "Fries and linguistic geography". In Peter Howard Fries & Nancy M. Fries, eds. *Towards an Understanding of Language: Charles Carpenter Fries in Perspective.* Amsterdam: Benjamins, 221-35.

1362 --- & ---. 1986. "Kentucky verb forms". In Montgomery & Bailey, 264-93.

1363 ---, ---, William A. Kretschmar, Jr., Theodore K. Lerud & Martha Rutcliff. 1986. "Inside a linguistic atlas". *Proceedings of the American Philosophical Society* 130:390-405.

1364 McDavid, Virginia G. 1988. "Sex-linked differences among atlas informants: irregular verbs". In *Thomas, 333-61.

1365 ---. 1990. "Irregular verb forms in Michigan, Wisconsin, and Minnesota: education attainment and gender differences". *KanQ* 22:31-43.

1366 McDonald, Marguerite Goodrich. 1985. "Cuban-American English: the second generation in Miami". Ph.D., University of Florida. DAI 47:2 (1986), 520-A. (Summary in *EWW* 8:290-1).

1367 ---. 1989. "Sociolinguistic variation and the multidimensional model of acculturation". *RLA: Romance Languages Annual* 1:677-81

1368 McKay, Sandra Lee. 1989. "The role of English in the Philippines, the United States, and South Africa". *TESOL Newsletter* 23:21,23.

1369 --- & Sau-ling Cynthia Wong, eds. 1988. *Language Diversity: Problem or Resource? A Social and Educational Perspective on Language Minorities in the United States.* Cambridge, Mass.: Newbury House.

1370 McMillan, James B. & Michael B. Montgomery. 1989. *Annotated Bibliography of Southern American English.* Tuscaloosa, Ala.: University of Alabama Press. (Rev. in *EWW* 10:345-8).

1371 Mahar, William J. 1985. "Black English in early blackface minstrelcy: a new interpretation of the sources of minstrel show dialect". *American Quarterly* 37:260-85.

1372 Manning, Alan & Robert Eatcock. 1982. "The influence of French on English in Quebec". *LACUS* 9:496-502.

1373 Manuel-Dupont, Sonia Sue. 1986. "Analysis of the English language use of Hualapai children in an academic setting". Ph.D., University of Kansas. DAI 47:7 (1987), 2565-A.

1374 Martin, Stefan Edmund. 1992. "Topics in the syntax of nonstandard English". Ph.D., University of Maryland College Park. DAI 53:7 (1993), 2351-A. (Summary in *EWW* 14:2).
1375 Martínez-Bartholomé, Marta Mateo. 1990. "La traduccíon del Black English y el argot negro norteamericano". *Revista Alicantina de Estudios Ingleses* 3:97-106.
1376 Maruta, Tadao. 1987. "A note on (V N) compounds in Newfoundland English". *RLS* 11:31-4.
1377 Mashbuon, Carolyn. 1989. "Multiple modals in an American English dialect". *CUNY Forum* 14:130-3.
1378 Maynor, Natalie. 1988. "Written records of spoken language: how reliable are they?". In *Thomas, 109-20.
1379 ---. 1991. "The WPA slave narratives revisited". *AS* 66:82-6.
1380 ---. 1993. "Reconstructing nineteenth-century Southern White English: more evidence from *The Tennessee Civil War Veterans Questionnaires*". In *Viereck 1993b:180-90.
1381 Mayo, Robert. 1991. "Vocal fundamental frequency and vowel formant frequency characteristics of normal African-American and European-American adults". Ph.D., Memphis State University. DAI 51:12 (1991), 5832-B.
1382 Medicine, Bea. 1987. "The role of American Indian women in cultural continuity and transition". In Joyce Penfield, ed. *Women and Language in Transition*. Albany, N.Y.: State University of New York Press, 159-66.
1383 Merril, Celia Dale. 1987. "Mexican-American English in McAllen, Texas: features of accentedness in the English of native Spanish bilinguals". Ph.D., University of Texas at Austin. DAI 48:5 (1987), 1192-3-A.
1384 Meseck, Birgit. 1986. "Die Amerikanisierung des kanadischen Englisch". In E. Bettinger & T. Meier-Fohrbeck, eds. *Von Shakespeare bis Chomsky*. Frankfurt/M.: Lang, 273-84.
1385 Metcalf, Allan, Luanne von Schneidemesser, *et al.* 1993. *An Index by Region, Usage, and Etymology to the Dictionary of American Regional English, Volumes I and II*. (PADS, 77). Tuscaloosa, Ala.: Univ. of Alabama Press.
1386 Middleton, Laverne Darnell. 1992. "An examination of language functions among selected African-American English speakers in the home setting: An ethnographic approach". Ph.D., Howard University. DAI 53:9 (1993), 3131-A. (Summary in *EWW* 14:2).

1387 Mille, Katherine Wyly. 1990. "A historical analysis of tense-mood-aspect in Gullah Creole: a case of stable variation". Ph.D., University of South Carolina. DAI 51:8 (1991), 2729-A. (Summary in *EWW* 12:294-5).

1388 Miller, Michael I. 1984a. "The city as a cause of morphophonemic change". *SECOLR* 8:28-59.

1389 ---. 1984b. "A Jacksonian view of American English". *RFEA* 8(18):397-403.

1390 ---. 1986. "The greatest blemish: plurals in *-sp*, *-st*, *-sk*". In Montgomery & Bailey, 235-53.

1391 ---. 1987a. "Evidence for a Virginia plantation creole?". *ZDL* 54:184-201.

1392 ---. 1987b. "Three changing verbs: *bite*, *ride*, and *shrink*". *JEngL* 20:3-12.

1393 ---. 1988. "Ransacking linguistic survey data with a number cruncher". In *Thomas, 464-79.

1394 ---. 1993a. "Beyond chi-square: nonparametric techniques for analyzing linguistic survey data". In *Viereck 1993a:268-78.

1395 ---. 1993b. "Yankee words in Chicago black speech". In Frazer, 157-72.

1396 Mills, Carl. 1990. *American Grammar: Sound, Form and Meaning*. New York: Lang.

1397 Minayo-Rowe, Liliana. 1986. "Sociocultural comparison of bilingual education policies and programmes in three Andean countries and the United States". *JMMD* 7:465-77.

1398 Mock, Carol C. 1991. "Impact of the Ozark drawl: its role in the shift of the diphthong /ey/". In *Eckert, 233-50.

1399 Moen, Per. 1988. "The English pronunciation of Norwegian-Americans in four Mid-Western states". *American Studies in Scandinavia* 20:105-21.

1400 Molesky, Jean. 1988. "Understanding the American linguistic mosaic: a historical overview of language maintenance and language shift". In McKay & Wong, 29-68.

1401 Montano-Harmon, Maria Rosario. 1989. "Discourse features in the compositions of Mexican, English-as-a-second-language, Mexican-American/Chicano, and Anglo High School students: considerations for the formulation of educational policies". Ph.D., University of Southern California. DAI 50:5 (1989), 1235-A.

1402 Montgomery, Michael B. 1987. "A questionnaire for the study of Tennessee English". *Tennessee Linguistics* 7(2):35-45.

1403 ---. 1988a. "The roots of Appalachian English". In *Thomas, 480-91.

1404 ---. 1988b. "Davy Crockett, the rhetoric of Tennessee politics, and the development of American English". *Tennessee Linguistics* 8(1):14-25.
1405 ---. 1988c. "The three grand dialects of Tennessee?". *Touchstone: Magazine of the Tennessee Humanities Council* 13:12-14.
1406 ---. 1989a. "Exploring the roots of Appalachian English". *EWW* 10:227-78.
1407 ---. 1989b. "A note on *Ya'll*". *AS* 64:273-5.
1408 ---. 1989c. "English language [in the South]". In Wilson & Ferris, 761-7.
1409 ---. 1989d. "Introduction to variable rule analysis". In *Kretzschmar, *et al.*, 111-8.
1410 ---. 1991a. "The linguistic value of the ex-slave recordings". In *Bailey, *et al.*, 173-89.
1411 ---. 1991b. "Descriptive terms for poor whites in the South". *Tennessee Folklore Society Bulletin* 55:116-33.
1412 ---. 1992. "The etymology of *y'all*". In *Hall, *et al.*, 356-69.
1413 ---. 1993. "Africanisms in the Deep South". In *Mufwene, 439-57.
1414 ---. fc.a. "The southern accent: alive and well". *Southern Cultures* 1.
1415 ---. fc.b. "Questionnaire for the study of South Carolina speech". In Wayne Glowka & Donald Lance, eds. *Ideas for Talking about Language Variation: American English and Related Topics*. New York: MLA.
1416 ---. fc.c. "Making the trans-Atlantic link between varieties of English: the case of plural verbal *-s*". *JEngL.*
1417 ---. fc.d. "The early work of Lorenzo Dow Turner". In *Montgomery fc.a.
1418 --- & Guy Bailey, eds. 1986a. *Language Variety in the South: Perspectives in Black and White*. University, Ala.: University of Alabama Press. (Rev. in *EWW* 7:324-7).
1419 --- & ---. 1986b. "Introduction". In Montgomery & Bailey, 1-29.
1420 --- & Curtis Chapman. 1992. "The pace of change in Appalachian English". In *Rissanen, *et al.*, 624-39.
1421 --- & Margaret Mishoe. fc. "The pragmatics of multiple modals in North and South Carolina". *AS.*
1422 --- & Stephen J. Nagle. fc. "Double modals and the southern United States: trans-Atlantic inheritance or independent development?". *Folia Linguistica Historica.*
1423 --- & Philip Robinson. fc. "Ulster English as Janus: language contact across the Irish Sea and across the North Atlantic". In P. Sture

Ureland, ed. *Language Contact across the North Atlantic*. Tübingen: Niemeyer.

1424 Mooney, Steve. 1991. "The myth of Appalachia as repository of old, middle or Elizabethan English". *University of Kentucky Studies* 8:53-8.

1425 Moonwomon, Birch. 1991. "Sound change in San Francisco English". Ph.D., University of California, Berkeley. DAI 53:2 (1992), 483-A. (Summary in *EWW* 14:2).

1426 Morgan, Marcyliena Hazel. 1989. "From down South to up South: the language behavior of three generations of Black women residing in Chicago". Ph.D., University of Pennsylvania. DAI 51:1 (1990), 154-A. (Summary in *EWW* 12:295-6).

1427 ---. 1993. "The Africanness of counterlanguage among Afro-Americans". In *Mufwene, 423-35.

1428 Morrison, Val, Bill Reimer & Frances M. Shaver. 1991. "English speakers in the Eastern townships of Quebec". *EWW* 12:63-74.

1429 Morrow, Daniel Hibbs. 1986. "The relationship between feature alternation and error in writing among University freshmen who select features of black American English in speech". Ph.D., University of Pittsburgh. DAI 47:6 (1986), 2063-A.

1430 Moulton, William G. 1990. "Some vowel systems in American English". In *Ramsaran, 119-36.

1431 Mufwene, Salikoko S. 1985. "The linguistic significance of African proper names in Gullah". *NWIG* 59:149-66.

1432 ---. 1986a. "Number delimitation in Gullah". *AS* 61:33-60.

1433 ---. 1986b. "Restrictive relativization in Gullah". *JPCL* 1:1-31.

1434 ---. 1989. "Equivocal structures in some Gullah complex sentences". *AS* 64:304-26.

1435 ---. 1991a. "Is Gullah decreolizing? A comparison of a speech sample of the 1930s with a sample of the 1980s". In Bailey, *et al.*, 213-30.

1436 ---. 1991b. "On the infinitive in Gullah". In *Edwards & Winford, 209-22.

1437 ---. 1991c. "Some reasons why Gullah is not dying yet". *EWW* 12:215-43.

1438 ---. 1992. "Ideology and facts on African American English". *Pragmatics* 2:141-66.

1439 ---. 1993a. "Africanisms in Gullah: A re-examination of the issues". In *Hall, *et al.*, 156-82.

1440 --- & Charles Gilman. 1987. "How African is Gullah, and why?". *AS* 62:120-39.

1441 Murray, Thomas E. 1985a. "The language of singles bars". *AS* 60:17-30.
1442 ---. 1985b. "Lapine lingo in American English: *Silflay*". *AS* 60:372-5.
1443 ---. 1986. *The Language of St. Louis, Missouri: Variation in the Gateway City*. New York: Lang. (Rev. in *EWW* 8:333-4).
1444 ---. 1987a. "'You $ # ^ % ? * & a Hoosier!': derogatory names and *the* derogatory name in St. Louis, Missouri". *Names* 35:1-7.
1445 ---. 1987b. "Appalachia on the move: *need* + [verb] + *-ed* in Ohio". In *Aspects of American English*. Reynoldsburg, Ohio: Advocate.
1446 ---. 1990a. "Appalachian/Ozarkian English on the plains". *KanQ* 22:45-73.
1447 ---. 1990b. "The ontogeny of a Southern folk argot". *Tennessee Folklore Society Bulletin* 54:91-9.
1448 ---. 1992. "Social structure and phonological variation on a Midwestern college campus". *AS* 67:163-74.
1449 ---. 1993a. "The language of St. Louis, Missouri: Dialect mixture in the urban Midwest". In Frazer, 125-36.
1450 ---. 1993b. "Positive *anymore* in the Midwest". In Frazer, 173-86.
1451 Mutt, Oleg. 1984. "American black English - some notes on its past, present and future". *Tartu riikliku ülikooli toimetised/ Ucenye zapiski Tartuskogo gosudarstuennogo universiteta* (Tartu) 684:90-6.
1452 Myhill, John. 1988a. "Postvocalic /r/ as an index of integration into the BEV speech community". *AS* 63: 203-13.
1453 ---. 1988b. "The rise of *be* as an aspect marker in Black English Vernacular". *AS* 63:304-25.
1454 ---. 1991. "The use of invariant *be* with verbal predicates in BEV". In *Edwards & Winford, 101-13.
1455 --- & Wendell A. Harris. 1986. "The use of the verbal *-s* inflection in BEV". In *Sankoff, 25-31.
1456 Nagle, Stephen J. 1993. "The English double modals: Internal or external change". In Jacek Fisiak, ed. *Language Contact and Linguistic Change*. Berlin: Mouton de Gruyter.
1457 Navarro, Richard. 1985. "The problems of language, education and society: who decides". In *Garcia & Padilla, 289-313.
1458 *Needed Research in American English (1983)*. 1984. (PADS, 71). University, Ala.: University of Alabama Press.
1459 Nelson-Barber, Sharon S. 1982. "Phonologic variations of Pima English". In Robert St. Clair & William Leap, eds. *Language Renewal Among American Indian Tribes: Issues, Problems, and Prospects*. Rossleyn, Va.: Nat. Clearinghouse for Bilingual Education, 115-31.

1460 Nichols, Patricia C. 1983. "Black and white speaking in the rural south: difference in the pronominal system". *AS* 58:201-15.
1461 ---. 1984. "Networks and hierarchies: language and social stratification". In *Kramarae, *et al.*, 23-42.
1462 ---. 1986. "Prepositions in black and white English of South Carolina". In Montgomery & Bailey, 73-84.
1463 ---. 1991. "Verbal patterns of black and white speakers of coastal South Carolina". In *Edwards & Winford, 114-28.
1464 Nichols, Steve. 1991. "English as a symbol of American culture". *ET* 7:31-5.
1465 Nylvek, Judith A. 1992a. "Is Canadian English in Saskatchewan becoming more American?". *AS* 67:268-78.
1465a ---. 1992b. "Canadian English in Saskatchewan: A sociolinguistic survey of four selected regions". Ph.D., University of Victoria.
1466 ---. 1993. "A sociolinguistic analysis of Canadian English in Saskatchewan: A look at urban versus rural speakers". In Clarke, 201-28.
1467 O'Barr, William M. 1993. "Professional varieties: the case of language and law". In Preston, 319-32.
1468 O'Connor, Jane Lorena. 1990. "Slang in the popular western novel". Ph.D, University of Tennessee. DAI 51:12 (1991), 4107-A. (Summary in *EWW* 12:298-9).
1469 Odmark, John. 1984. The American idiom and the semiotics of culture". In Tibor Frank, ed. *The Origins and Originalities of American Culture*. Budapest: Akadémiai Kiadó, 665-73.
1470 O'Hearn, Carolyn. 1988. "*Swingletree*, *singletree*, and the *OED*". *AS* 63:285-8.
1471 Oomen, Ursula. 1985. "'I tell you just like I been know it' - Die Entwicklung einer kreolischen Konstruktion im Black English". In Manfred Pfister, ed. *Anglistentag 1984. Vorträge*. Giessen: Hoffmann, 105-15.
1472 --- & Monika Lissewski. 1989. "Pronoun variation in South Carolinian 'Early Black English'". In *Pütz & Dirven, 109-33.
1473 Ornstein-Galicia, Jacob, ed. 1984a. *Form and Function in Chicano English*. Rowley, Mass.: Newbury House. (Rev. in *EWW* 5:312-3).
1474 ---. 1984b. "Networking: a needed research direction". In Ornstein-Galicia, 160-65.
1475 ---. 1987/1988. "The U.S. Southwest as a sociolinguistic problem area". In *Ammon, *et al.*, 1405-13.

1476 ---, Betty Lou Duboi & Bates Hoffer. 1984. "The El Paso sociolinguistic microsurvey as bilingualism". In Ornstein-Galicia, 143-59.

1477 Orr, Eleanor Wilson. 1987. *Twice as Less: Black English and the Performance of Black Students in Mathematics and Science*. New York: Norton.

1478 Owens, Thompson W. & Paul M. Baker. 1984. "Linguistic insecurity in Winnipeg: validation of a Canadian index of linguistic insecurity". *LinS* 13:337-50.

1479 Paddock, Harold. 1984. "Mapping lexical variants in Newfoundland English". In Helmut Zobl, ed. *Papers from the Seventh Annual Meeting of the Atlantic Provinces Linguistics Association*. Moncton, N.B.: University of Moncton, 84-103.

1480 ---. 1991. "Linguistic vs. non-linguistic conditioning of linguistic variables". *Journal of the Atlantic Provinces Linguistic Association* 13:71-83.

1481 Padilla, Raymond V. 1984. "Federal policy shifts and the implementation of bilingual education programs". In Garcia, *et al.*, 90-110.

1482 Padolsky, Enoch & Ian Pringle. 1984. "Demographic analysis and regional dialect surveys in Canada: data collection and use". *Canadian Papers in Rural History* 1984:240-75.

1483 Patterson, Janet Lee. 1992. "The development of sociolinguistic phonological variation patterns for (ING) in young children". Ph.D., The University of New Mexico. DAI 53:9 (1993), 3196-A. (Summary in *EWW* 14:2).

1484 Pederson, Lee. 1985. "Systematic phonetics". *JEngL* 18:14-24.

1485 ---. 1986a. "A graphic plotter grid". *JEngL* 19:25-41.

1486 ---. 1986b. "Rewriting dialect literature: The wonderful tar-baby story". *Atlanta Historical Journal* 30:57-70.

1487 ---. 1987. "An Automatic Book Code (ABC)". *JEngL* 20:48-71.

1488 ---. 1988a. "Zum Einsatz von Schnelldruckerkarten in der Dialektkartographie: rechnergestützte Sprachdatenbearbeitung im Rahmen des 'Linguistic Atlas of the Gulf States'". *ZDL* 55:306-31.

1489 ---. 1988b. "Electronic matrix maps". *JEngL* 21:149-74.

1490 ---. 1989. "AAM phonology". In *Kretzschmar, *et al.*, 54-62.

1491 ---. 1992. "A Georgia word geography". In *Hall, *et al.*, 384-99.

1492 ---. 1993. "An approach to linguistic geography: The Linguistic Atlas of the Gulf States". In Preston, 31-92.

1493 --- & Michael W. Madsen. 1989. "Linguistic geography in Wyoming". In *Kretzschmar, *et al.*, 17-24.

1494 ---, Susan Leas McDaniel & Marvin Bassett. 1984. "The LAGS concordance". *AS* 59:332-9.

1495 ---, *et al.*, eds. 1986. *Linguistic Atlas of the Gulf States, Vol. I: Handbook for the Linguistic Atlas of the Gulf States.* Athens, Ga.: University of Georgia Press.

1496 ---, *et al.*, eds. 1988. *Linguistic Atlas of the Gulf States, Vol. II: General Index for the Linguistic Atlas of the Gulf States.* Athens, Ga.: University of Georgia Press.

1497 ---, *et al.*, eds. 1989. *Linguistic Atlas of the Gulf States, III: Technical Index for the Linguistic Atlas of the Gulf States.* Athens, Ga.: University of Georgia Press.

1498 ---, *et al.*, eds. 1990. *Linguistic Atlas of the Gulf States, IV: Regional Matrix for the Linguistic Atlas of the Gulf States.* Athens, Ga.: University of Georgia Press.

1499 ---, *et al.*, eds. 1991a. *Linguistic Atlas of the Gulf States, V: Regional Pattern for the Linguistic Atlas of the Gulf States.* Athens, Ga.: University of Georgia Press.

1500 ---, *et al.*, eds. 1991b. *Linguistic Atlas of the Gulf States, VI: Social Matrix for the Linguistic Atlas of the Gulf States.* Athens, Ga.: University of Georgia Press.

1501 ---, *et al.*, eds. 1991c. *Linguistic Atlas of the Gulf States, VII: Social Pattern for the Linguistic Atlas of the Gulf States.* Athens, Ga.: University of Georgia Press.

1502 Peñalosa, Fernando. 1985. "A world-system perspective for Chicano sociolinguistics". *IJSL* 53:7-19.

1503 ---. 1986. "Trilingualism in the barrio: Mayan Indians in Los Angeles". *LPLP* 10:229-53.

1504 Penfield, Joyce. 1984. "Prosodic patterns: some hypotheses and findings from fieldwork". In Ornstein-Galicia, 49-59.

1505 ---. 1989. "Social and linguistic parameters of prosody in Chicano English". In *García & Otheguy, 387-401.

1506 --- & Jacob L. Ornstein-Galicia. 1985. *Chicano English: An Ethnic Contact Dialect.* Amsterdam: Benjamins.

1507 Pfeffer, J. Alan. 1985. "Comparative subordinating conjunctions in American English". *IRAL* 23:323-30.

1508 Philips, Susan Urmston. 1983. *The Invisible Culture: Communication in Classroom and Community on the Warm Springs Indian Reservation.* New York & London: Longman.

1509 Pierce, James Alfred. 1989. "Sociolinguistic relationships in attitudes toward Anglo and Mexican American varieties of English in Corpus Christi, Texas". Ph.D., University of Texas at Austin. DAI 50:6 (1989), 1649-A.

1510 Pigadas, George. 1990. "Class formation and language maintenance in British Canada, 1880-1970". Ph.D., York University. DAI 53:1 (1992), 140-A. (Summary in *EWW* 13:288-9).

1511 Piper, David. 1989. "Socio-political influence on cultural identity in Canada: implications for cross-cultural communication in English". In *García & Otheguy, 161-83.

1512 Pitts, Anne. 1986. "Flip-flop prestige in American *tune*, *duke*, *news*". *AS* 61:130-8.

1513 Pitts, Walter Franklin. 1986a. "Linguistic variation as a function of ritual frames in the Afro-Baptist church in Central Texas". Ph.D., University of Texas at Austin. DAI 47:5 (1986), 1715-A. (Summary in *EWW* 8:292-3).

1514 ---. 1986b. "Contrastive use of verbal -*z* in slave narratives". In *Sankoff, 73-82.

1515 ---. 1988. "'Keep the fire burnin': Language and ritual in the Afro-Baptists church". *Journal of American Folklore* 56:77-97.

1516 ---. 1989. "West African poetics in the black preaching style". *AS* 64:137-49.

1517 Pons-Ridler, Suzanne & Neil B. Ridler. 1989. "The territorial concept of official bilingualism: a cheaper alternative for Canada?". *Language Sciences* 11:147-58.

1518 Poplack, Shana. 1983. "Intergenerational variation in language use and structure in a bilingual context". In Charlene Rivera, ed. *An Ethnographic/Sociolinguistic Approach to Language Proficiency Assessment*. Clevedon: Multilingual Matters, 42-7.

1519 ---. 1988. "Language status and language accommodation along a linguistic border". In *Lowenberg, 90-118.

1520 ---. 1993. "Variation theory and language contact: concepts, methods and data". In Preston, 251-86.

1521 --- & David Sankoff. 1987. "The Philadelphia story in the Spanish Caribbean". *AS* 62:291-314.

1522 --- & Sali Tagliamonte. 1989. "There's no tense like the present: verbal *–s* inflection in early black English". *LVC* 1:47-84.

1523 --- & ---. 1993. "African American English in the diaspora: Evidence from old-line Nova Scotians". *LVC* 5:301-39. (Reprinted in Clarke, 109-50).

1524 Poulsen, Richard C. 1985. *The Mountain Man Vernacular: Its Historical Roots, Its Linguistic Nature, and Its Literary Uses*. New York: Lang.

1525 Pratt, T.K. 1984. "I dwell in possibility: variable (ay) in Prince Edward Island". *Journal of the Atlantic Provinces Linguistic Association* 4:27-35.

1526 ---. 1988. *Dictionary of Prince Edward Island English*. Toronto: UP. (Rev. in *EWW* 10:175-6).

1527 ---. 1993. "The hobgoblin of Canadian English spelling". In Clarke, 45-64.

1528 Preston, Dennis R. 1985a. "The Li'l Abner syndrome: written representations of speech". *AS* 60:328-36.

1529 ---. 1985b. "Southern Indiana perceptions of 'correct' and 'pleasant' speech". In *Warkentyne, 387-412.

1530 ---. 1986. "Five visions of America". *LinS* 15:221-40.

1531 ---. 1988. "Methods in the study of dialect perceptions". In *Thomas, 373-95.

1532 ---. 1989a. *Perceptual Dialectology: Nonlinguists' Views of Areal Linguistics*. Dordrecht: Foris. (Rev. in *EWW* 11:139-41).

1533 ---. 1989b. "Standard English spoken here: the geographical foci of linguistic norms". In *Ammon, 324-54.

1534 ---. 1989c. "Folk speech [in the South]". In Wilson & Ferris, 768-9.

1535 ---. 1992. "Talking black and talking white: a study in variety imitation". In *Hall, *et al.*, 327-55.

1536 ---, ed. 1993a. *American Dialect Research: An Anthology Celebrating the 100th Anniversary of the American Dialect Society*. Amsterdam, Philadelphia: Benjamins.

1537 ---. 1993b. "Folk dialectology". In Preston, 333-78.

1538 ---. 1993c. "Two Heartland perceptions of language variety". In Frazer, 23-48.

1539 Pringle, Ian. 1983. "The concept of dialect and the study of Canadian English". *Queen's Quarterly* 90:100-21. (Reprinted in *Allen & Linn 1986:217-36).

1540 ---. 1985. "Attitudes to Canadian English". In *Greenbaum, 183-205.

1541 ---. 1986. "The complexity of the concept of standard". In Lougheed, 20-38.

1542 --- & Enoch Padolsky. 1983. "The linguistic survey of the Ottawa valley". *AS* 58:325-44.

1543 ---, *et al.* 1985. "Procedures to solve a methodological problem in the Ottawa Valley". In *Warkentyne, 477-94.

1544 Raith, Joachim. 1981. "Phonologische Interferenzen im amerikanischen Englisch der anabaptistischen Gruppen deutscher Herkunft in Lancaster County (Pennsylvania): Unter Berücksichtigung von Sprachgemeinschaftstyp und Erwerbskontext". *ZDL* 48:35-52.

1545 ---. 1986. "Variation, linguistic continua and related issues: data from Anabaptist groups in Lancaster County, Pennsylvannia". In Enninger, 37-45.

1546 Ramirez, Manuel III. 1984. "The Chicano bilingual, cultural democracy and the multicultural personality in a diverse society". In Ornstein-Galicia, 99-114.

1547 Ramos, Joseph. 1991. "'No ... because': A study of pragmatic transfer in refusals among Puerto Rican teenagers speaking English". Ph.D., Columbia University. DAI 52:7 (1992), 2533-A. (Summary in *EWW* 13:289-90).

1548 Ray, George B. 1987. "An ethnography of nonverbal communication in an Appalachian community". *Research on Language & Social Interaction* 21:171-88.

1549 Read, Allen Walker. 1986. "An American ABC: remarks on DARE at MLA". *NADS* 18:6-7.

1550 ---. 1987. "The embattled dominance of English in the United States". In *Levitt, *et al.*, 221-30.

1551 Richards, Craig. 1985. "Bilingualism and Hispanic employment: school reform or social control". In *Garcia & Padilla, 269-88.

1552 Richards, Donna Jean. 1988. "Prestige and standard in Canadian English: evidence from the Survey of Vancouver English". Ph.D., The University of British Columbia. DAI 49:12 (1989), 3708-A. (Summary in *EWW* 11:287-8).

1552a ---. fc. "The Survey of English: Attitudes and awareness". In de Wolf fc.a.

1553 Richardson, Carmen. 1991. "Habitual structures among blacks and whites in the 1990s". *AS* 66:292-302.

1554 Richardson, Gina. 1984. "Can *y'all* function as a singular pronoun in Southern dialect?". *AS* 59:51-9.

1555 Rickford, John R. 1985. "Ethnicity as a sociolinguistic boundary". *AS* 60:99-125.

1556 ---. 1986. "Some principles for the study of black and white speech in the South". In Montgomery & Bailey, 38-62.

1557 ---. 1988. "Language contact, variation and diffusion: microlevel community perspectives". In *Lowenberg, 25-44.

1558 ---. 1990. "Number delimitation in Gullah: a reponse to Mufwene". *AS* 65:148-63.

1559 ---. 1991. "Representativeness and reliability of the ex-slave materials, with special reference to Wallace Quarterman's recording and transcript". In *Bailey, *et al.*, 191-212.

1560 ---. 1992. "Grammatical variation and divergence in Vernacular Black English". In M. Gerritsen & D. Stein, eds. *Internal and External Factors in Syntactic Change*. Berlin: Mouton de Gruyter, 175-200.

1561 ---, Arnetha Ball, Renée Blake, Raina Jackson & Nomi Martin. 1991. "Rappin on the copula coffin: theoretical and methodological issues in the analysis of copula variation in African-American Vernacular English." *LVC* 3:103-32.

1562 Riney, Timothy J. 1993. "Linguistic controversies, VBE structures, and Midwest attitudes". In Frazer, 81-96.

1563 Roberts, Roda P. 1989. "Translating and interpreting in Canada's far north: a true intercultural challenge". *BACLA* 11:97-108.

1564 Rogers, Phillip W. 1984. "The *Dictionary of Newfoundland English*". *Queen's Quarterly* 91:823-37.

1565 Romero, Mary. 1988. "Chicano discourse about language use". *LPLP* 12:110-29.

1566 Rot, Sándor. 1986. "Varieties of American English in the macrostructure of American culture and semiotic problems of cultural pluralism". In Charlotte Kretzoi, ed. *High and Low in American Culture*. Budapest: Department of English, Roland Eötvös University, 133-55.

1567 ---. 1987. "Non-standard varieties of American English in the macrostructure of American culture". *Annales Universitatis Scientiarium Budapestinensis. Sectio Linguistica* 18:191-210.

1568 Roy, John D. 1987. "The linguistic and sociolinguistic position of black English and the issue of bidialectalism in education". In *Homel, *et al.*, 231-42.

1569 Rudin, Ronald. 1988. "English-speaking Québec and the Canadian constitution". *LVC* 1:215-24.

1570 Rudnyckyj, J.B. 1983. *Multiculturalism and Multilingualism in Canada.* Ottawa: Ukrainian Language Association.

1571 ---. 1990. *Multilingual Canada.* Ottawa & Montreal.

1572 Ruiz, Richard. 1985. "La crise de l'anglais aux États-Unis". In Jacques Maurais, ed. *La Crise des Langues.* Québec: Gouvernement du Québec, Conseil de la langue française, 147-88.

1573 ---. 1988. "Bilingualism and bilingual education in the United States". In *Paulston, 539-60.

1574 Sachdev, Itesh, *et al.* 1987. "Language attitudes and vitality perceptions: intergenerational effects among Chinese Canadian communities". *JLSP* 6:287-307.

1575 Sagarin, Edward & Robert J. Kelly. 1985. "Polylingualism in the United States of America: a multitude of tongues amid a monolingual majority". In William R. Beer & James E. Jacob, eds. *Language Policy and National Unity.* Totowa, N.J.: Rowman & Allanheld, 20-44.

1576 Sahlmann-Karlsson, Siiri. 1986. "Nagra iakttagelser rörande amerika-finnarnas finska och engelska". *Finno-Ugrica Suedana* 8:101-22.

1577 Salmons, Joe. 1988. "On the social function of some southern Indiana German-American dialect stories". *Humor* 1:159-75.

1578 Sánchez, Francisca. 1986. "*Of* reduction in black English: a quantitative study". In *Sankoff, 59-72.

1579 Sanchez, Rosaura. 1983. *Chicano Discourse: Sociohistoric Perspective.* Rowley, Mass.: Newbury House.

1580 Sankoff, David. 1988. "Sociolinguistics and syntactic variation". In *Newmeyer, 140-61.

1581 San Miguel, Guadalupe. 1984. "Bitter struggles: Mexican Americans and the revision of the Texas bilingual education bill in 1981". In García, *et al.*, 111-30.

1582 Santa Ana A., Otto. 1991. "Phonetic simplification processes in the English of the Barrio: a cross-generational sociolinguistic study of the Chicanos of Los Angeles". Ph.D., University of Pennsylvania. DAI 52:7 (1992), 2534-A. (Summary in *EWW* 13:290-1).

1583 Santoyo, Julio-César. 1984. "Spanish loan-words in American English: a testimony against some historical prejudice". In Tibor Frank, ed. *The Origins and Originalities of American Culture.* Budapest: Akadémiai Kiadó, 717-26.

1584 Sato, Charlene J. 1989a. "A non-standard approach to standard English". *TESOLQ* 23:259-82.

1585 ---. 1989b. "Language attitudes and sociolinguistic variation in Hawaii". *University of Hawaii Working Papaers in ESL* 8:191-216.

1586 ---. 1991. "Sociolinguistic variation and language attitudes in Hawaii". In *Cheshire, 647-63.

1587 Schneider, Edgar W. 1985. "Regional variation in nineteenth century Black English in the American South". In *Fisiak, 467-87.

1588 ---. 1986. "'How to speak Southern' - An American English dialect stereotyped". *Amerikastudien/American Studies* 31:425-39.

1589 ---. 1987. "Dialect analysis and automatic cartography by means of a microcomputer". *Literary and Linguistic Computing* 2:80-5.

1590 ---. 1988. "Qualitative vs. quantitative methods of area delimitation in dialectology: a comparison based on lexical data from Georgia and Alabama". *JEngL* 21:175-212.

1591 ---. 1989. *American Earlier Black English. Morphological and Syntactic Variables*. Tuscaloosa, Ala.: The University of Alabama Press. (Rev. in *EWW* 10:344-5).

1592 ---. 1990. "Strategien des Computereinsatzes in der nordamerikanischen Dialektologie am Ende der achtziger Jahre". *ZDL* 57:273-94.

1593 ---. 1993. "Africanisms in the grammar of Afro-American English: Weighing the evidence". In *Mufwene, 209-21.

1594 ---. fc.a. "Appalachian mountain vocabulary: Its character, sources, and distinctiveness". In *Viereck.

1595 ---. fc.b. "The Chattahoochee River - a dialect boundary?". In *Montgomery fc.b.

1596 ---. fc.c. "Black-white language contact through the centuries: Diachronic aspects of linguistic convergence or divergence in the USA". In Jacek Fisiak, ed. *Language Contact and Linguistic Change*. Berlin: Mouton de Gruyter.

1597 --- & William A. Kretzschmar, Jr. 1990. "LAMSAS goes SASsy: statistical methods and Linguistic Atlas data". In *Kretzschmar, *et al.*, 129-41.

1598 Schneider, Harald Johann. 1990. "Das Vorkommen lexikalischer Afrikanismen im amerikanischen ("Black") Englisch: Eine empirische Untersuchung". ("Lexical Africanisms in American (Black) English: An empirical study"). Ph.D., Innsbruck University (Austria). DAI 53:3 (1992), 395-C. (Summary in *EWW* 14:2).

1599 Schoeck, Richard J. 1982-83. "The Canadian experiment: bilingualism and biculturalism in Canada, 1982". *Council of National Literature/ World Report* 6:8-13.

1600 Schofield, David Stuart. 1991. "Texas prison slang". *Verbatim* 18(2):11.

1601 Schrock, E.F. 1986. "Some features of the *be* verb in the speech of blacks of Pope County, Arkansas". In Montgomery & Bailey, 202-15.

1602 Scott, Jerrie Cob. 1985. "The King case: implications for educators". In Brooks, 63-71.

1603 ---. 1986. "Mixed dialects in the composition classroom". In Montgomery & Bailey, 333-47.

1604 --- & Geneva Smitherman. 1985. "Language attitudes and self-fulfilling prophecies in the elementary school". In *Greenbaum, 302-14.

1605 Sebastian, Richard J. & Ellen Bouchard Ryan. 1985. "Speech cues and social evaluation: Markers of ethnicity, social class, and age". In Howard Giles & Robert N. St. Clair, eds. *Recent Advances in Language, Communication, and Social Psychology*. London: Erlbaum, 112-43.

1606 Sengova, Joko. fc. "Recollections of African language patterns in an American speech variety: an assessment of Mende influences in Lorenzo Dow Turner's Gullah data". In *Montgomery fc.a.

1607 Shannon, Sheila M. 1987. "English in el Barrio: a sociolinguistic study of second language contact". Ph.D., Stanford University. DAI 48:11 (1988), 2825-6A. (Summary in *EWW* 9:308-9).

1608 Shapson, Stanley & Vincent D'Oyley, eds. 1984. *Bilingual and Multicultural Education: Canadian Perspectives*. Clevedon: Multilingual Matters.

1609 Shields, Kenneth, Jr. 1985. "Germanisms in Pennsylvania English: an update". *AS* 60:228-37.

1610 ---. 1987. "Germanisms in the English of Eastern Pennsylvania". *JEngL* 20:163-80.

1611 ---. 1989. "A note on the *greasy/greazy* isogloss in east-central Pennsylvania". *AS* 64:280-4.

1612 Shipley, E.F. 1991. "Farewell to 'thee'". In *Napoli & Kegl, 171-81.

1613 Shockey, Linda. 1984. "All in my flap: long-term accommodation in phonology". *IJSL* 46:87-95.

1614 Shores, David L. 1984. "The stressed vowels of the speech of Tangier Island, Virginia". *JEngL* 17:37-56.

1615 ---. 1985. "Vowels before /l/ and /r/ in Tangier dialect". *JEngL* 18:124-6.

1616 ---. 1986. "*Porchmouth* for *Portsmouth*". *AS* 61:147-52.
1617 ---. 1989a. "Chesapeake Bay dialect". In Wilson & Ferris, 785-6.
1618 ---. 1989b. "Outer banks dialect". In Wilson & Ferris, 790-1.
1619 Shorrocks, Graham. 1991. "Memorial University of Newfoundland research centres and repositories: new developments". *RLS* 13:14-9.
1620 ---. 1993. "A supplement to the bibliography of Newfoundland folklore and language". *RLS* 14:32-9.
1621 --- & Beverly Rodgers. 1993. "Non-standard dialect in Percy James' novel *House of Hate*". *RLS* 14:2-25.
1622 Shuman, R. Baird. 1985. "English language in the secondary school". In *Greenbaum, 315-26.
1623 Simon, Beth. 1990. "Style, dialect switching, and the notion of 'standard' in Missouri and adjoining areas". *KanQ* 22:143-62.
1624 Simpson, David. 1986. *The Politics of American English, 1776-1850*. Oxford: UP.
1625 Siudek, Margaret. 1988. "A study of some factors affecting the sequence and rate acquisition of ESL by adult refugees in Western Pennsylvania". *PSCL* 22:203-25.
1626 Sledd, Andrew. 1993. "Black English and Standard English in Chicago". In Frazer, 67-80.
1627 Sledd, James. 1986. "Permanence and change in standard American English: the making of 'literacy crises'". In *Nickel & Stalker, 59-70.
1628 Sledge, Mailande Cheney. 1986. "The representation of the Gullah dialect in Francis Griswold's *A Sea Island Lady*". Ph.D., University of Alabama. DAI 46:7 (1986), 1917-A.
1629 ---. 1988. "The verisimilitude of the Gullah dialect in Francis Griswold's *A Sea Island Lady*". In *Thomas, 625-36.
1630 Smitherman, Geneva. 1984. "Black language as power". In *Kramarae, *et al.*, 101-15.
1631 ---. 1985. "What go round come round: *King* in perspective". In Brooks, 41-62.
1632 ---. 1991. "'What is Africa to me?': Language, ideology, and *African American*". *AS* 66:115-32.
1633 Smitherman-Donaldson, Geneva. 1988. "Discriminatory discourse on Afro-American speech". In Geneva Smitherman-Donaldson & Teun A. van Dijk, eds. *Discourse and Discrimination*. Detroit: Wayne State UP, 144-75.

1634 Snipper, Grace Capizzi. 1986. "Real Americans don't speak Spanish: some Hispanic parents' views on bilingual education". *Bilingual Review* 13:13-25.

1635 Sobel, Mechal. 1987. *The World They Made Together: Black and White Values in Eighteenth-century Virginia.* Princeton, N.J.: Princeton UP.

1636 Sohn, Joong-Dong. 1989. "American English dialects in Hawaii". *Journal of English Language and Literature* 30:219-37.

1637 Sommer, Elisabeth. 1986. "Variation in southern urban English". In Montgomery & Bailey, 180-201.

1638 ---. 1991. "Prepositions in Black English Vernacular". *SECOLR* 15:183-99.

1639 Southard, Bruce. 1983. "The Linguistic Atlas of Oklahoma and computer cartography". *JEngL* 16:65-77.

1640 ---. 1993. "Elements of Midwestern speech in Oklahoma". In Frazer, 229-44.

1641 Spears, Arthur K. 1988. "Black American English". In Johnetta B. Cole, ed. *Anthropology for the Nineties.* New York: Free, 96-113.

1642 ---. 1991. "Teaching language and culture to minorities". *CUNY Forum* 16:138-54.

1643 ---. 1992. "Reassessing the status of Black English (Review article of Butters 1989)". *LinS* 21:675-82.

1644 Speicher, Barbara L. & Seane M. McMahon. 1992. "Some African-American perspectives on Black English Vernacular". *LinS* 21:383-407.

1645 Stadler, Beatrice. 1983. *Language Maintenance and Assimilation: The Case of Selected German-Speaking Immigrants in Vancouver, Canada.* Vancouver: Canadian Association of University Teachers of German.

1646 Stanback, Marsha Houston. 1985. "Language and black woman's place: evidence from the black middle class". In Paula A Treichler, *et al.*, eds. *For Alma Mater: Theory and Practice in Feminist Scholarship.* Urbana: University of Illinois Press, 177-93.

1647 Starks, Judith A. 1983. "The black English controversy and its implications for addressing the educational needs of black children: the cultural linguistic approach". In Chambers, 97-132.

1648 Stein, Roberta. 1990. "Closing the 'achievement gap' of Mexican Americans: a question of language, learning style, or economics?". *JMMD* 11:405-19.

1649 Steinmetz, Sol. 1986. *Yiddish and English: A Century of Yiddish in America*. University, Ala.: University of Alabama Press.
1650 Stewart, William A. 1987. "Coping or groping? Psycholinguistic problems in the acquisition of receptive and productive competence across dialects". In *Homel, *et al.*, 281-98.
1651 ---. 1989a. "Structural mimicry in decreolization and its effect on pseudo-comprehension". In *García & Otheguy, 263-80.
1652 ---. 1989b. "Whence the nominal dual in Gullah?". *CUNY Forum* 14:211-8.
1653 Stockman, Ida J. & Fay Vaughn-Cooke. 1989. "Addressing new questions about black children's language". In *Fasold & Schiffrin, 275-300.
1654 Story, G.M. 1986. "The role of the dictionary in Canadian English". In Lougheed, 41-53.
1655 --- & William J. Kirwin, 1987. *Linguistic Atlas of Newfoundland Dialect Questionnaire*. 2nd ed. St. John's: Memorial University of Newfoundland.
1656 ---, --- & John D.A. Widdowson, eds. 1983. 2nd ed. with supplement 1990. *Dictionary of Newfoundland English*. Toronto: UP. (Rev. in *EWW* 4:114-5).
1657 Sullivan, Nancy Mae. 1991. "Evaluational reactions to ethnic groups in Chicago". Ph.D., University of Texas at Austin. DAI 52:4 (1991), 1312-3-A.
1658 Surs, Zlili. 1981. "Lexical features of American dialects". *Waiguoyu* 6(16):9-14. [in Chinese]
1659 Tabbert, Russell. 1984. "Terms for 'not Alaska' in Alaskan English". *AS* 59:256-8.
1660 ---. 1985a. "The term *native* in Alaskan English". *AS* 59:378.
1661 ---. 1985b. "*Visqueen* in Alaskan English". *AS* 59:379.
1662 ---. 1985c. "*Berm* in Alaskan English". *AS* 60:93-4.
1663 ---. 1985d. "*Wanigan* and *Leanto* in Alaskan English". *AS* 60:94-5.
1664 ---. 1991. *Dictionary of Alaskan English*. Juneau, Alaska: The Denali Press. (Rev. in *EWW* 12:330-1).
1665 Tagliamonte, Sali & Shana Poplack. 1988. "How Black English *past* got to the present: Evidence from Samaná". *LinS* 17:513-33. [= 2630]
1666 Taylor, Donald. 1989. "Language attitudes in a multilingual northern community". *Canadian Journal of Native Studies* 9:85-119.

1667 Taylor, Hanni Ulrike. 1986. "Dialectism in a small literal arts college". Ph.D., Northern Illinois University. DAI 47:6 (1986), 2147-A. (Summary in *EWW* 8:294-5).
1668 ---. 1989. "Standard English, black English and bidialectalism: a controversy". *American University Studies* 13:9.
1669 Taylor, Orlando L. 1983. "Black English: an agenda for the 1980's". In Chambers, 133-43.
1670 ---. 1985. "Standard English as a second dialect". *ET* 2:9-12.
1671 Thees, Petra. 1991. "Zur Widerspiegelung der Besiedelungsgeschichte Kanadas in der Lexik des kanadischen Englisch". In *Hansen, 86-94.
1672 Thomas, Erik R. 1989. "The implications of /o/ fronting in Wilmington, North Carolina". *AS* 64:327-33.
1673 ---. 1991. "The origin of Canadian raising in Ontario". *CJL* 36:147-70.
1674 ---. 1993. "The use of *all the* + comparative structure". In Frazer, 257-66.
1675 --- & Guy Bailey. 1992. "A case of competing mergers and their resolution". *SECOLR* 16:179-200.
1676 Thomas, Gerald & J.D.A. Widdowson, eds. 1991. *Studies in Newfoundland Folklore: Community and Process*. St. John's: Breakwater Books for the Department of Folklore, Memorial University of Newfoundland.
1677 Thompson, Roger M. 1985. "Revisiting a dialect: validating the checklist". *SECOLR* 9:170-84.
1678 Tokuma, Shin'ichi. 1989. "Syllabic nasals in American English: a study by experimental phonetics". *Sophia Linguistica* (Tokyo) 27:165-72.
1679 Toohey, Kelleen. 1985. "Domain analysis and second language instruction in Northern Ontario native communities". *CMLR* 41:652-88.
1680 Tottie, Gunnel & Gerd Övergaard. 1984. "The author's *would*: a feature of American English". *SL* 38:148-64.
1681 Tousignant, Claude. 1987. "Relations sociales entre le /r/ vélaire et le /r/ rétroflexe anglais de Montréal". *Revue Québécoise de Linguistique théorique et appliquée* 6:39-55.
1682 Troike, Rudolph C. 1983. "The Texas dialect survey: responses from Austin, Texas". *Southwest Journal of Linguistics* 6:145-54.
1683 ---. 1986. "McDavid's law". *JEngL* 19:177-205.
1684 Troutman-Robinson, Denise Eloise. 1987. "Oral and written discourse: a study of feature transfer". Ph.D., Michigan State University. DAI 48:3 (1987), 641-A. (Summary in *EWW* 9:309-10).

1685 Trudgill, Peter. 1985. "New-dialect formation and the analysis of colonial dialects: the case of Canadian Raising". In *Warkentyne, 35-45.

1686 Tucker, G. Richard. 1984. "Toward the development of a language-competent American society". *IJSL* 45:153-60.

1687 Tugwell, R. Michael. 1990. "Presentation of the analysis of Linguistic Atlas data: another view". *LACUS* 17:498-503.

1688 Ture, Sue. 1984-85. "Milwaukee medical maledicta". *Maledicta* 8:117-8.

1689 Turner, Darwin T. 1985. "Black students, language, and classroom teachers". In Brooks, 30-40.

1690 Underwood, Gary Neal. 1983. "Mid-south English, midwestern teachers, and middle-of-the-road textbooks". In Chambers, 81-96.

1691 ---. 1988. "Accent and identity". In *Thomas, 406-27.

1692 Urcinoli, Bonnie. 1985. "Bilingualism as code and bilingualism as practice". *AnL* 27:363-86.

1693 Valdés, Guadalupe. 1988. "The language situation of Mexican Americans". In McKay & Wong, 111-39.

1694 Vance, Timothy J. 1987. "'Canadian raising' in some dialects of the northern United States". *AS* 62:195-210.

1695 Van Halsema, Tess. 1983. "Language observation by long distance". In *Edmondson, 58-71.

1696 Vaughn-Cooke, F.B. 1986. "Lexical diffusion: evidence from a decreolizing variety of Black English". In Montgomery & Bailey, 111-30.

1697 Veatch, Thomas Clark. 1991. "English vowels: their surface phonology and phonetic implementation in vernacular dialects". Ph.D., University of Pennsylvania. DAI 52:7 (1992), 2535-A. (Summary in *EWW* 13:292-3).

1698 Veltman, Calvin. 1983a. "Anglicization in the United States: language environment and language practice of American adolescents". *IJSL* 44:99-114.

1699 ---. 1983b. *Language Shift in the United States*. Berlin: Mouton de Gruyter. (Rev. in *EWW* 5:136-8).

1700 Verma, Shivendra K. 1986. "What is American about American English?". *International Journal of Dravidian Linguistics* 15:278-89.

1701 Viereck, Wolfgang. 1985. "On the origin and developments of American English". In *Fisiak, 561-9.

1701a ---. 1986. "American English: What has been achieved and what remains to be done". In Sándor Rot, ed. *English in Function II*. Vol IV. Budapest, 206-18.

1702 ---. 1988a. "Invariant *be* in an unnoticed source of American early Black English". *AS* 63:291-303.

1703 ---. 1988b. "Notes on black and red American English". In *Duncan-Rose & Vennemann, 145-57.

1704 ---. 1989a. "A linguistic analysis of recordings of 'early' American Black English". In *Fries & Heusser, 179-96.

1705 ---. 1989b. "In need of more evidence on American Black English: the ex-slave narratives revisited". *NM* 92:247-62.

1705a ---. 1991. "Whither dialectology I/Dove va la dialettologia? I". *Quaderni di Semantica* 12:325-7.

1705b ---. fc. "Verbal *-s* inflection in 'early' American Black English". In Jacek Fisiak, ed. *Language Contact and Linguistic Change*. Berlin: Mouton de Gruyter.

1706 Vilá-Barreto, Joaquín Salvador. 1991. "Socio-affective factors, learning strategies in pidginization: A study of the learning of English in Puerto Rico". Ph.D., Michigan State University. DAI 53:1 (1992), 138-A. (Summary in *EWW* 13:293-4).

1707 von Schneidemesser, Luanne. 1983. "The *Dictionary of American Regional English* and its use of computers: considerations for a large-scale project". In Sarah K. Burton & Douglas D. Short, eds. *Sixth International Conference on Computers and the Humanities*. Rockville, Md.: Computer Science, 619-23.

1708 ---. 1988. "The foundations of the *Dictionary of American Regional English*". *Lexicographica* 4:34-59.

1709 ---. 1990. "Linguistic recollections of a Kansas childhood, from the view of a dictionary editor". *KanQ* 22:109-32.

1710 ---. 1993. "DARE's completion: a beginning?". In *Viereck 1993b:529-41.

1711 Wachal, Robert S. fc. "The capitalization of color names and other terms for ethnic groups". In Little & Montgomery.

1712 Waddell, Eric. 1986. "Les anglophones du Québec: une nouvelle minorité ethnique?". In *Séminaires 1985*. Talence: Centre de recherches sur l'Amér. Anglophone, Maison des Sciences de l'Homme d'Aquitaine, 7-20.

1713 Wade-Lewis, Margaret. 1988. *Lorenzo Dow Turner: First African-American Linguist*. Philadelphia: Temple University Institute of African and African-American Affairs, Occasional Paper no. 2.

1714 ---. 1989. "The African substratum in American English". Ph.D., New York University. DAI 49:10 (1989), 3016-A.

1715 Waggoner, Dorothy. 1988. "Language minorities in the United States in the 1980s: the evidence from the 1980 census". In McKay & Wong, 69-108.

1716 Wainstein, Nancy. 1990. "Parental attitudes toward languages and their role in understanding, explaining and predicting English reading achievement of Hispanic background students". Ph.D., University of Washington. DAI 52:5 (1991), 1697-A. (Summary in *EWW* 13:295).

1717 Wald, Benji. 1984. "The Status of Chicano English as a dialect of American English". In Ornstein-Galicia, 14-31.

1718 ---. 1985. "Motivation for language choice behavior of elementary Mexican American children". In *Garcia & Padilla, 71-95.

1719 ---. 1987. "Spanish-English grammatical contact in Los Angeles: the grammar of reported speech in the East Los Angeles English contact vernacular". *Linguistics* 25:53-80.

1720 Ward, James Wesley. 1990. "Judges' attitudes toward Standard English and black English in the State of Texas". Ph.D., Wayne State University. DAI 50:7 (1990), 1850-A.

1721 Wardhaugh, Ronald. 1983. *Language and Nationhood: The Canadian Experience*. Vancouver: New Star Books.

1722 Warkentyne, H.J. 1983. "Attitudes and language behaviour". *CJL* 28:71-6.

1723 ---. 1985. "On the position of Canadian English". In *Berry & Acheson, 177-88.

1724 --- & A.C. Brett. 1993. "Statistical analysis of variation in Canadian English". In *Viereck 1993a:496-506.

1725 Washington, Gerald Robert. 1991. "From the spoken to the written word: an analysis of the writing of selected African-American junior high school students". Ph.D., Howard University. DAI 51:11 (1991), 3657-A.

1726 Washington, Trudy Lynne. 1986. "An investigation of teachers' attitudes toward nonstandard and black language as related to language program participation". Ph.D., United States International University. DAI 47:3 (1986), 1332-B.

1727 Welleford, David. 1988. "A pin is not a pen; is a pan? Is southern pronunciation incorrect?". *The English Journal* 77(6):25-8.

1728 Wescott, Roger W. 1987. "Zazzification in American slang". *WWays* 20:216-7.

1729 White, Grover Gene. 1986. "Black dialect in student writing: a correlation analysis of reading achievement, syntactic maturity, intelligence, grade level, and sex". Ph.D., Auburn University. DAI 46:12 (1986), 3639-A.

1730 Widdowson, John D.A. 1991. "Lexical retention in Newfoundland dialect". In Thomas & Widdowson, 245-58.

1731 Wild, Joy, *et al.* 1983. "Sociolinguistic aspects of Native Indian speech". *Sociolinguistic Newsletter* 14:6-8.

1732 Williams, Cratis D. 1992. *Southern Mountain Speech*. Edited with an introduction and glossary by Jim Wayne Miller and Loyal Jones. Berea, Ky.: Berea College Press.

1733 Williams, John Roger. 1985. "Appalachian migrants in Cincinnati, Ohio: the role of folklore in the reinforcement of the ethnic identity". Ph.D., Indiana University. DAI 47:2 (1986), 624-A. (Summary in *EWW* 8:296-7).

1734 Williams, Lanis III. 1991. "Vernacular speech, ethnicity, and employability". Ph.D., University of Texas at Austin. DAI 53:1 (1992), 21-A. (Summary in *EWW* 13:296).

1735 Williams, Patrice Dale. 1991. "Tense-aspect in African-American English: a sociolinguistic perspective". Ph.D., University of Florida. DAI 52:10 (1992), 3595-A. (Summary in *EWW* 13:297).

1736 Williams, Selase W. 1993. "Substantive Africanisms at the end of the African linguistic diaspora". In *Mufwene, 406-22.

1737 Willinsky, John. 1988. *The Well-Tempered Tongue: The Politics of Standard English in the High School*. New York & London: Teachers College Press.

1738 Willmorth, Michael John. 1988. "The representation of American dialects in prime time network television dramatic programs". Ph.D., University of Pennsylvania. (Summary in *EWW* 11:290-1).

1739 Wilson, Charles Reagan & William Ferris, eds. 1989. *Encyclopedia of Southern Culture*. Chapel Hill, London: University of North Carolina Press.

1740 Winford, Donald. 1988. "The creole continuum and the notion of the community as locus of language". *IJSL* 71:95-105.

1741 Winter, Kate H. 1985. "North Country voices". In Frank Bergmann, ed. *Upstate Literature Essays in Memory of Thomas F. O' Dannell*. Syracuse: Syracuse UP, 143-64.

1742 Wölck, Wolfgang. 1984. "Sounds of a city: types and characteristics of the speech of Buffalo and its ethnic groups". *New York Folklore* 10:7-22.

1743 Wolfram, Walt. 1984a. "Is there an 'Appalachian English'?". *Appalachian Journal* 11:215-24.

1744 ---. 1984b. "Unmarked tense in American Indian English". *AS* 59:31-50.

1745 ---. 1985. "Variability in tense marking? A case for the obvious". *LL* 35:229-53.

1746 ---. 1986a. "Black-white dimensions in sociolinguistic text [recte: test] bias". In Montgomery & Bailey, 373-85.

1747 ---. 1986b. "Language variation in the United States". In Orlando L. Taylor, ed. *Nature of Communication Disorders in Culturally and Linguistically Diverse Populations*. San Diego: College-Hill, 73-156.

1748 ---. 1986c. "Walt Wolfram replies". *AS* 61:329-31.

1749 ---. 1988. "Reconsidering the semantics of *a*-prefixing". *AS* 63:247-53.

1750 ---. 1989. "Structural variability in phonological development: final nasals in vernacular black English". In *Fasold & Schiffrin, 301-32.

1751 ---. 1990. "Re-examining vernacular black English. (Review article of Schneider 1989 and Butters 1989)". *Language* 66:121-33.

1752 ---. 1993. "Identifying and interpreting variables". In Preston, 193-222.

1753 --- & Anthony Cavendar. 1992. "Dialect and special-interest domains: conceptual and methodological issues in collecting a medical lexicon". *AS* 67:406-20.

1754 --- & Donna Christian. 1988. "Dialects, society, and education". In Bixler-Marquez & Ornstein-Galicia, 9-28.

1755 --- & ---. 1989. *Dialects and Education: Issues and Answers*. Englewood Cliffs, N.J.: Prentice Hall.

1756 --- & Deborah Hatfield. 1984. "Tense marking in interlanguage: the case of Vietnamese English". Final Report, NIE project no. NIE-G-83.0035.

1757 --- & ---. 1986. "Interlanguage fads and linguistic reality: the case of tense unmarking". In Deborah Tannen & James E. Alatis, eds. *Language and Linguistics: The Interdependence of Theory, Data, and Application*. (GURT '85). Washington, D.C.: Georgetown UP, 17-34.

1758 Wolfson, Nessa. 1989. *Perspectives: Sociolinguistics and TESOL*. Cambridge, Mass.: Newbury House.

1759 Wood, Gordon R. 1989. "[Southern] drawl". In Wilson & Ferris, 786-7.

1760 Woods, Howard B. 1986. "Variation in English as a second language in Canada". In Lougheed, 139-51.

1761 ---. 1987. *The Ottawa Survey of Canadian English*. Montreal, Quebec: Didier.

1762 ---. 1991. "Social differentiation in Ottawa English". In *Cheshire, 134-49.

1763 ---. 1993. "A synchronic study of English spoken in Ottawa: Is Canadian English becoming more American?". In Clarke, 151-78.

1764 Woods, Ronald C. 1983. "Law, ideology and social perception: the *King* decision and other language-related litigation". In Chambers, 56-70.

1765 Wright, Barbara Helen White. 1985. "Hypercorrections and dialect forms in the compositions of native born college students from Georgia". Ph.D., City University of New York. DAI 46:11 (1986), 3340-A. (Summary in *EWW* 7:284-5).

1766 Wright, Sandra. 1984. "A description of the variance between the oral and written language patterns of a group of black college students". Ph.D., Wayne State University. DAI 46:5 (1985), 1267-A. (Summary in *EWW* 7:285-6).

1767 Wyatt, Toya Annette. 1991. "Linguistic constraints on copula production in Black English child speech". Ph.D., University of Massachusetts. DAI 52:2 (1991), 781-B.

1768 Yan, Weiming. 1984. "American history and American language". *Waiguoyu* 1(29):24-9. [in Chinese]

1769 Yip, Virginia Choy-Yin. 1989. "Aspects of Chinese/English interlanguage: syntax, semantics and learnability". Ph.D., University of Southern California. DAI 51:1 (1990), 155-A. (Summary in *EWW* 12:302-3).

1770 Youmans, Gilbert. 1986. "Any more on *anymore*?: evidence from a Missouri dialect survey". *AS* 61:61-75.

1771 Zeigler, Mary Elizabeth Brown. 1984. "The lexicon of Richard Malcom Johnston's Middle Georgia dialect". Ph.D., University of Georgia. DAI 44:11 (1984), 3375-A. (Summary in *EWW* 5:245-6).

1772 Zeller, Christine. 1993. "Linguistic symmetries, asymmetries and border effects within a Canadian/American sample". In Clarke, 179-99.

1773 Zentella, Ana Celia. 1987. "Language and female identity in the Puerto Rican community". In Joyce Penfield, ed. *Women and Language in Transition*. Albany, N.Y.: State University of New York Press, 167-79.

1774 ---. 1990. "Integrating qualitative and quantitative methods in the study of bilingual code-switching". In Edward H. Bendix, ed. *The Uses of Linguistics*. New York: New York Academy of Sciences, 75-92.

1775 Zuo, Biao. 1987. "Fragmentary observations on black English". *Waiguoyu* 4(50):42-4. [in Chinese]

Part IV: Writings on Englishes in the rest of the world

MANFRED GÖRLACH

The decision on what, and what not, to list follows the same principles as Viereck, Schneider & Görlach (1984). Titles of the following type are, then, generally omitted:

- reprints of earlier works, if there were no changes or only minimal alterations;
- inclusive dictionaries (like the various forms of the *Macquarie Dictionary*);
- journalistic papers, notes and queries, replies and rejoinders, entries in encyclopedias, etc.;
- unprinted conference papers and similar contributions (but Ph.D. theses *are* included);
- papers in which the focus appeared to be on education, pragmatics, language in society, multilingualism, onomastics, etc., rather than on variation in English. (As a compromise, I have included a few *collections* of papers, but not the individual contributions.)

Krio, Sranan and Tok Pisin cannot be considered forms of English; I have therefore listed titles devoted to these only selectively, especially if they have a particular relevance for the *English* of the region.

I have seen many, but by no means all, of the publications listed. Many of my entries come from more specialised bibliographies or reference sections in recent books on relevant topics (such as Cheshire 1991, Romaine 1991, Schmied 1991, etc.).

I am grateful to Robert Baumgardner, Beat Glauser, Anthea Fraser Gupta, Josef Schmied, Edgar Schneider, Christoph Stephan, Brian Taylor, Wolfgang Viereck and Helen Weiss for help with this section.

For relevant collections of papers or contrastive studies on varieties of English spoken outside Great Britain, Ireland, the USA and Canada see in particular entries 12, 35, 37-8, 40, 42-3, 52, 99, 113-4, 145, 166, 206, 229, 251, 268, 271, 286 and 297.

1776 Abdulaziz, Mohamed M.H. 1988. "A sociolinguistic profile of East Africa". In *Ammon, *et al.*, 1347-53.

1777 ---. 1991. "East Africa (Tanzania and Kenya)". In *Cheshire, 391-401.

1778 Abu-Jarad, Hassan Ali. 1986. "English interlanguage of Palestinian university students in Gaza strip: an analysis of relative clauses and verb tense". Ph.D., Ball State University. DAI 47:2 (1986), 518-A. (Summary in *EWW* 8:277-8).

1779 Adegbija, Efurosibina. 1987. "Speech act functions: dimensions of communication and meaning". *ITL* 76:43-62.

1780 ---. 1989a. "Lexico-semantic variation in Nigerian English". *WE* 8:165-77.

1781 ---. 1989b. "The implications of the language of instruction for nationhood: an illustration with Nigeria". *ITL* 85/86:25-50.

1782 Afolayan, Adebisi. 1984. "The English language in Nigerian education as an agent of proper multilingual and multicultural development". *JMMD* 5:1-22.

1783 --- & Obafemi Awolowo. 1987. "English as a second language: a variety or a myth?". *JESL* 1:4-16.

1784 Africa, H.P. 1983. "Zambian English: myth or reality". Lusaka: University of Zambia, Department of Literature and Languages.

1785 Aggarwal, Kailash S. 1988. "English and India's three-language formula: an empirical perspective". *WE* 7:289-90.

1786 Agheyisi, Rebecca N. 1984. "Linguistic implications of the changing role of Nigerian Pidgin English". *EWW* 5:211-33.

1787 ---. 1988. "The standardization of Nigerian Pidgin English". *EWW* 9:227-41.

1788 Agnihotri, Rama Kant & Anju Sahgal. 1985. "Is Indian English retroflexed and r-full?". *IJAL* 11:97-108.

1789 ---, *et al.* 1984. "The use of articles in Indian English: errors and pedagogical implications". *IRAL* 22:115-29.

1790 ---, *et al.* 1988. *Tense in Indian English. A Sociolinguistic Perspective.* Report of the Indian Council of Social Science Research, ICSSR. (SELL, 12). New Delhi: Bahri Publications.

1790a Ahulu, Samuel. 1992. "English in Ghana". Ph.D., University of Cambridge. (Summary in *EWW* 14:2).

1791 Aitchison, Jean. 1984. "Social networks and urban New Guinea Pidgin (Tok Pisin)". In Sebba & Todd, 9-18.

1792 --- & Rama Kant Agnihotri. 1985. "'I deny that I'm incapable of not working all night': divergence of negative structures in British and Indian English". In *Eaton, *et al.*, 3-14.

1793 Aksornkool, N. 1985. *An Historical Study of Language Planning*. Singapore: UP.

1794 Aldridge, Maurice V. 1988. "South Africa". In *Ammon, *et al.*, 1400-5.

1795 Algeo, John. 1991. "A meditation on the varieties of English". *ET* 27:3-6.

1796 ---. 1992. "New Zealand English and the dictionary". In *Blank, II:209-23.

1797 Ali, Ahmed. 1993. "English in South Asia: A historical perspective". In Baumgardner, 1-10.

1798 Alisjahbana, S. Takdir. 1990. "The teaching of English in Indonesia". In *Britton, *et al.*, 315-27.

1799 Allan, K. 1984. "The component functions of the high-rise terminal contour in Australian declarative sentences". *AJL* 4:19-32.

1800 Allan, Scott. 1990. "The rise of New Zealand intonation". In Bell & Holmes, 115-28.

1801 Allsopp, Jeanette. 1992. "French and Spanish loan words in Caribbean English". *ET* 29:12-20.

1802 Allsopp, Richard. 1984a. "Cross-referencing many standards: some sample entries for the *Dictionary of Caribbean English Usage* (DCEU)". *EWW* 4:187-97.

1803 ---. 1984b. "Caribbean English as a challenge to lexicography". In Reinhard R.K. Hartmann, ed. *LEXeter '83. Papers from the International Conference on Lexicography at Exeter, 9-12 Sept. 1983*. Tübingen: Niemeyer, 31-41.

1804 ---. 1987. "'Like if say you see a jumbie or a duppy': problems of definitional differentiae in a complex of Anglophone cultures". In *Bailey, 75-98.

1804a ---. 1993. *A Concise Dictionary of Caribbean English & Usage*. With a French and Spanish supplement by Jeanette Allsopp. Oxford: UP.

1805 Alo, Moses. 1984. "A lexical study of educated Yoruba English". Ph.D., University of Reading.

1806 ---. 1989. "A prototype approach to the analysis of meanings of kinship terms in non-native English". *Language Sciences* 11:159-76.

1807 Alqazweeni, Ali. 1990. "Pronunciation difficulties as experienced by Kuwaiti students learning English as a foreign language". Ph.D., The Florida State University. DAI 51:2 (1990), 492-A. (Summary in *EWW* 12:280).

1808 Amoabeng, Kwaku. 1986. "The English language in Ghana: a comprehensive annotated bibliography". Ph.D., State University of New York. DAI 47:6 (1986). (Summary in *EWW* 8:278-9).

1809 Amuda, Atoye A. 1986. "Yoruba/English code-switching in Nigeria: aspects of its functions and form". Ph.D., University of Reading.

1810 Aniche, Godfrey C. 1982. "Standard Nigerian English and the educated user". *IJAL* 8:71-81.

1811 Arends, Jaques. 1993. "Towards a gradualist model of creolization". In *Byrne & Holm, 371-80.

1812 Atoye, Raphael O. 1991. "Word stress in Nigerian English". *WE* 10:1-6.

1813 Austin, Paddy. 1990. "Politeness revisited: the dark side". In Bell & Holmes, 276-93.

1814 Awonusi, Victor O. 1985. "Sociolinguistic variation in Nigerian (Lagos) English". Ph.D., University of London.

1815 ---. 1990. "Coming of age: English in Nigeria". *ET* 22:31-5.

1816 Ayodele, Samuel O. 1982. "Nigerian primary school teachers' mastery of English language pronunciation". *ITL* 57:41-52.

1817 ---. 1983. "A description of the varieties of Nigerian English for pedagogic purposes". *British Journal of Language Teaching* 21:101-8.

1818 Azuike, Macpherson N. 1984. "Style, context and the written text: a linguistic examination of written English in Nigeria today". Ph.D., University of Exeter.

1819 Bailey, Richard W. 1984. "Notes on South African English". *South African Journal of Linguistics* 2(3):1-35.

1820 ---. 1985a. "South African English slang: form, function and origins". *South African Journal of Linguistics* 3(1):1-42.

1821 ---. 1985b. "The idea of world English". *ET* 1:3-6.

1822 ---. 1990. "English at its twilight". In *Ricks & Michaels, 83-94.

1823 ---. fc. "Attitudes toward English: the future of English in South Asia". In Baumgardner.

1824 Baker, Philip. 1987. "The historical developments in Chinese Pidgin English and the nature of the relationships between the various pidgin Englishes of the Pacific region". *JPCL* 2:163-207.

1825 ---. 1990a. "Off target?". *JPCL* 5:107-19.

1826 ---. 1990b. "Pacific reorientations". *JPCL* 5:253-69.

1827 --- & Peter Mühlhäusler. fc. "From business to pidgin". *Journal of Asian Communication* 1.

1828 Baker, Stephen B. 1983. "Some thoughts on English language teaching in Zambia". *World Language English* 2:225-8.

1829 Baldauf, Richard B., Jr. 1990. "Education and language planning in the Samoas". In Baldauf & Luke, 259-76.

1830 --- & Allan Luke, eds. 1990. *Language Planning and Education in Australia and the South Pacific*. Clevedon: Multilingual Matters. (Rev. in *EWW* 11:324-5).

1831 Ball, Peter. 1983. "Stereotypes of Anglo-Saxon and non Anglo-Saxon accents: some exploratory Australian studies with the matched guise technique". *Language Sciences* 5:163-83.

1832 ---, C. Gallois & V. Callan. 1989. "Language attitudes: a perspective from social psychology". In Collins & Blair, 89-102.

1833 Balla, Malik E. 1991. "The prospect of Sudanese institutions of higher education changing the language of instruction from English to Arabic, in the light of the Syrian experience". Ph.D., Michigan State University. DAI 53:1 (1992), 26-A. (Summary in *EWW* 13:277).

1834 Bamgbose, Ayo. 1991. *Language and the Nation. The Language Question in Sub-Saharan Africa*. Edinburgh: UP for the International African Institute. (Rev. in *EWW* 13:329-31).

1835 Bamiro, Edmund O. 1991a. "Nigerian Englishes in Nigerian English literature". *WE* 10:7-17.

1836 ---. 1991b. "The social and functional power of Nigerian English". *WE* 10:275-86.

1837 Banda, Felix. 1992. "A lexical-semantic and syntactic-grammatical analysis of Zambian English: towards a 'meaning-to-grammar hypothesis' of classroom second language instruction". *JMMD* 13:341-57.

1838 Barron, C. 1986. *Lexical Nativisation in Papua New Guinean English*. Research Report No. 7. Department of Language and Communication Studies. Papua New Guinea University of Technology, Lae.

1839 Baskaran, Loga M. 1987. "Aspects of Malaysian English syntax". Ph.D., University of London. (Summary in *EWW* 9:294-5).

1840 Bauer, Anton. 1992. "The origin and modification of Pidgin English: sociocultural background and linguistic hybridization". In *Blank, II:185-97.

1841 Bauer, Laurie 1986. "Notes on New Zealand English phonetics and phonology". *EWW* 7:225-58.

1842 ---. 1987a. "New Zealand English morphology: some experimental evidence". *TeReo* 30:37-53.

1843 ---. 1987b. "Approaching New Zealand English grammar". *New Zealand English Newsletter* 1:12-15.

1844 ---. 1988. "Number agreement with collective nouns in New Zealand English". *AJL* 8:247-59.

1845 ---. 1989a. "The verb *have* in New Zealand English". *EWW* 10:69-83.

1846 ---. 1989b. "Marginal modals in New Zealand English". *TeReo* 32:3-16.
1847 ---. 1992. "The Second Great Vowel Shift revisited". *EWW* 13:253-68.
1848 ---. fc. "English in New Zealand". In *Burchfield.
1849 Baumgardner, Robert J. 1987. "Utilizing Pakistani newspaper English to teach grammar". *WE* 6:241-52.
1850 ---. 1990. "The indigenization of English in Pakistan". *ET* 21:59-65. (Reprinted in Baumgardner 1993:37-50).
1851 ---. 1992. "'*To Shariat* or not *to Shariat*?': bilingual functional shifts in Pakistani English". In *Smith & Sridhar, 129-40.
1852 ---, ed. 1993a. *The English Language in Pakistan*. Karachi: Oxford UP.
1852a ---. 1993b. "Utilizing Pakistani newspaper English to teach grammar". In Baumgardner, 246-64.
1853 ---, ed. fc. a. *South Asian English: Structure, Use and Users*. Urbana & Chicago: University of Illinois Press.
1854 ---. fc. b. "Innovation in Pakistani English political lexis". In Baumgardner.
1854a --- & Audrey E.H. Kennedy. 1993. "The use of local contexts in the design of EST materials". In Baumgardner, 265-73.
1854b ---, --- & Fauzia Shamim. 1993. "The urduization of English in Pakistan". In Baumgardner, 76-196.
1855 --- & Ray Tongue. 1988. "The problems and the potential of exploiting the English language press as an aid to language teaching in South Asia". In Dick Chamberlain & R.J. Baumgardner, eds. *ESP in the Classroom: Practice and Evaluation*. (ELT Documents, 128). London: Macmillan.
1856 Bayard, Donn. 1987. "Class and change in New Zealand English: a summary report". *TeReo* 30:3-36.
1857 ---. 1989. "'Me say that? No way!': The social correlates of American lexical diffusion in New Zealand English". *TeReo* 32:17-60.
1858 ---. 1990a. "'God help us if we all sound like this!': Attitudes to New Zealand and other English accents". In Bell & Holmes, 67-96.
1859 ---. 1990b. "Minder, mork and mindy? (-t) glottalisation and post-vocalic (-r) in younger New Zealand English speakers". In Bell & Holmes, 149-64.
1860 ---. 1991a. "Social constraints on the phonology of New Zealand English". In *Cheshire, 169-86.
1861 ---. 1991b. "Antipodean accents and the 'cultural cringe': New Zealand and American attitudes toward New Zealand English and other English accents". *TeReo* 34:15-52.

1862 Bayer, Jennifer Marie. 1986. *A Sociolinguistic Investigation of the English Spoken by the Anglo-Indians in Mysore City*. (CIIL Sociolinguistic Series, 1). Mysore: Central Institute of Indian Languages. (Rev. in *EWW* 9:347-9).
1863 Bell, Allan. 1983. "Broadcast news as a language standard". *IJSL* 40:29-42.
1864 ---. 1984. "Good copy - bad news: the syntax and semantics of news editing". In Peter Trudgill, ed. *Applied Sociolinguistics*. London: Academic Press, 73-116.
1865 ---. 1985. "One rule of news English: geographical, social and historical spread". *TeReo* 28:95-117.
1866 ---. 1988. "The British base and the American connection in New Zealand media English". *AS* 63:326-44.
1867 ---. 1990. "Audience and referee design in New Zealand media language". In Bell & Holmes, 165-94.
1868 --- & Janet Holmes, eds. 1990a. *New Zealand Ways of Speaking English*. Clevedon: Mulilingual Matters, 65. (Rev. in *EWW* 12:164-6).
1869 --- & ---. 1990b. "Attitudes, varieties, discourse: an introduction to the sociolinguistics of New Zealand English". In Bell & Holmes, 1-20.
1870 --- & ---. 1991. "New Zealand". In *Cheshire, 153-68.
1871 Bell, Roger & Larry Peng Quee Ser. 1983. "'Today la? Tomorrow lah!': the LA particle in Singapore English". *RELC Journal* 14:1-18.
1872 Benson, Philip. 1990. "A language in decline?". *ET* 24:19-23.
1873 Benton, Richard A. 1985. "Maori, English, and Maori English". In J.B. Pride, ed. *Cross-Cultural Encounters: Communication and Mis-Communication*. Melbourne: River Seine Publications, 110-20.
1874 ---. 1991. "Maori English: a New Zealand myth?". In *Cheshire, 187-99.
1875 Bernard, J.R. 1989a. "Quantitative aspects of the sounds of Australian English". In Collins & Blair, 187-204.
1876 ---. 1989b. "Regional variation in Australian English: a survey". In Collins & Blair, 255-9.
1877 --- & A.L. Lloyd. 1989. "The indeterminate vowel in Sydney and Rockhampton English". In Collins & Blair, 288-300.
1878 Bhatia, Tej K. 1987. "English in advertising: multiple mixing and media". *WE* 6:33-48.
1879 Bhatia, Vijay K. 1992. "The bilingual's orthodoxy in professional genres". In *Smith & Sridhar, 225-34.
1880 ---. fc. "Nativization of job applications in South Asia". In Baumgardner.

1881 "Bibliography of English in Singapore/Malaysia". 1988. In Foley, 192-234.

1882 Bilby, Kenneth M. 1983. "How the 'Older heads' talk: a Jamaican Maroon spirit possession language and its relationship to the creole of Surinam and Sierra Leone". *NWIG* 57:37-88.

1883 ---. 1993. "Latent intervocalic liquids in Aluku: links to the phonological past of a Maroon Creole". In *Byrne & Holm, 25-35.

1884 Bisang, W. 1985. *Das chinesische Pidgin-Englisch: ein bilinguales Pidgin im Spannungsfeld von Superstrat, Substrat und eigener Kreativität*. (Amsterdam Asia Studies 58). University of Amsterdam: Department of South and Southeast Asian Studies.

1885 Blair, David. 1989. "The development and current state of Australian English: a survey". In Collins & Blair, 171-5.

1886 Blake, Barry J. 1985. "'Short a' in Melbourne English". *JIPA* 15:6-20.

1887 Bloom, D. 1986. "The English language and Singapore: a critical survey". In Basant K. Kapur, ed. *Singapore Studies: Critical Surveys of the Humanities and Social Sciences*. Singapore: University, 337-458.

1888 Bock, Sylvia Martina. 1984. "Fronting in Caribbean creoles". Ph.D., University of Southern California. DAI 46:2 (1985), 412-A. (Summary in *EWW* 7:272).

1889 Bokamba, Eyamba G. 1984. "Language and literacy in West Africa". *ARAL* 4 (*Literacy Issues*):40-74.

1890 ---. 1989. "Are there syntactic constraints on code-mixing?". *WE* 8:277-92.

1891 ---. 1991. "West Africa". In *Cheshire, 493-508.

1892 Bradley, David. 1989. "Regional dialects in Australian English phonology". In Collins & Blair, 260-70.

1893 ---. 1991. "/æ/ and /a:/ in Australian English". In *Cheshire, 227-34.

1894 ---. 1992. "Regional distribution of /æ/ and /a:/ in Australian English". In Dutton, *et al.*, 49-55.

1895 --- & M. Bradley. 1992. *English in Australia*. Melbourne: Oxford UP.

1896 Branford, Jean. 1986. "Some surprises from the corpus of the *Dictionary of South African English on Historical Principles*". *CRUX* 20:68-72.

1897 Branford, William. fc. "English in Southern Africa". In *Burchfield.

1898 --- & Penny Silva. fc. *A Dictionary of South African English on Historical Principles*. Cape Town/Oxford: Oxford UP.

1899 Brann, Conrad Max Benedict. 1980. *Mother Tongue, Other Tongue, and Further Tongue*. Maiduguri: Maiduguri UP.

1900 ---. 1984. "Afro-Saxons and Afro-Romans: language policies in Sub-Saharan Africa". *History of European Ideas* 5:307-21.

1901 ---. 1985. *Official and National Languages in Africa: Complementarity or Conflict?* Québec: Centre International de Recherche sur le Bilinguisme.

1902 ---. 1988. "West Africa". In *Ammon, *et al.*, 1414-29.

1903 Brathwaite, Edward Kaman. 1984. *History of the Voice: The Development of Nation Language in Anglophone Caribbean Poetry.* London: New Beacon Books.

1904 Brauner, S., *et al.*, eds. 1985. *Verkehrs- und Nationalsprachen in Afrika.* (Ost-)Berlin.

1905 Breinburg, Petronella. 1986. "Language attitudes: the case of Caribbean language". In *Sutcliffe & Wong, 136-48.

1906 Breitborde, Lawrence B. 1988. "The persistence of English in Liberia: sociolinguistic factors". *WE* 7:15-23.

1907 Bretton, Roland. 1991. "The handicaps of language planning in Africa". In *Marshall, 153-74.

1908 British Council. 1986. *Proceedings of the Conference on English in East Africa. 24-27 March 1986.* Nairobi.

1909 Broderick, S. Modupe. 1985. "Time and structure in a Krio oral narrative". In *Hancock, 94-115.

1910 Brown, Adam. 1986. "Pedagogical importance of consonantal features of the English of Malaysia and Singapore". *RELC Journal* 17:1-25.

1911 ---. 1988a. "The staccato effect in the pronunciation of English in Malaysia and Singapore". In Foley, 115-28.

1912 ---. 1988b. "Vowel differences between Received Pronunciation and the English of Malaysia and Singapore: which ones really matter?". In Foley, 129-47.

1913 ---. 1992a. *Making Sense of Singapore English.* Singapore: Federal Press. (Rev. in *EWW* 14:1).

1914 ---. 1992b. "Representing pronunciations in a dictionary of Singapore English". In Pakir, 37-46.

1915 Brown, Robert Harry. 1989. "A sociolinguistic study of language attitudes among selected tertiary Liberian bilinguals and their attained proficiency in ESL". Ph.D., University of Essex. DAI 51:1 (1990), 151-A. (Summary in *EWW* 12:284-5).

1916 Bryant, Pauline. 1985. "Regional variation in the Australian English lexicon". *AJL* 5:55-66.

1917 ---. 1989a. "Regional variation in the Australian English lexicon". In Collins & Blair, 301-14.

1918 ---. 1989b. "The south-east lexical region in Australian English". *AJL* 9:85-134.

1919 ---. 1991. "A survey of regional usage in the lexicon of Australian English". In Romaine, 287-303.

1920 ---. 1992. "Eastern mainland sub-regions of Australian English". In Dutton, *et al.*, 57-74.

1921 Buffet, Alice I. 1992. "The writing of Norfolk". In Dutton, *et al.*, 75-80.

1922 --- & Donald C. Laycock. 1988. *Speak Norfolk today*. Norfolk Island: Himii Publishing. (Rev. in *EWW* 9:352-3).

1922a Burchfield, Robert W. 1988. "Some unedited New Zealand words". In T.L. Burton & Jill Burton, eds. *Lexicographical and Linguistic Studies: Essays in Honour of G.W. Turner*. Woodbridge: Boydell & Brewer, 185-97.

1923 Butler, Susan. 1992a. "The publishing history of the *Macquarie Dictionary* - a personal narrative". In Pakir, 7-14.

1924 ---. 1992b. "Achieving goals in English language dictionary publishing in Singapore and the region". In Pakir, 15-28.

1925 ---. 1992c. "The range of lexical items in Singapore English and the structure of dictionary entries". In Pakir, 117-38.

1926 Byrne, Francis. 1984a. "Instrumental in Saramaccan". In Sebba & Todd, 39-50.

1927 ---. 1984b. "*Fi* and *fu*: origins and functions in some Caribbean English-based creoles". *Lingua* 62:97-120.

1928 ---. 1987. *Grammatical Relations in a Radical Creole: Verb Complementation in Saramaccan*. Amsterdam: Benjamins.

1929 --- & Alexander Caskey. 1993. "A few observations on the creole aspectual marker *ta* and some implications for finiteness". In *Byrne & Holm, 207-16.

1930 --- & John Holm. 1993. "Introduction: perspectives on the Atlantic and Pacific ... and beyond". In *Byrne & Holm, 1-22.

1931 Campbell, Stuart, *et al*. 1990. "Term bank design: work in progress on a computerised glossary of health and welfare terms". *SHLRC Working Papers*; *Lexicology Report*. Macquarie University: School of English and Linguistics, 1-12.

1932 Carls, Uwe. 1991. "Kriterien für die Abgrenzung national markierter Lexik von der Common-core-Lexik am Beispiel des Indischen Englisch". In *Hansen, 60-73.

1933 Carrington, Lawrence D. 1987. "The substance of creole studies: a reappraisal". In *Gilbert, 77-92.

1934 ---. 1992. "Images of creole space". *JPCL* 7:93-9.

1935 Carrington, Lois, *et al.* 1983. *Papers in Pidgin and Creole Linguistics*, No. 3. (*PacL* A-65). Canberra: ANU. (Rev. in *EWW* 6:343-4).

1936 Carter, Hazel. 1987. "Suprasegmentals in Guyanese: some African comparisons". In *Gilbert, 213-63.

1937 Casamada Ribera, Pilar. 1987. "The role of English in India since independence: 1947-1980. A study in language planning". Ph.D., University of Barcelona. (Summary in *EWW* 11:281-2).

1938 Cassidy, Frederic G. 1986a. "Etymology in Caribbean Creoles". In Görlach & Holm, 133-40.

1939 ---. 1986b. "Barbadian Creole - possibility and probability". *AS* 61:195-205.

1940 Chan, Mimi & Helen Kwok. 1985. *A Study of Lexical Borrowing from Chinese into English with Special Reference to Hong Kong*. Hong Kong: Centre of Asian Studies. (Rev. in *EWW* 7:166-9).

1941 Charpentier, Jean-Michel. 1984. "Le pidgin bichelamar avant et après l'indépendance de Vanuatu (cas d'une dépidginisation avant créolisation)". In Sebba & Todd, 51-62.

1942 Chaudhary, Shreesh Chandra. 1989. *Some Aspects of the Phonology of Indian English*. Ranchi: Jayaswal Press.

1943 Cheshire, Jenny. 1991. "Introduction: sociolinguistics and English around the world". In *Cheshire, 1-12.

1944 Cheung, Y.S. 1984. "The uses of English and Chinese languages in Hong Kong". *Language Learning and Communication* 3:273-83.

1945 Chick, J. Keith. 1985. "The international accomplishment of discrimination in South Africa". *LinS* 14:299-326.

1946 ---. 1989. "Intercultural miscommunication as a source of friction in the workplace and in educational settings in South Africa". In *García & Otheguy, 139-60.

1947 ---. 1991. "Sources and consequences of miscommunication in Afrikaans English - South African English encounters". In *Cheshire, 446-61.

1948 Chisanga, Teresa. 1987. "An investigation into the form and function of educated English in Zambia as a possible indigenized non-native variety". Ph.D., University of York.

1949 ---. 1989. "'Non-problematic Zambianisms' and their implications for the teaching of English in Zambia". In Schmied, 63-84.

1950 Chishimba, Maurice M. 1982. "Language teaching and literacy: East Africa". *ARAL* 3:168-88.

1951 ---. 1983. "African varieties of English: text in context". Ph.D., University of Illinois at Urbana-Champaign. (Summary in *EWW* 4:285-6).

1952 ---. 1984. "Language policy and education in Zambia". *International Education Journal* 1:151-80.

1953 ---. 1985. *Deviation and Innovation in English: Zambian Examples.* Lusaka: University of Zambia.

1954 ---. 1991. "Southern Africa". In *Cheshire, 435-45.

1955 Christie, Pauline. 1986. "Evidence for an unsuspected habitual marker in Jamaican". In Görlach & Holm, 183-190.

1956 ---. 1989. "Questions of standards and intra-regional differences in Caribbean examinations". In *García & Otheguy, 243-62.

1957 Chumbow, B. 1987. "Pidgin-English and the role of simplification and restructuring in pidginization and creolization". *Orbis* 32:118-33.

1958 Chutisilp, Pornpimol. 1984. "A sociolinguistic study of an additional language: English in Thailand". Ph.D., University of Illinois at Urbana-Champaign. (Summary in *EWW* 6:280-1).

1959 Clark, J.E., ed. 1985. *The Cultivated Australian: Festschrift in Honour of Arthur Delbridge*. Hamburg: Buske.

1960 ---. 1989. "Some proposals for a revised phonetic transcription of Australian English". In Collins & Blair, 205-13.

1961 Clark, Ross. 1990. "Pidgin English and Pidgin Maori in New Zealand". In Bell & Holmes, 97-114.

1962 Cline-Bailey, Jerry. 1992. "Creole-source language linguistic relatedness: Implications for Krio and English". Ph.D., The University of Texas at Austin. DAI 53:4 (1992), 1142-A. (Summary in *EWW* 14:2).

1963 Cluver, August D. de V. 1991. "A systems approach to language planning: the case of Namibia". *LPLP* 15:43-64.

1964 Clyne, Michael G., ed. 1985. *Australia - Meeting Place of Languages.* (PacL C-92). Canberra: ANU.

1965 ---, ed. 1991. *Linguistics in Australia: Trends in Research*. Canberra: Academy of the Social Sciences in Australia.

1966 Cochrane, G.R. 1989. "Origins and development of the Australian accent". In Collins & Blair, 176-86.

1967 Collins, Peter. 1988. "The semantics of some modals in contemporary Australian English". *AJL* 8:261-86.

1968 ---. 1989a. "Sociolinguistics in Australia: a survey". In Collins & Blair, 3-20.

1969 ---. 1989b. "Divided and debatable usage in Australian English". In Collins & Blair, 138-149.

1970 ---. 1991a. "*Will* and *shall* in Australian English". In Stig Johansson & Anna-Brita Stenström, eds. *English Computer Corpora*. Berlin: Mouton de Gruyter, 181-99.

1971 ---. 1991b. "The modals of obligation and necessity in Australian English". In *Aijmer & Altenberg, 145-65.

1972 --- & David Blair, eds. 1989. *Australian English. The Language of a New Society*. St. Lucia: The University of Queensland Press. (Rev. in *EWW* 12:309-13.)

1973 --- & Pamela Peters. 1988. "The Australian Corpus Project". In Merja Kytö, *et al.*, eds. *Corpus Linguistics, Hard and Soft*. (Proceedings of the Eighth International Conference on English Language Research on Computerized Corpora). Amsterdam: Rodopi, 103-20.

1974 [entry deleted]

1975 Cooper, Robert L. 1985. "Fantasti! Israeli attitudes towards English". In *Greenbaum, 242-51.

1976 Corson, David. 1991. "Social class differences in the lexicon". In Romaine, 349-61.

1977 Craig, Dennis R. 1984. "Communication, creole and conceptualization". *IJSL* 45:21-37.

1978 ---. 1986. "Social class and the use of language: a case study of Jamaican children". In Görlach & Holm, 71-116.

1979 ---. 1988. "Cognition and situational context: explanations from English-lexicon creole". *IJSL* 71:11-23.

1980 ---. 1989. "Creolistics and education". In *Ahrens, 265-77.

1981 Criper-Friedman, Lindsay. 1990. "The tone system of West African English". *WE* 9:63-77.

1982 Crowley, Terry. 1989a. "English in Vanuatu". *WE* 8:37-46.

1983 ---. 1989b. "Referential and expressive expansion in Bislama". *EWW* 10:85-118.

1984 ---. 1989c. "Sources and structures in Melanesian Pidgin". *Multilingua* 8:397-409.

1985 ---. 1990a. "The position of Melanesian Pidgin in Vanuatu and Papua New Guinea". In Verhaar, 1-18.

1986 ---. 1990b. *An Illustrated Bislama-English and English-Bislama Dictionary*. Vila, Vanuatu: Pacific Languages Unit, University of the South Pacific. (Rev. in *EWW* 12:138-42).

1987 ---. 1990c. *Beach-la-Mar to Bislama. The Emergence of a National Language in Vanuatu*. Oxford: Clarendon. (Rev. in *EWW* 12:171-3).

1988 ---. 1992. "Derivational morphology and structural complexity in nineteenth century Melanesian Pidgin". *Te Reo* 35:3-18.

1989 Dalphinis, Morgan. 1985. *Caribbean and African Languages. Social History, Language, Literature and Education*. London: Karia Press.

1990 ---. 1986. "African language influences in creoles lexically based on Portuguese, English and French, with special reference to Casamance Kriul, Gambian Krio and St. Lucian Patwa". Ph.D., University of London. DAI 46:10 (1986), 3017-A. (Summary in *EWW* 8:280-1).

1991 Das, Sisir Kumar. 1990. "The teaching of English in India, 1945-1985". In *Britton, *et al*., 297-314.

1992 ---. 1992. "The sounds of Indian English". In *Blank, II:149-54.

1993 Dasgupta, Probal. 1986. "On the sociolinguistics of English in India". *Indian Journal of Linguistics* 13:61-88.

1994 ---. 1993. *The Otherness of English. India's Auntie Tongue Syndrome*. London: SAGE. (Rev. in *EWW* 14:2).

1995 Davies, Alan. 1989. "Is international English an interlanguage?". *TESOL Quarterly* 23:447-67.

1996 Davy, Derek. fc. "History of New Zealand English". In *Burchfield.

1997 D'Costa, Jean C. 1984. "Louise Bennett's dialect poetry: problems of variation along a creole continuum in a literary text". In *Enninger & Haynes, 135-58.

1998 --- & Barbara Lalla, eds. 1989. *Voices in Exile. Jamaican Texts of the 18th and 19th Centuries*. Tuscaloosa: University of Alabama Press.

1999 DeBose, C.E. 1983. "Samaná English: a dialect that time forgot". *Proceedings of the Ninth Annual Meeting of the Berkeley Linguistics Society*, 47-53.

2000 De Klerk, Vivian & Barbara Bosch. 1993. "English in South Africa: the Eastern Cape perspective". *EWW* 14:2.

2001 Delbridge, Arthur. 1987. "Cultural, national and modal labels in dictionaries of English". In R. Steele & T. Threadgold, eds. *Language Topics: Essays in Honour of Michael Halliday*, Vol. 2. Amsterdam/Philadelphia: Benjamins, 65-9.

2002 ---. 1988. "Australian English". In L. Hergenhan, ed. *New Literary History of Australia*. Ringwood, Vic.: Penguin, 47-59.

2003 ---. 1989. "The *Macquarie*, an international national dictionary". In H.–J. Müllenbrock & R. Noll-Wiemann, eds. *Anglistentag 1988. Göttingen*. Tübingen: Niemeyer, 66-79.

2004 ---. 1990. "Australian English now". In *Ricks & Michaels, 66-76.
2005 Dennis, James Peter Lindsay. 1984. "A semantic study of aspect in Krio". Ph.D., University of Michigan. DAI 45:7 (1985), 2083-A. (Summary in *EWW* 7:275-6).
2006 Desai, Gaurav. 1993. "English as an African language". *ET* 34:4-11.
2007 Deverson, A.J. 1985. "'Home loans': Maori input into current New Zealand English". *English in New Zealand* 33:4-10.
2008 ---. 1988. "The pronunciation of Maori words in New Zealand English". *Occasional Papers in Language and Linguistics* 1:25-31.
2009 ---. 1990. "Considering Kiwi: a survey of teachers' attitudes to New Zealand English". *New Zealand English Newsletter* 4:10-15.
2010 Deverson, Tony. 1991. "The Maori dimension". *ET* 26:18-25.
2011 Devonish, Hubert. 1984. "Creole language standardisation in Guyana: race, class and urban-rural factors". In Sebba & Todd, 63-73.
2012 ---. 1986a. *Language and Liberation: Creole Language Politics in the Caribbean*. London: Karia Press. (Rev. in *EWW* 8:316-9).
2013 ---. 1986b. "The decay of neo-colonial official language policies. The case of the English-lexicon creoles of the Commonwealth Caribbean". In Görlach & Holm, 23-52.
2014 ---. 1991. "Standardisation in a creole continuum situation: the Guyana case". In *Cheshire, 585-94.
2015 --- & Jean-Charles Pochard. 1988. "On the diversification in the function of deictic markers: a study of *a*, *da* and *dem* in the Jamaican Creole noun phrase". *EWW* 9:213-26.
2016 --- & Walter Seiler. 1991. "A reanalysis of the phonological system of Jamaican Creole". (*SCL* 24). St. Augustine, Trinidad: Society for Caribbean Linguistics.
2017 Diensberg, Bernhard. 1986. "Aspects of sociolectal variation in present-day Australian English". In "Carstensen & Grabes, 404-16.
2018 Dineen, Anne. 1992. "High rise tones and Australian English intonation: a descriptive problem". In Dutton, *et al.*, 115-24.
2019 Dissanayake, Wimal. 1985. "Towards a decolonized English: South Asian creativity in fiction". *WE* 4:233-42.
2020 Dixon, R.M.W. n.d. "Some observations on the grammar of Indian English". In B.L. Bai & B.R. Reddy, eds. *Studies in Dravidian and General Linguistics*. (Osmania University Publications in Linguistics, 6), 437-47.

2021 ---, W.S. Ramson & Mandy Thomas. 1990. *Australian Aboriginal Words in English. Their Origin and Meaning*. Melbourne: Oxford UP. (Rev. in *EWW* 13:168-71).

2022 Drayton, Kathleen. 1990. "'The most important agent of colonization': teaching English in the West Indies". In *Britton, *et al.*, 200-25.

2023 D'Souza, Jean. 1987. "English in India's language modernization". *WE* 6:63-70.

2024 ---. 1988. "International strategies in South Asian languages: their implications for teaching English internationally". *WE* 7:159-72.

2025 ---. 1990. "English: one or many? An experimental study". *WE* 9:371-82.

2026 ---. 1991. "Speech acts in Indian English fiction". *WE* 10:307-16.

2027 ---. 1992. "The relationship between code-mixing and the new varieties of English: issues and implications". In *Smith & Sridhar, 217-23.

2028 Dua, Hans R. 1990. "Patterns of language use and print media: implications for language spread". In *Laforge & McConnell, 139-58.

2029 ---. 1991. "Language planning in India: problems, approaches and prospects". In *Marshall, 105-33.

2030 Dubey, Vinod S. 1983. "Style of English newspapers in India: a linguistic study". Ph.D., Bhagalpur. (Summary in *EWW* 4:291-2).

2031 ---. 1989. *Newspaper English in India*. (SELL, 13). New Delhi: Bahri Publications.

2032 ---. 1991. "The lexical style of Indian English newspapers". *WE* 10:19-32.

2033 Dutton, Thomas E. 1983. "The origin and spread of Aboriginal Pidgin English in Queensland: a preliminary account". *Aboriginal History* 7:90-122.

2034 ---, Malcolm Ross & Darrell Tryon, eds. 1992. *The Language Game: Papers in Memory of Donald C. Laycock*. (PacL C-110). Canberra: ANU. (Rev. in *EWW* 14:2).

2035 Eades, Diana. 1991. "Communicative strategies in Aboriginal English". In Romaine, 84-93.

2036 Eagleson, Robert D. 1985. "Urban Aboriginal English: misunderstandings and misconceptions". *Australian Review of Applied Linguistics* 8:131-40.

2037 ---. 1989. "Popular and professional attitudes to prestige dialects". In Collins & Blair, 150-7.

2038 ---. 1991. "Plain English: some sociolinguistic revelations". In Romaine, 363-72.

2039 Eastman, Carol M. 1991. "The political [sic] and sociolinguistics of status planning in Africa". In *Marshall, 135-51.

2040 Edwards, Walter F. 1984. "A community-based approach to the provenance of urban Guyanese Creole". In Sebba & Todd, 83-94.

2041 ---. 1985. "Intra-style shifting and linguistic variation in Guyanese speech". *AnL* 27:86-93.

2042 ---. 1990. "Morphosyntactic acculturation at the rural/urban interface in Guyana". *AS* 65:99-113.

2043 Eisikovits, Edina. 1987. "Variation in the lexical verb in Inner-Sydney English". *AJL* 7:1-24. (Reprinted in *Trudgill & Chambers, 120-42).

2044 ---. 1989a. "Girl-talk/boy-talk: sex differences in adolescent speech". In Collins & Blair, 35-54.

2045 ---. 1989b. "Variation in the perfective in Inner-Sydney English". *AJL* 9:3-20.

2046 ---. 1991. "Variation in subject-verb agreement in Inner-Sydney English". In *Cheshire, 235-55.

2047 Eka, David. 1985. "A phonological study of Standard Nigerian English". Ph.D., Zaria University. (Summary in *EWW* 8:282-3).

2048 Eltis, K.J. 1989. "Pupils' speech style and teacher reaction". In Collins & Blair, 103-10.

2049 *ELT in China*. (Papers presented at the International Symposium on Teaching English in the Chinese Context (ISTEC), Guanzhou, China 1985). 1990. Beijing: Foreign Language Teaching and Research Press.

2050 Escure, Geneviève. 1984. "The acquisition of Creole by urban and rural black Caribs in Belize". In Sebba & Todd, 95-106.

2051 ---. 1988. "Topic structures as language universals". *JPCL* 3:159-76.

2052 ---. 1991. "Gender roles and linguistic variation in the Belizean Creole community". In *Cheshire, 595-608.

2053 Evans, Daniel William. 1982. "Relationships between attitudes of Korean businessmen and three types of attainment in English: global proficiency, intonative performance, and discrete-point academic achievement". Ph.D., University of Texas at Austin. DAI 43:3 (1982), 787-A. (Summary in *EWW* 4:298-9).

2054 Faigley, Lester. fc. "The impact of electronic communication technologies on World Englishes". Paper Islamabad 1989, to appear in Baumgardner (?).

2055 Faraclas, Nicholas. 1984. "Rivers Pidgin English: tone, stress, or pitch-accent language?". In E. Bokamba, ed. *Language in African Culture and Society. Studies in the Linguistic Sciences* 14(2):67-76.

2056 ---. 1986a. *Reading and Writing Nigerian Pidgin*. Rivers Readers Project. University of Port Harcourt.

2057 ---. 1986b. "Pronouns, creolization, and decreolization in Nigerian Pidgin". *Journal of West African Languages* 16:3-8.

2058 ---. 1987. "Creolization and tense-aspect-modality system of Nigerian Pidgin". *Journal of African Languages and Linguistics* 9:45-59.

2059 ---. 1988. "Nigerian Pidgin and the languages of southern Nigeria". *JPCL* 3:177-97.

2060 ---. 1989. "A grammar of Nigerian Pidgin". Ph.D., University of California, Berkeley. DAI 51:5 (1990), 1595-A. (Summary in *EWW* 12:286-7).

2061 ---. 1990. "From Old Guinea to Papua New Guinea: a comparative study of Nigerian Pidgin and Tok Pisin". In Verhaar, 91-169.

2062 ---. 1991. "The pronoun system in Nigerian Pidgin: a preliminary study". In *Cheshire, 509-18.

2063 ---, *et al.* 1984. "Rivers State Pidgin English". *Journal of the Linguistic Society of Nigeria* 2:187-98.

2064 Fayer, Joan M. 1986. "Pidgins as written languages: evidence from 18th century Old Calabar". *AnL* 28:313-9.

2065 ---. 1990. "Nigerian Pidgin English in Old Calabar in the eighteenth and nineteenth centuries". In *Singler, 185-202.

2066 Ferguson, Charles A. fc. "English in South Asia: imperialist legacy and regional asset". In Baumgardner.

2067 Fernando, Chitra. 1985. "Australian idiom". In Clark, 349-60.

2068 ---. fc. "The ideational function of English in Sri Lanka". In Baumgardner.

2069 Fernando, Siromi. 1989. "Style range in Sri Lankan English fiction: an analysis of four texts". *WE* 8:119-32.

2070 Fishman, Joshua A. & Alma Rubal-Lopez. 1992. "Cross-polity analysis of factors affecting English language spread: predicting three criteria of spread from a large pool of independent variables". In *Smith & Sridhar, 309-29.

2071 Flint, K. 1989. "Some morphological variants in Australian English". *Working Papers of the Speech, Hearing and Language Research Centre, Macquarie University*, 131-6.

2072 Foley, Joseph A., ed. 1988a. *New Englishes. The Case of Singapore*. Singapore: UP. (Rev. in *EWW* 10:176-8).

2073 ---. 1988b. "Studies in Singapore English: looking back and looking forward". In Foley, 1-26.

2074 ---. 1988c. "The English language syllabus and the pre-school child". In Foley, 51-69.

2075 ---. 1991. "Developmental features of children's writing in Singapore". In Kwan-Terry, 255-81.

2076 ---. 1992. "The English Language Survey: an overview of the pilot study". In Pakir, 74-83.

2077 Forbes, Duncan. 1993. "Singlish". *ET* 34:18-21.

2078 Freeman, R. & Munzali Jibril, eds. 1984. *English Language Studies in Nigerian Higher Education. Papers of the Nigeria English Studies Association/British Council Conference held at Bayero University, Kano, Nigeria, 23 to 27 September 1984*. London: The British Council. (Rev. in *EWW* 9:124-7).

2079 Gallois, Cynthia & Victor J. Callan. 1989. "Attitudes to spoken Australian English: judgements of ingroup and ethnic outgroup speakers". *AJL* 9:149-60.

2080 ---, *et al*. 1984. "Personality judgements of Australian Aborigine and white speakers: ethnicity, sex, and context". *JLSP* 3:39-57.

2081 Ghadessy, Mohsen. 1992. "Singapore written business communication". In Pakir, 89-101.

2082 Gibbons, John. 1987. *Code-mixing and Code Choice. A Hong Kong Case Study*. Clevedon: Multilingual Matters. (Rev. in *EWW* 8:336-7).

2083 Gibson, Kean. 1984. "Evidence against an anterior tense system in Guyanese and Jamaican Creoles". In Sebba & Todd, 123-30.

2084 ---. 1988. "The habitual category in Guyanese and Jamaican Creoles". *AS* 63:195-202.

2085 Gilbert, Glenn C. 1985a. "Hugo Schuchardt and the Atlantic creoles: a newly discovered manuscript 'On the Negro English of West Africa'". *AS* 60:31-63. [cf. 2664]

2086 ---. 1985b. "The first systematic survey of the world's pidgins and creoles: Hugo Schuchardt, 1882-1885". *YPL* 11:131-40.

2087 Gillam, D. 1980-81. "'Defensively Australian': some Australian attitudes to Australian English". *Studia Germanica Gandensia* 21:153-69.

2088 Gilman, Charles. 1985. "Proto-creole /r/". In *Hancock, 33-43.

2089 Görlach, Manfred. 1984a. "A selective bibliography of English as a world language (1965-1983)". In *Viereck, Schneider & Görlach, 225-319.

2090 ---. 1984b. "English in Africa - African English?". *Revista Canaria de Estudios Ingleses* (La Laguna, Tenerife) 8:33-56. (Reprinted in *Görlach 1991:122-43).

2091 ---. 1985. "Lexicographical problems of New Englishes and English-related pidgin and creole languages". *EWW* 6:1-36. (Reprinted in

*Görlach 1991:36-68; shorter version in *Hyldgaard-Jensen & Zettersten, 223-44).

2092 ---. 1986. "Bottom - thou art translated: problems of 'creolizing' a German children's book". In N. Boretzky, *et al.*, eds. *Beiträge zum 2. Essener Kolloquium über "Kreolsprachen und Sprachkontakte"*. Bochum: Brockmeyer, 83-101. (Reprinted in *Görlach 1991:174-91).

2093 ---. 1987. "Englisch - Formen einer Weltsprache. Bericht und Standortbestimmung". *Forschung in Köln* 1:44-7.

2094 ---. 1988a. "Sprachliche Standardisierungsprozesse im englischsprachigen Raum". *Standardisierungsentwicklungen in europäischen Nationalsprachen: Romania, Germania. Sociolinguistics* 2. Tübingen: Niemeyer, 131-85. English version in Manfred Görlach. 1990. *Studies in the History of the English Language*. (Anglistische Forschungen, 210). Heidelberg: Winter, 9-64.

2095 ---. 1988b. "English as a world language - the state of the art". *EWW* 9:1-32. (Reprinted in *Görlach 1991:10-35).

2096 ---. 1989a. "The sociolinguistics of English as a world language". In Dieter Riemenschneider, ed. *Critical Approaches to the New Literatures in English*. Essen: Blaue Eule, 116-30.

2097 ---. 1989b. "From an Indian letter-writer". *EWW* 10:135-40.

2098 ---. 1990. "Lexical problems of English in Africa". In Schmied, 27-46.

2099 ---. 1991a. "Scotland and Jamaica - bilingual or bidialectal?". In *Görlach 1991:69-89.

2100 ---. 1991b. "Australian English: standards, stigmata, stereotypes and statistics". In *Görlach 1991:144-73.

2101 ---. 1991c. "Blurbs from an Indian book catalogue (1990)". *EWW* 12:261-6.

2102 ---. 1992. "Englishes. A selective bibliography 1984-1991 (excluding Britain, Ireland and the USA/Canada)". *EWW* 13:59-109.

2103 --- & John Holm. 1986. *Focus on the Caribbean*. (VEAW, G8). Amsterdam: Benjamins. (Rev. in *EWW* 8:311-16).

2104 Goke-Pariola, B. 1987. "Language transfer and the Nigerian writer of English". *WE* 6:127-36.

2105 Gonzalez, Andrew B. 1984. "Philippine English across generations: the sound system". *DLSU Dialogue* 20:1-23.

2106 ---. 1985. *Studies on Philippine English*. (Occ. Papers, 39). Singapore: RELC.

2107 ---. 1990. "Evaluating bilingual education in the Philippines: towards a multidimensional model of evaluation in language planning". In Baldauf & Luke, 319-34.

2108 ---. 1991. "Stylistic shifts in the English of the Philippine print media". In *Cheshire, 333-63.

2109 Gordon, Elizabeth. 1983a. "New Zealand English pronunciation: an investigation into some early written records". *TeReo* 26:29-42.

2110 ---. 1983b. "'The flood of impure vocalisation' - A study of attitudes towards New Zealand speech". *The New Zealand Speech-Language Therapists' Journal* 38:16-29.

2111 ---. 1989. "That colonial twang: New Zealand speech and New Zealand identity". In D. Novitz & W. Wilmott, eds. *Culture and Identity in New Zealand*. Wellington: Government Printer Books, 77-90.

2112 ---. 1992. "Finding their own voice: the evolution of New Zealand English". In *Blank, II:198-208.

2113 --- & Marcia Abell. 1990. "'This objectionable colonial dialect': historical and contemporary attitudes to New Zealand speech". In Bell & Holmes, 21-48.

2114 --- & A.J. Deverson. 1985. *New Zealand English: An Introduction to New Zealand Speech and Usage*. Auckland: Heinemann. (Rev. in *EWW* 7:349-50).

2115 --- & ---. 1989. *Finding a New Zealand Voice: Attitudes towards English Used in New Zealand*. Auckland: New House Publishers.

2116 --- & Margaret A. Maclagan. 1985. "A study of the /i/~/e/ contrast in New Zealand English". *The New Zealand Speech-Language Therapists' Journal* 40:16-26.

2117 --- & ---. 1989. "*Beer* and *bear*, *cheer* and *chair*: a longitudinal study of the *ear*/*air* contrast in New Zealand English". *AJL* 9:203-20.

2118 --- & ---. 1990. "A longitudinal study of the 'ear/air' contrast in New Zealand speech". In Bell & Holmes, 129-48.

2119 Gordon, Ian A. 1988. "British regional survivals in New Zealand English." In T.L. Burton & Jill Burton, eds. *Lexicographical and Linguistic Studies: Essays in Honour of G.W. Turner*. Woodbridge: Boydell & Brewer, 179-84.

2120 Grabe, William. 1988. "English, information access, and technology transfer: a rationale for English as an international language". *WE* 7:63-72.

2121 Graber, Philip. 1987. "Thematic participation in a Kriol story". *JPCL* 2:209-27.

2122 Green, E. & Pam Peters. 1991. "The Australian Corpus Project and Australian English". *ICAME Journal* 15:37-54.

2123 Greichen, H. 1989. "Regionale, soziale und funktionelle Differenzierung des Englischen am Beispiel des australischen Englisch". In *Graustein & Thiele, 66-72.

2124 Griffin, Ron. 1992. "Comprehension and sentence complexity in Tanzanian classrooms". In Schmied, 57-73.

2125 Gunn, John S. 1989. "The shearing shed society". In Collins & Blair, 78-88.

2126 ---. 1992. "Social contexts in the history of Australian English". In *Machan & Scott, 204-29.

2127 Gupta, Anthea Fraser. 1986. "A standard for written Singapore English?". *EWW* 7:75-99. (Reprinted in Foley 1988:27-50).

2128 ---. 1989. "Singapore Colloquial English and Standard English". *Singapore Journal of Education* 10:33-9.

2129 ---. 1990. "A study of the acquisition and use of interrogatives and questions in the English of pre-school Chinese Singaporeans". D.Phil., University of York. (Summary in *EWW* 12:288-9).

2130 ---. 1991a. "Acquisition of diglossia in Singapore English". In Kwan-Terry, 119-60.

2131 ---. 1991b. "Contact features of Singapore colloquial English". In Bolton & Kwok, 323-45.

2132 ---. 1991c. "Almost a creole: Singapore Colloquial English". *California Linguistic Notes* 23(1):9-21.

2133 ---. 1992a. "The pragmatic particles of Singapore Colloquial English". *Journal of Pragmatics* 17(3):39-65.

2134 ---. 1992b. "Restrictive labels for a dictionary of Singapore and Malaysian English". In Pakir, 139-42.

2135 ---. fc. *The Step Tongue: Children's English in Singapore*. Clevedon: Multilingual Matters.

2136 Guy, Gregory R. 1991. "Australia". In *Cheshire, 213-26.

2137 ---, *et al.* 1986. "An intonational change in progress in Australian English". *LinS* 15:23-52.

2138 --- & Julia Vonwiller. 1989. "The high rising tone in Australian English". In Collins & Blair, 21-34.

2139 Gyasi, Ibrahim K. 1991. "Aspects of English in Ghana". *ET* 26:26-31.

2140 Halim, A. 1985. *The Status and Role of English in Indonesia*. A report prepared for the United States Information Service, Jakarta.

2141 Hammarström, Göran. 1987. "Irritating expressions in Australian English". *Language and Speech* 30:357-72.

2142 Haque, Anjum Riyazul. 1993. "The position and status of English in Pakistan [1983]". In Baumgardner, 11-6.

2143 Harlech-Jones, Brian. 1989. "Politics and policies: language planning in Namibia, with special reference to English". (L.A.U.D., Series B, Paper No. 205). Duisburg: University.

2144 ---. 1990. *'You Taught Me Language'*. The implementation of English as a medium of instruction in Namibia. Oxford: UP. (Rev. in *EWW* 13:335-6).

2145 Harris, John W. 1984. "Language contact, pidgins and the emergence of Kriol in the Northern Territory: theoretical and historical perspectives". Ph.D., University of Queensland. (Summary in *EWW* 7:277-9).

2146 ---. 1985. "Contact languages at the Northern Territory British military settlements". *Aboriginal History* 9:148-69.

2147 ---. 1986a. *Northern Territory Pidgins and the Origins of Kriol*. (PacL C-89). Canberra: ANU.

2148 ---. 1986b. "Creoles - new languages and an old debate". *Journal of Christian Education* 85:9-21.

2149 ---. 1988a. "Northern Territory pidgin English: a lexical study". *EWW* 9:77-99.

2150 ---. 1988b. "North Australian Kriol and the Kriol 'Holi Baibul'". In T. Swain & D.B. Rose, eds. *Aboriginal Australians and Christian Missions*. Bedford Park, SA: Australian Society for the Study of Religions, 412-21.

2151 ---. 1989. "North Australian Kriol: historical perspectives and new directions". *Australian Review of Applied Linguistics* 11:1-8.

2152 ---. 1991. "Kriol - the creation of a new language". In Romaine, 195-203.

2153 --- & John Sandefur. 1985a. "Kriol and multilingualism". In Clyne, 257-64.

2154 --- & ---. 1985b. "The creole language debate and the use of creoles in Australian schools". *The Aboriginal Child at School* 12:8-29.

2155 Harrison, Shirley. 1984. "Variation in present Norfolk Island speech. A study of stability and instability in diglossia". Ph.D., Macquarie University. (Summary in *EWW* 6:281-3).

2156 ---. 1985. "The social setting of Norfolk speech". *EWW* 6:131-53.

2156a Hartford, Beverly S. fc. "The relationship of New Englishes and linguistic theory: A cognitive-based grammar of Nepali English". In Baumgardner.

2157 Hauptfleisch, T. 1983. *Language Loyalty in South Africa. Vol. 4: Language Loyalty and Language Shift: Some Trends among White Adults in Urban Areas*. Pretoria: Human Sciences Research Council. (Rev. in *EWW* 5:152).

2158 Hawkins, R.E. 1984. *Common Indian Words in English*. Delhi: Oxford UP. (Rev. in *EWW* 8:334-5).

2159 Haynes, Lilith M. 1984. "Language variation in *Island Voices*". *EWW* 5:25-42.

2160 Haynes, R. 1984. *A Pilot Study into the Emergence of a Non-Standard Dialect of English in Zambia. Part 1: Possibilities*. Lusaka: University of Zambia.

2161 Hellinger, Marlis. 1985. *Englisch-orientierte Pidgin- und Kreolsprachen: Entstehung, Geschichte und sprachlicher Wandel*. Darmstadt: Wissenschaftliche Buchgesellschaft. (Rev. in *EWW* 6:341-3).

2162 ---. 1986. "On writing English-related creoles in the Caribbean". In Görlach & Holm, 53-70.

2163 ---. 1990. "Creolistics and sociolinguistics". *EWW* 11:59-77.

2164 Herbert, Robert K., ed. fc. *Proceedings of the Colloquium on Sociolinguistics in Africa*. Johannesburg: Witwatersrand UP.

2165 Herzfeld, Anita. 1985. "A sociolinguistic view towards a creole continuum: the study of Limon English Creole". In P.H. Nelde, ed. *Methoden der Kontaktlinguistik*. Bonn: Dümmler, 75-86.

2166 Hirsh, W., ed. 1987. *Living Languages: Bilingualism and Community Languages in New Zealand Today*. Auckland: Heinemann.

2167 Ho, Mian-Lian. 1986. "The verb phrase in Singapore English". Ph.D., Monash University, Melbourne.

2168 ---. 1992a. "The language bioprogram hypothesis and Singaporean English". *RELC Journal* 23:1-14.

2169 ---. 1992b. "The semantics of some verbs of movement in Singapore English: bring/take, send, follow and fetch". In Pakir, 52-61.

2170 --- & John T. Platt. 1993. *Dynamics of a Contact Continuum. Singaporean English*. Oxford: Clarendon.

2171 Holm, John. 1984. "Central American English: our hemisphere's best-kept secret". *Geolinguistics*.

2172 ---. 1986. "The spread of English in the Caribbean area". In Görlach & Holm, 1-22.

2173 ---. fc. "English in the Caribbean". In *Burchfield.

2174 Holmes, Janet. 1986. "Compliments and compliment responses in New Zealand English". *AnL* 28:485-508.

2175 ---. 1988a. "'Sort of' in New Zealand women's and men's speech". *Studia Linguistica* 42:85-121.

2176 ---. 1988b. "'Of course': a pragmatic particle in New Zealand women's and men's speech". *AJL* 8:49-74.

2177 ---. 1990a. "Politeness strategies in New Zealand women's speech". In Bell & Holmes, 252-75.

2178 ---. 1990b. "Apologies in New Zealand English". *LinS* 19:155-99.

2179 --- & Allan Bell. 1988b. "Learning by experience: notes for New Zealand". *TeReo* 31:19-49.

2180 Holzknecht, Susanne. 1989. "Sociolinguistic analysis of a register: birthday notices in Papua New Guinea *Post Courier*". *WE* 8:179-92.

2181 Hong, Chua Seok. 1990. "A language for the people: a history of English language teaching in Singapore". In *Britton, *et al.*, 249-68.

2182 Horvath, Barbara M. 1985. *Variation in Australian English: The Sociolects of Sydney*. (Cambridge Studies in Linguistics, 45). Cambridge: UP. (Rev. in *EWW* 7:140-3).

2183 ---. 1991. "Finding a place in Sydney: migrants and language change". In Romaine, 304-17.

2184 --- & D. Sankoff. 1987. "Delimiting the Sydney speech community". *LinS* 16:179-204.

2185 Hosali, Priya & Jean Aitchison. 1986. "Butler English: a minimal pidgin?". *JPCL* 1:51-79.

2186 Howard, E. 1983. "Pitcairn and Norfolk: the saga of *Bounty*'s children". *National Geographic* 164:510-41.

2187 Hudson, B. & L. Pickering. 1986. *The First Australian Dictionary of Vulgarities and Obscenities*. Frenchs Forest, NSW: Lilyfield Publishers. (Reprinted 1987, Newton Abbot & London: David & Charles).

2188 Hudson, Diana & Josef Schmied. 1992. "Deviation and language awareness in Kenyan popular literature". In Schmied, 1-20.

2189 Huebner, Thom. 1986. "Vernacular literacy, English as a language of wider communication, and language shift in American Samoa". *JMMD* 7:393-411.

2190 ---. 1989. "Language and schooling in Western and American Samoa". *WE* 8:59-72.

2191 Hughes, Joan. 1989. *Australian Words and Their Origins*. Melbourne: Oxford UP. (Rev. in *EWW* 13:167-8).

2192 --- & Bill Ramson. 1990. "A dinkum dialogue with the demon drink". *ET* 6:66-9.

2193 --- & ---. 1992. "Lexicographic evidence of a popular pursuit". In Dutton, *et al.*, 187-90.
2194 Hume, A. 1986. "F.W.C. Gerstäcker: an overlooked informant on language in mid-19th century Australia". *AUMLA* 66:272-85.
2195 Husain, Abbas M. 1992. "Varieties of verbosity in Pakistani English". *WE* 11:51-60.
2196 Huttar, George & Evert Koanting. 1993. "Are Ndjuká comparative markers verbs?". In *Byrne & Holm, 165-74.
2197 Huygens, I. & G. Vaughan. 1983. "Language attitudes, ethnicity and social class in New Zealand". *JMMD* 4:207-23.
2198 Ingram, J.C.L. 1989. "Connected speech processes in Australian English". *AJL* 9:21-49.
2199 ---, *et al.* 1985. "Developmental and sociolinguistic variation in the speech of Brisbane schoolchildren". *AJL* 5:233-46.
2200 Jafre Bin Zainol Abidin, Mohamad. 1992. "The English language needs of students at the Science University of Malaysia". Ph.D., University of Keele (UK). DAI 53:3 (1992), 745-A. (Summary in *EWW* 14:2).
2201 Janks, Hilary & Jonathan Paton. 1990. "English and the teaching of English literature in South Africa". In *Britton, *et al.*, 226-48.
2202 Jennings, Isabel Yumol. 1984. "Filipino English: Contrastive analysis and interference in three syntactic structures". Ph.D., University of Texas at Austin. DAI 45:7 (1985), 2083-A. (Summary in *EWW* 7:282-3).
2203 Jibril, Munzali. 1986. "Sociolinguistic variation in Nigerian English". *EWW* 7:47-74.
2204 ---. 1987. "Language in Nigerian education". *IJAL* 13:38-51.
2205 ---. 1991. "The sociolinguistics of prepositional usage in Nigerian English". In *Cheshire, 519-44.
2206 ---, *et al.* "Nigerian primary school teachers' mastery of English stress and intonation". *Journal of English Studies* 3:23-35.
2207 Johansen, L.M. 1988. *The Dinkum Dictionary. A Ripper Guide to Aussie English*. Ringwood, Vic.: Viking O'Neill/Penguin.
2208 Johnson, Alex C. 1985. "Multilingualism and language policy in Sierra Leone". BASS 5:115-44.
2209 Jones, Eldred D., *et al.*, eds. 1992. *Reading and Writing Krio. Proceedings of a Workshop (...)*. (Acta Universitatis Upsaliensis, 77). Uppsala & Stockholm: Almqvist & Wiksell. (Rev. in *EWW* 13:331-2).
2210 Jones, Frederick C.V. 1984. "Aspects of the morphology of English-derived words in Sierra Leone Krio". In Sebba & Todd, 181-90.

2211 ---. 1990a. "The development of #s plural in Sierra Leone Krio". In *Edmondson, *et al.*, 309-22.

2212 ---. 1990b. "The grammatical items *bin*, *fɔ* and *mɔs* in Sierra Leone Krio". *Linguistics* 28:845-66.

2213 Jourdan, Christine. 1985a. "Sapos Iumi Mitim Iumi: the social context of creolization in the Solomon Islands". Ph.D., Australian National University, Canberra. (Summary in *EWW* 9:299).

2214 ---. 1985b. "Creolisation, nativisation or substrate influence: what is happening to *bae* in Solomon Islands Pijin". In Romaine, *et al.*, 67-96.

2215 ---. 1989. "Nativization and anglicization in Solomon Pijin". *WE* 8:25-35.

2216 ---. 1990. "Solomon Pijin: an unrecognized national language". In Baldauf & Luke, 166-81.

2217 Jowitt, David. 1991. *Nigerian English Usage. An Introduction.* Ikeja: Longman Nigeria. (Rev. in *EWW* 13:333-5).

2218 --- & S. Nuamonu. 1985. *Common Errors in English.* London: Longman.

2219 Kachru, Braj B. 1983a. *The Indianization of English: the English Language in India.* New Delhi: Oxford UP.

2220 ---. 1983b. "The bilingual's creativity: discoursal and stylistic strategies in contact literatures in English". *Studies in the Linguistic Sciences* 13(2):37-55. (Reprinted in Kachru 1986:159-73).

2221 ---. 1984a. "The alchemy of English: social and functional power of non-native varieties". In *Kramarae, *et al.*, 176-93. (Reprinted in Kachru 1986:1-15).

2222 ---. 1984b. "Regional norms". In Sandra J. Savignon & Margie S. Berns, eds. *Initiatives in Communicative Language Teaching: A Book of Readings.* New York: Addison-Wesley, 55-78. (Reprinted in Kachru 1986:83-99).

2223 ---. 1985a. "Institutionalized second language varieties". In *Greenbaum, 211-26. (Reprinted in Kachru 1986:16-32).

2224 ---. 1985b. "Standards, codification and sociolinguistic realism: the English language in the outer circle". In *Quirk & Widdowson, 11-30.

2225 ---. 1986. *The Alchemy of English: The Spread, Functions and Models of Non-Native Englishes.* Oxford: Pergamon Press. (Rev. in *EWW* 7:329-30).

2226 ---. 1987. "English education in India: a sociolinguistic profile of Indian English". *Nagoya Gakuin University (Japan) Round Table* 15:11-30.

2227 ---. 1988a. "ESP and non-native varieties of English: toward a shift in paradigm". In Dick Chamberlain & R.J. Baumgardner, eds. *ESP in the*

Classroom: Practice and Evaluation. (ELT Documents, 128). London: Macmillan.
2228 ---. 1988b. "The spread of English and sacred linguistic cows". In Lowenberg, 207-28. (Cf. also: "The sacred cows of English". *ET* 16:3-8).
2229 ---. 1988c. "India". In *Ammon, *et al.*, 1282-7.
2230 ---. 1988d. "Toward expanding the English canon: Raja Rao's credo for creativity". *World Literatures Today* 62:582-6.
2231 ---. 1991. "Liberation linguistics and the Quirk concern". *ET* 25:3-13.
2232 ---. 1992. "The second diaspora of English". In *Machan & Scott, 230-52.
2233 ---. fc. a. "English in South Asia". In *Burchfield.
2234 ---. fc. b. "South Asian English: toward an identity in diaspora". In Baumgardner.
2235 ---. fc. c. "Indian English: linguistic analysis". In E. Benson, *et al.*, eds. *Encyclopedia of Commonwealth Literature*. London: Routledge & Kegan Paul.
2236 Kachru, Yamuna. 1985. "Discourse analysis, non-native Englishes and second language acquisition research". *WE* 4:223-32.
2237 ---. 1991. "Speech acts in world Englishes: toward a framework for research". *WE* 10:299-306.
2238 ---. 1992. "Speech acts in the other tongue: an integrated approach to cross-cultural research". In *Smith & Sridhar, 235-40.
2239 ---. fc. "Language and cultural meaning: expository writing in South Asian English". In Baumgardner.
2240 Kadeghe, Michael Y. 1992. "Establishing educational bilingual programmes in Tanzania: an alternative option". In Schmied, 46-56.
2241 Källgård, Anders. 1993. "Present-day Pitcairnese". *EWW* 14:71-114.
2242 Kaldor, Susan & Ian G. Malcolm. 1985. "Aboriginal children's English - educational implications". In Clyne, 223-40.
2243 --- & ---. 1991. "Aboriginal English - an overview". In Romaine, 67-83.
2244 Kale, Joan. 1990. "Language planning and the language of education in Papua New Guinea". In Baldauf & Luke, 182-96.
2245 Kandiah, Thiru. 1987/90. "New varieties of English: the creation of the paradigm and its radicalisation". Sections I-III *Navasilu* 9:31-42 and Sections IV-VII *Navasilu* 10:126-39.
2246 ---. 1991. "South Asia". In *Cheshire, 271-87.
2247 ---. fc. "Syntactic 'deletion' in Lankan English: learning from a new variety of English about ----". In Baumgardner.

2248 Kanyoro, Musimbi R.A. 1991. "The politics of the English language in Kenya and Tanzania". In *Cheshire, 402-19.

2249 Kapili, Lily V. 1988. "Requiem for English?". *ET* 16:30-5.

2250 Kaplan, Robert B. 1987. "English in the language policy of the Pacific rim". *WE* 6:137-48.

2251 Kassulamemba, Frederick T. 1984. "The learning of postmodification structure by adult second language learners of English: a case for Tanzania". Ph. D., University of Reading.

2252 Katikar, Pratibha. 1984. "The meanings of the modals in Indian English". Ph.D., Shivaji University, Kolhapur. (Summary in *EWW* 8:285-7).

2253 Keesing, N. 1982. *Lily on the Dustbin: Slang of Australian Women and Families*. Ringwood, Vic.: Penguin.

2254 Keesing, Roger M. 1985. "Subject pronoun and tense-marking in Southeast Solomonic languages and Solomon Pijin: grounds for substratomania?". In Romaine, *et al.*, 97-132.

2255 ---. 1986. "Plantation networks, plantation culture: the hidden side of colonial Melanesia". *Journal de la Société des Océanistes* 82-83:163-70.

2256 ---. 1988a. *Melanesian Pidgin. The Oceanic Substrate*. Stanford: UP.

2257 ---. 1988b. "Solomons Pidgin pronouns: a further look". *EWW* 9:271-92.

2258 ---. 1990. "Solomon Pijin: colonial ideologies". In Baldauf & Luke, 149-65.

2259 Kennedy, Audrey E.H. 1993. "Of dacoits and desperados: crime reporting in Pakistani English". In Baumgardner, 65-75.

2259a ---. 1993. "A bribe by any other name...: Terms of gratification in Pakistani English". In Baumgardner, 197-204.

2260 Kephart, Ronald F. 1986. "'It have more soft words': a study of creole English and reading in Carriacou, Grenada". Ph.D., University of Florida. DAI 47:1 (1986), 166-A. (Summary in *EWW* 8:287-8).

2261 Khan, Farhat. 1989. "Linguistic variation in Indian English: a sociolinguistic study". Ph.D., University of Reading. DAI 50:12 (1990), 3934-A. (Summary in *EWW* 12:292).

2262 ---. 1991. "Final consonant cluster simplification in a variety of Indian English". In *Cheshire, 288-98.

2263 Khan, Shayan Afzal & Jane Ann Lindley. 1993. "English language publishing in Pakistan". In Baumgardner, 17-28.

2264 Khiralla, Mohamed Nagy A.K. 1990. "The development of a computer-assisted Maritime English learning programme: Describing, testing and teaching some stylistic features of international maritime conventions". Ph.D., University of Exeter. DAI 52:4 (1991), 1310-A. (Summary in *EWW* 13:281-2).

2265 Khoo, Rosemary. 1992. "The A to Z of Singapore life - the selection of lexical entries". In Pakir, 105-15.

2266 Khubchandani, Lachman M., ed. 1988. *Language in a Plural Society*. Motilal Banarsidass.

2267 Kirpal Singh. 1984. "An approach to Singapore writing in English". *Ariel* 15:5-24.

2268 Knight, Anne. 1988. "South Australian Aboriginal words surviving in Australian English". In T.L. Burton & Jill Burton, eds. *Lexicographical and Linguistic Studies: Essays in Honour of G.W. Turner*. Woodbridge: Boydell & Brewer, 151-62.

2269 Koch, Harold. 1991. "Language and communication in Aboriginal land claim hearings". In Romaine, 94-103.

2270 Kramer, Johannes. 1986. *English and Spanish in Gibraltar*. Hamburg: Buske. (Rev. in *EWW* 9:142-3).

2271 Kuiper, Koenraad. 1991. "Sporting formulae in New Zealand English: two models of male solidarity". In *Cheshire, 200-9.

2272 --- & Paddy Austin. 1990. "They're off and racing now: the speech of the New Zealand race caller". In Bell & Holmes, 195-220.

2273 Kujore, Obafemi. 1985. *English Usage. Some Notable Nigerian Variations*. Ibadan: Evans Brothers (Nigeria Publishers). (Rev. in *EWW* 11:323-4).

2274 Kumar, Ashok. 1987. "Certain aspects of the form and functions of Hindi-English code-switching". Ph.D., Hyderabad: CIEFL. (Summary in *EWW* 9:304-5).

2275 Kuo, E.C.Y. 1985. "Language and social mobility in Singapore". In *Wolfson & Manes, 337-54.

2276 Kwan-Terry, Anna. 1986a. *The Simultaneous Acquisition of English and Chinese by a Pre-School Child in Singapore*. RELC Research Report.

2277 ---. 1986b. "The acquisition of word order in English and Cantonese interrogative sentences: a Singapore case study". *RELC Journal* 17:14-39.

2278 ---, ed. 1991a. *Child Language Development in Singapore and Malaysia*. Singapore: UP.

2279 ---. 1991b. "Home language and school language: a study of children's language use in Singapore". In Kwan-Terry, 12-34.

2280 ---. 1992a. "Code-switching and code-mixing: the case of a child learning English and Chinese simultaneously". *JMMD* 13:243-59.

2281 ---. 1992b. "Towards a dictionary of Singapore English - issues relating to making entries for particles in Singapore English". In Pakir, 62-72.

2282 Kwo, Ora & Mark Bray. 1987. "Language and education in Hong Kong: new policies but unresolved problems". *RELC Journal* 18:98-108.

2283 Labru, G.L. 1984. *Indian Newspaper English*. Delhi: B.R. Publishing. (Rev. in *EWW* 9:145-6).

2284 Laitin, David & Edward Mensah. 1991. "Language choice among Ghanaians". *LPLP* 15:139-61.

2285 Lalla, Barbara. 1983. "The consonant system of early Jamaican Creole". *Carib* 3:31-7.

2286 ---. 1986. "Tracing elusive phonological features of Early Jamaican Creole". In Görlach & Holm, 117-32.

2287 --- & Jean D'Costa, eds. 1990. *Language in Exile. Three Hundred Years of Jamaican Creole*. Tuscaloosa: University of Alabama Press. (Rev. in *EWW* 13:134-8).

2288 Lane, Chris. 1990. "The sociolinguistics of questioning in district court trials". In Bell & Holmes, 221-51.

2289 Lanham, L.W. 1984. "Stress and intonation and the intelligibility of South African Black English". *African Studies* 43:217-30.

2290 ---. 1985. "The perception and evaluation of varieties of English". In *Greenbaum, 242-51.

2291 Lass, Roger. 1987. "How reliable is Goldswain? On the credibility of an early South African English source". *African Studies* 46:156-62.

2292 ---. 1990. "Where do extraterritorial Englishes come from? Dialect input and recodification in transported Englishes". In *Adamson, *et al.*, 245-80.

2293 --- & Susan Wright. 1985. "The South African chain shift: order out of chaos?". In *Eaton, *et al.*, 137-61.

2294 --- & ---. 1986. "Endogeny vs. contact: 'Afrikaans influence' on South African English". *EWW* 7:201-24.

2295 Lawrence, Lorraine. 1992a. "Assessing second language learner proficiency in Zambia". In Schmied, 74-92.

2296 ---. 1992b. "The role of English in education in Southern Africa". In Schmied, 103-13.

2297 --- & Charles Sarvan. 1983. "Zambian English: an enquiry". *Zambia Educational Review* 4:27-39.

2298 Lawton, David. 1984. "Grammar of the English-based Jamaican proverb". *AS* 59:123-30.

2299 ---. 1985. "Code-shifting in Jamaican Creole". In *Hancock, 68-88.

2300 Laycock, Donald C. 1989. "The status of Pitcairn-Norfolk: creole, dialect or cant?". In *Ammon, 608-29.

2301 ---. 1990. "The interpretation of variation in Pitcairn-Norfolk". In *Edmondson, *et al.*, 621-8.

2302 Lee, David. 1984. "Image and speech-style in the Australian television commercial". *AUMLA* 61:52-68.

2303 ---. 1989. "Sociolinguistic variation in the speech of Brisbane adolescents". *AJL* 9:51-72.

2304 Leek, R.-H. & J. Greenwood. 1991. "Broadcasting and New Zealand English: styling the news in the nineties". *New Zealand English Newsletter* 5:5-10.

2305 Leitner, Gerhard. 1983a. "Indian English - a critique of the ethnography of speaking". *IJSL* 43:153-67.

2306 ---. 1983b. "Indian English - a critique of ethnographic analysis". *Proceedings of the XIIIth International Conference of Linguistics*, Tokyo, 809-12.

2307 ---. 1984a. "Australian English or English in Australia - linguistic identity or dependence in broadcast language". *EWW* 5:55-85.

2308 ---. 1984b. "A diachronic study of broadcast communication". *Australian Journal of Communication* 5/6:57-64; also in G. Bentele & E.W.B. Hess-Lüttich, eds. *Zeichengebrauch in Massenmedien*. Tübingen: Niemeyer, 1985:376-94.

2309 ---. 1986. "Das Englische in Indien - ein Überblick über die Literatur seit ca. 1975". *ACOLIT*, Frankfurt/Main, 18-38.

2310 ---. 1987. "Zur Grammatik des Englischen in Indien". *ZAA* 35:338-50.

2311 ---. 1988. "Wie anders ist das Englische in Indien?". In H. Ludwig, ed. *Anglistentag 1987. Tübingen*. Gießen: Hoffmann, 385-96.

2312 ---. 1989a. "'You're not supposed to say nothing to nobody' - about Australian English grammar". In Dieter Riemenschneider, ed. *Critical Approaches to the New Literatures in English*. Essen: Blaue Eule, 142-54.

2313 ---. 1989b. "Der Tempusgebrauch im indischen Englisch als Problem für das 'international English'". In *Graustein & Thiele, 43-52.

2314 ---. 1990a. "International Corpus of English. Corpus design - problems and suggested solutions". *CCE Newsletter* 4:25-49.

2315 ---. 1990b. "Ist das australische Englisch wirklich wie das Londoner Cockney?". In G. Stilz & H. Lamping, eds. *Australienstudien in Deutschland. Grundlagen und Perspektiven*. Frankfurt/M.: Lang, 185-200.

2316 ---. 1990c. "Divergence and similarity in English - Australian English in contrast with Indian English". In *Edmondson, *et al.*, 323-50.
2317 ---. 1991a. "The *Kolhapur Corpus of Indian English* - intravarietal description and/or intervarietal comparison". In Stig Johansson & Anna-Brita Stenström, eds. *English Computer Corpora*. Berlin: Mouton de Gruyter, 215-32.
2318 ---. 1991b. "Have I your permission to leave, sir? Die Herausforderung der neuen Formen des Englischen für die Anglistik". *Die Neueren Sprachen* 90:23-38.
2319 ---. 1991c. "International Corpus of English and the text encoding initiative". *CCE Newsletter* 5:31-46.
2320 LePage, Robert B. 1984. "Retrospect and prognosis in Malaysia and Singapore". *IJSL* 45:113-26.
2321 ---. 1987. "The need for a multidimensional model". In *Gilbert, 113-29.
2322 ---. 1988. "Some premises concerning the standardization of languages, with special reference to Caribbean Creole English". *IJSL* 71:25-36.
2323 --- & Andrée Tabouret-Keller. 1985. *Acts of Identity: Creole-Based Approaches to Language and Ethnicity*. London: Cambridge UP. (Rev. in *EWW* 7:143-6).
2324 --- & ---. 1992. "What can we learn from the case of Pitcairnese?". In Rosemarie Tracy, ed. *Who Climbs the Grammar-Tree*. Tübingen: Niemeyer.
2325 Lim, Catherine. 1986. "English in Singapore: a study of its status and its solidarity and attitudes to its use". Ph.D., National University of Singapore. (Summary in *EWW* 8:289-90).
2326 Lim, Gerard & Alain Polguère. 1992. "Can lexical functions help to characterize Singapore English". In Pakir, 154-71.
2327 Lim, Helen Rojas. 1991. "An ethnographic study of English/Pilipino code-switching in bilingual classrooms in Manila". Ph.D., University of Illinois at Urbana-Champaign. DAI 52:7 (1992), 2531-A. (Summary in *EWW* 13:285-6.)
2328 Lipski, John M. 1992. "Pidgin English usage in Equatorial Guinea (Fernando Poo)". *EWW* 13:33-57.
2329 Llamzon, Teodoro A., ed. 1983. *Varieties of English and Their Implications for ELT in South East Asia*. (RELC Occ. Papers, 29). Singapore: RELC.
2330 ---. 1984. "The status of English in metro Manila today". In Andrew B. Gonzalez, ed. *PANAGANI: Essays in Honor of Bonifacio P. Sibayan*

on His Sixty-Seventh Birthday. Manila: Linguistic Society of the Philippines, 106-21.

2331 ---. 1986. "Life cycle of new Englishes: Restriction phase of Filipino English". *EWW* 7:101-25.

2332 Lowenberg, Peter H. 1984. "English in the Malay Archipelago: nativisation and its functions in a sociolinguistic area". Ph.D., University of Illinois at Urbana-Champaign. (Summary in *EWW* 6:287-8).

2333 ---. 1986a. "Sociolinguistic context and second-language acquisition: acculturation and creativity in Malaysian English". *WE* 5:71-84.

2334 ---. 1986b. "Non-native varieties of English: nativization, norms and implications". *Studies in Second Language Acquisition* 8:1-18.

2335 ---. 1991a. "Variation in Malaysian English: the pragmatics of language in contact". In *Cheshire, 364-75.

2336 ---. 1991b. "English as an additional language in Indonesia". *WE* 10: 127-38.

2337 ---. 1992. "The marking of ethnicity in Malaysian English literature: nativization and its functions". In *Smith & Sridhar, 251-8.

2338 Lu, Jung-Ying. 1991. "Code-switching between Mandarin and English". *WE* 10:139-51.

2339 Lubega, Stephen. 1987. "English as an international language: the concept and misconceptions". *JESL* 1:62-73.

2340 Luke, Kang-Kwong. 1984. "Expedient and oriental language mixing in Hong Kong". In Sebba & Todd, 191-202.

2341 Lukmani, Yasmeen. 1992. "Indian English: the written record". In *Blank, II:155-65.

2342 Lynch, John. 1987. "The French legacy in Bislama". In *Laycock & Winter, 411-20.

2343 McAndrew, Alex. 1992. "*Hosties* and *garbos*: a look behind diminutives and pejoratives in Australian English". In *Blank, II:166-84.

2344 McConvell, P. 1988. "Mix-im-up: Aboriginal codeswitching, old and new". In *Heller, 97-124.

2345 McGinley, Kevin. 1987. "The future of English in Zimbabwe". *WE* 6:159-64.

2346 Madaki, Rufa'i Omar. 1983. "A linguistic and pragmatic analysis of Hausa-English code-switching". Ph.D., University of Michigan. DAI 44:2 (1983), 478-A. (Summary in *EWW* 5:242).

2347 Magura, B.J. 1984. "Style and meaning in Southern African English". Ph.D., University of Illinois at Urbana-Champaign. (Summary in *EWW* 6:288-9).

2348 ---. 1985. "Southern African Black English". *WE* 4:251-6.

2349 Mair, Christian. 1992. "Problems in the compilation of a corpus of standard Caribbean English: A pilot study". In *Leitner, 75-96.

2350 Mann, Charles C. 1993. "Polysemic functionality of prepositions in pidgins and creoles: the case of *fò* in Anglo-Nigerian Pidgin". In *Byrne & Holm, 57-67.

2351 Marchese, Lynell & Anna Shnukal. 1982. "Nigerian Pidgin English of Warri". *JOLAN* 1:213-9.

2352 Marivate, Cynthia Nkhensani. 1992. "The evolution of language policy for Africans in South Africa, 1948-1989". Ed.D., Harvard University. DAI 53:5 (1992), 1501-A. (Summary in *EWW* 14:2).

2353 Mason, Gloria Jane. 1991. "Bilingual education in Cameroon: a case study of the anglophone region". Ph.D., Harvard University. DAI 52:6 (1991), 2054-A. (Summary in *EWW* 13:286-7).

2354 Matthews, Stephen. 1993. "Creole aspect and morphological typology". In *Byrne & Holm, 233-41.

2355 Mawasha, A.L. 1984. "Your English, our English: English in Black South Africa". *English Usage in Southern Africa* 15(2):12-8.

2356 Mazzon, Gabriella. 1988. "English in Malta". Ph.D., University of Naples. (Summary in *EWW* 10:316). Published in Italian as *L'Inglese di Malta*. Napoli: Liguori, 1992.

2357 ---. 1992. "A chapter in the worldwide spread of English: Malta". In *Rissanen, *et al.*, 592-601.

2358 Mbangwana, Paul. 1987. "Some characteristics of sound patterns of Cameroon Standard English". *Multilingua* 6:411-24.

2359 ---. 1989. "Flexibility in lexical usage in Cameroon English". In *García & Otheguy, 319-33.

2360 ---. 1991. "Invigorative and hermetic innovations in English in Yaoundé". *WE* 10:53-63.

2361 ---. 1992. "Some grammatical sign-posts in Cameroon Standard English". In Schmied, 93-102.

2362 Medeiros, Regina Del Negri. 1982. "American Brazilian English". *AS* 57:150-2.

2362a Meraj, Shaheen. 1993. "The use of English in Urdu advertising in Pakistan". In Baumgardner, 214-45.

2363 Mesthrie, Rajend. 1985. "Indian English - a lexical study". In *Proceedings of the 21st Congress of the Linguistic Society of Southern Africa*. Pietermauritzburg: University of Natal.

2364 ---. 1987. "From OV to VO in language shift: South African Indian English and its OV substrates". *EWW* 8:263-76.

2365 ---. 1988. "Toward a lexicon of South African Indian English". *WE* 7:5-14.

2366 ---. 1990. "Did the butler do it?: on an analogue of Butler English in Natal, South Africa". *WE* 9:281-8.

2367 ---. 1991. "Syntactic variation in South African Indian English: the relative clause". In *Cheshire, 462-73.

2368 ---. 1992. *A Lexicon of South African Indian English*. Leeds: Peepal Tree Press. (Rev. in *EWW* 14:2).

2369 ---. 1992b. *English in Language Shift*. The history, structure and socio-linguistics of South African Indian English. Cambridge: UP. (Rev. in *EWW* 14:139-40).

2369a ---. 1993a. "English in South Africa". *ET* 33:27-33.

2370 ---. 1993b. "South African Indian English". *ET* 34:12-16, 63.

2371 --- & Timothy T. Dunne. 1990. "Syntactic variation in language shift: the relative clause in South African Indian English". *LVC* 2:31-56.

2371a Meyerhoff, Miriam. 1993. "Lexical shift in working class New Zealand English: variation in the use of lexical pairs". *EWW* 14:2.

2372 Millar, J. Bruce, *et al*. 1989. "Design, collection, and description of a data base of spoken Australian English". *AJL* 9:165-89.

2373 Mohanan, K.P. 1992. "Describing the phonology of non-native varieties of a language". In *Smith & Sridhar, 111-28.

2374 Montgomery, Michael & Cecil Ataide Melo. 1990. "The phonology of the lost cause. The English of the Confederados in Brazil". *EWW* 11:195-216. [= 205]

2375 Moore, Clive. 1985. *Kanaka: A History of Melanesian Mackay*. Port Moresby: Institute of Papua New Guinea Studies and University of Papua New Guinea Press.

2376 Morrison, Andrew. 1989. "World Englishes: implications for English language teaching in Zimbabwe". In Ngara & Morrison, 190-9.

2377 Morrow, Phillip R. 1987. "The users and uses of English in Japan". *WE* 6:49-62.

2378 Mühlhäusler, Peter. 1985a. "The number of pidgin Englishes in the Pacific". In Romaine, *et al*., 25-51.

2379 ---. 1985b. "Remnants of Kanaka English in Queensland". In Clyne, 241-55.

2380 ---. 1985c. "Internal development of Tok Pisin". In Wurm & Mühlhäusler, 75-166.

2381 ---. 1985d. "Variation in Tok Pisin". In Wurm & Mühlhäusler, 233-73.
2382 ---. 1985e. "Syntax of Tok Pisin". In Wurm & Mühlhäusler, 341-421.
2383 ---. 1985f. "The scientific study of Tok Pisin: language planning and the Tok Pisin lexicon". In Wurm & Mühlhäusler, 595-664.
2384 ---. 1985g. "Synonymy and communication across lectal boundaries in Tok Pisin". In *Hancock, 134-53.
2385 ---. 1986a. "Pidgins and creoles of Australia and the Pacific: current research for an atlas of languages of intercultural communication". *AJL* 6:181-99.
2386 ---. 1986b. "English in contact with Tok Pisin". In *Viereck & Bald, 549-70.
2387 ---. 1987a. "Tracing predicate markers in Pacific Pidgin English". *EWW* 8:97-121.
2388 ---. 1987b. "The politics of small languages in Australia and the Pacific". *Language and Communication* 7:1-24.
2389 ---. 1987c. "The history of research into Tok Pisin 1900-1975". In *Gilbert, 177-209.
2390 ---. 1988. "Toward an atlas of the pidgins and creoles of the Pacific area". *IJSL* 71:37-50.
2391 ---. 1989. "Creolistics and theoretical linguistics". In *Ahrens, 225-34.
2392 ---. 1991a. "Overview of the pidgin and creole languages of Australia". In Romaine, 159-73.
2393 ---. 1991b. "Queensland Kanaka English". In Romaine, 174-9.
2394 ---, *et al.* 1979. *Papers in Pidgin and Creole Linguistics* 2. (PacL A-57). Canberra: ANU. (Rev. in *EWW* 5:108-11).
2395 Mufwene, Salikoko S. 1986. "Notes on durative constructions in Jamaican and Guyanese Creole". In Görlach & Holm, 167-82.
2396 Murray-Smith, S. 1987. *Right Words: A Guide to English Usage in Australia*. Ringwood, Vic.: Viking Press. (²1989).
2397 Myers-Scotton, Carol. 1989. "Codeswitching with English: types of switching, types of communities". *WE* 8:333-46.
2398 ---. 1993. *Social Motivations for Codeswitching*. Evidence from Africa. Oxford: Clarendon.
2399 Nadkarni, Mangesh V. 1992. "On liberating English to be a world language". In *Smith & Sridhar, 331-9.
2400 Ndebele, Njabulo S. 1985. "The English language and social change in South Africa". *TriQuarterly* 69:217-35.

2401 Nelson, Cecil Linwood. 1984. "Intelligibility: the case of non-native varieties of English". Ph.D., University of Illinois at Urbana-Champaign. (Summary in *EWW* 4:301).
2402 ---. 1985. "My language, your culture: whose communicative competence?". *WE* 4:243-50; repr. in *Kachru 1992:327-39.
2403 ---. 1988. "The pragmatic dimension of creativity in the other tongue". *WE* 7:173-81.
2404 ---. 1991. "New Englishes, new discourse: new speech acts". *WE* 10:317-23.
2405 Newbrook, Mark, ed. 1987. *Aspects of the Syntax of Educated Singaporean English. Attitudes, Beliefs and Usage.* Frankfurt/M.: Lang. (Rev. in *EWW* 9:322-4).
2406 ---. 1992. "Unrecognised grammatical and semantic features typical of Australian English". *EWW* 13:1-32.
2407 ---. fc. "Shared features of South Asian English and South-East Asian English: diffusion or independent origin?". Paper Islamabad 1989, to appear in Baumgardner (?).
2408 Ney, J.W. 1985. "Australian English dialect studies". *Orbis* 31:101-6.
2409 Ngara, Emmanuel & Andrew Morrison, eds. 1989. *Literature, Language and the Nation.* Harare: ATOLL in association with Baobab Books.
2410 Niang, Sada. 1987. "Creole features of three West Indian Writers - V. Rieg, R. Mais and D. Walcott: a functional approach". Ph.D., York University.
2411 Nihalani, Narsu K. 1985. "English in the Third World: changing attitudes". In G.S. Amur, *et al.*, eds. *Indian Readings in Commonwealth Literature.* New York & New Delhi: Apt, Sterling, 38-43.
2412 Nihalani, Paroo. 1988. "Communication: Received Pronunciation and Third World". *ITL* 79-80:61-75.
2413 ---. 1991. "Co-articulation and social acceptability: pragmatic implications for world Englishes". *WE* 10:287-98.
2414 Noss, R.B., ed. 1984. *An Overview of Language Issues in Southeast Asia: 1950-1980.* Singapore: Oxford UP.
2415 Nsakala, Lengo Kiese Kiawu. 1990. "Errors in the speech of Zairean students of English: with special reference to rate and lexical diversity". Ph.D., University of York. DAI 52:8 (1992), 2909-A. (Summary in *EWW* 13:287-8).
2416 Nwoye, Onuigbo G. 1992. "Obituary announcements as communicative events in Nigerian English". *WE* 11:15-27.

2417 Nyaggah, Lynette Behm. 1990. "Cross-linguistic influence in Kenyan English: the impact of Swahili and Kikuyu on syntax". Ph.D., University of California, Los Angeles. DAI 51:5 (1990), 1598-A. (Summary in *EWW* 12:297-8).

2418 Nylander, Dudley. 1983. "A unified analysis of Krio *na*". In B.L. Collins ed. *Proceedings of the Linguistic Circle, 23*. North Dakota: UP.

2419 Oasa, Hiroaki. 1989. "Phonology of current Adelaide English". In Collins & Blair, 271-87.

2420 Obilade, Anthony O. 1984. "On the nativization of the English language in Nigeria". *AnL* 26:170-85.

2421 Odumuh, Adama E. 1984. "Educated Nigerian English as a model of standard Nigerian English". *World Language English* 3:231-5.

2422 ---, ed. 1987. *Nigerian English (NigE). Selected Essays*. Zaria: Ahmadu Bello UP.

2423 Ofuani, Ogo A. 1984. "On the problem of time and tense in Nigerian Pidgin". *AnL* 26:293-304.

2424 Okanlawon, Bidemi O. 1984. "A study of the acquisition of some aspects of English by Nigerian learners". Ph.D., University of Edinburgh.

2425 ---. 1987. "A study of the acquisition of the article system of English by Nigerian learners". *JESL* 1:47-60.

2426 Oloruntoba, Christiana Iyetunde. 1992. "Sociocultural dimensions of Nigerian Pidgin usage (western Niger Delta of Nigeria)". Ph.D., Indiana University. DAI 53:6 (1992), 1893-A. (Summary in *EWW* 14:2).

2427 Omamor, Augusta. 1990. "Research into English and African languages in Nigeria". In Schmied, 47-66.

2428 Orsman, H.W. 1987. "A New Zealand National Dictionary". *New Zealand English Newsletter* 1:10-1.

2429 Ożóg, Conrad K. 1990. "The English language in Malaysia and its relationship with the national language". In Baldauf & Luke, 305-18.

2430 --- & Peter W. Martin. 1990. "The *bah* particle in Brunei English". *RELC Journal* 21:14-28.

2430a Ozolins, Uldis. 1993. *The Politics of Language in Australia*. Cambridge: UP. (Rev. in *EWW* 14:2).

2431 Pachori, Satya S. 1990. "The language policy of the East India Company and the Asiatic Society of Bengal". *LPLP* 14:104-18.

2432 Pakir, Anne. 1991. "The range and depth of English-knowing bilinguals in Singapore". *WE* 10:167-79.

2433 ---, ed. 1992. *Words in a Cultural Context.* (Proceedings of the Lexicography Workshop). Singapore: Unipress. (Rev. in *EWW* 14:2).

2434 Pandharipande, Rajeshwari. 1987. "On nativization of English". *WE* 6:149-58.

2435 ---. 1992. "Defining politeness in Indian English". In *Smith & Sridhar, 241-50.

2436 Parakrama, Arjuna. 1990. "De-hegemonizing language standards: learning from (post)colonial Englishes about 'English'". Ph.D., University of Pittsburgh. DAI 52:2 (1991), 523-A. (Summary in *EWW* 14:2).

2437 Parasher, S.V. 1988. "Certain stylistic features of Indian English and their relationship to degrees of formality". *IJAL* 14:95-122.

2438 Pascasio, E.M. 1984. "Philippine bilingualism and code-switching". In A.B. Gonzalez, ed. *PANAGANI: Essays in Honor of Bonifacio P. Sibayan on His Sixty-Seventh Birthday*. Manila: Linguistic Society of the Philippines, 122-34.

2439 Patrick, Peter Lumpkin. 1992. "Linguistic variation in urban Jamaican creole: A sociolinguistic study of Kingston, Jamaica". Ph.D., University of Pennsylvania. DAI 53:5 (1992), 1502-A. (Summary in *EWW* 14:2).

2440 Pattanayak, Debi Prasanna, ed. 1990. *Multilingualism in India*. Clevedon: Multilingual Matters, 61. (Rev. in *EWW* 12:162-3).

2441 Pauwels, Anne, ed. 1987. *Language, Gender and Society in Australia and New Zealand.* Sydney: Australian Professional Publications.

2442 ---. 1991. "Gender differences in Australian English". In Romaine, 318-26.

2443 Peirce, Bronwyn Norton. 1989. "Toward a pedagogy of possibility in the teaching of English internationally: people's English in South Africa". *TESOLQ* 23:401-20.

2444 Pemagbi, Joe. 1989. "Still a deficient language? A description and glossary of the 'New English' of Sierra Leone". *ET* 17:20-4.

2445 Peters, Pam, ed. 1990. *Frontiers of Style: Proceedings of Style Councils 87 and 88*. Macquarie University: for the Dictionary Research Centre. (Rev. in *EWW* 12:163-4).

2446 --- & Arthur Delbridge. 1989. "Standardisation in Australian English". In Collins & Blair, 127-37.

2447 --- & Margaret Fee. 1989. "New configurations: the balance of British and American English features in Australian and Canadian English". *AJL* 9:135-47.

2448 ---, *et al.* 1990. "Word frequencies from the Macquarie corpus: the newspaper files". *SHLRC Working Papers*; *Lexicology Report*. Macquarie University: School of English and Linguistics, 13-92.

2449 Phillipson, Robert, *et al.* 1986. "Namibian educational language planning: English for liberation or neo-colonialism?". In *Spolsky, 77-95.

2450 Philps, Dennis. 1991. "Linguistic security in the syntactic structures of air traffic control English". *EWW* 12:103-24.

2451 Pittam, Jeffery. 1987. "Listeners' evaluations of voice quality in Australian English speakers". *Language and Speech* 30:99-113.

2451a Plag, Ingo. fc. *Sentential Complementation in Sranan. On the Formation of an English-based Creole Language*. Tübingen: Niemeyer. (Ph.D., University of Marburg, 1992. Summary in *EWW* 14:2).

2452 Platt, John. 1986. "Quantitative analysis and the New Englishes". *WE* 5:85-7.

2453 ---. 1987. "Substratum influences in Basilectal Singaporean English". In *Laycock & Winter, 535-44.

2454 ---. 1988. "Singapore". In *Ammon, *et al.*, 1384-8.

2455 ---. 1991. "Social and linguistic constraints on variation in the use of two grammatical variables in Singapore English". In *Cheshire, 376-87.

2456 ---. 1992. "Not pidgin, not creole - but is it English? The nature of basilectal Singaporean English". In Dutton, *et al.*, 335-43.

2457 --- & Mian Lian Ho. 1988. "Language universals or substratum influences? Past tense marking in Singapore English". *EWW* 9:65-75.

2458 --- & ---. 1989. "Discourse particles in Singaporean English: substratum influences and universals". *WE* 8:215-22.

2459 --- & Kirpal Singh. 1984. "The use of localized English in Singapore poetry". *EWW* 5:43-54.

2460 ---, H. Weber & Mian Lian Ho. 1984. *The New Englishes*. London: Routledge & Kegan Paul. (Rev. in *EWW* 6:155-60).

2461 Pochard, J.-C. & Hubert Devonish. 1986. "Deixis in Caribbean English-lexicon Creole. A description of *a*, *da* and *de*". *Lingua* 69:105-20.

2462 Pollard, Velma. 1984. "Rastafarian language in St. Lucia and Barbados". In Sebba & Todd, 253-64.

2463 ---. 1986. "Innovation in Jamaican Creole: the speech of Rastafari". In Görlach & Holm, 157-66.

2464 ---. 1989. "The particle *en* in Jamaican creole: a discourse-related account". *EWW* 10:55-68.

2465 ---. 1990. "The speech of the Rastafarians of Jamaica, in the eastern Caribbean: the case of St. Lucia". *IJSL* 85:81-90.

2466 Poplack, Shana & David Sankoff. 1987. "The Philadelphia story in the Spanish Caribbean". *AS* 62:291-314.

2467 Poynton, Cate. 1989. "Terms of address in Australian English". In Collins & Blair, 55-69.

2468 Quirk, Randolph. 1986. "Speculations on the future role of English in Hong Kong and the implications for educational policy". In Verner Bickley, ed. *Future Directions in English Language Teacher Education: Asia and Pacific Perspectives*. Hong Kong: Institute of Language in Education, 3-8.

2469 Rahim, Syed A. 1986. "Language as power apparatus: observations on English and cultural policy in nineteenth-century India". *WE* 5:231-40.

2469a Rahman, A.M.M. Hamidur. fc. "Acceptability and English curriculum change in Bangladesh". In Baumgardner.

2470 Rahman, Tariq. 1990. *Pakistani English: The Linguistic Description of a Non-Native Variety of English*. (NIPS Monograph Series, III). Islamabad: Quaid-i-Azam University. (Rev. in *EWW* 12:336-7).

2471 ---. 1991a. "The use of words in Pakistani English". *ET* 26:32-8.

2472 ---. 1991b. "Pakistani English: some phonological and phonetic features". *WE* 10:83-95.

2473 Ralston, Lenore D. 1985. "A historical account of 'country talk' on St. Vincent Island: problems and new directions". In *Hancock, 13-32.

2474 Ramachandran, N. 1988. "Malayalam-influenced English - a study based on lexis and syntax as found in the English written by Malayalam-speaking writers". Ph.D., University of Kerala. (Summary in *EWW* 9:306-8).

2475 Ramaiah, L.S. 1988. *Indian English: A Bibliographical Guide to Resources*. Gian.

2476 Ramson, William S. 1987. "The *Australian National Dictionary*: a foretaste". In *Burchfield, 136-55.

2477 ---, ed. 1988. *The Australian National Dictionary. A Dictionary of Australianisms on Historical Principles*. Melbourne: OUP. (Rev. in *EWW* 10:145-9).

2478 ---. 1989. "Regionalism in Australian English: the value of newspaper evidence". *AJL* 9:73-83.

2479 Reagan, Timothy. 1986. "The role of language policy in South African education". *LPLP* 10:1-13.

2480 ---. 1987. "The politics of linguistic apartheid: language policies in black education in South Africa". *The Journal of Negro Education* 56:299-312.

2481 Reeve, Janice L. 1982. "Attitudes to Australian English revealed in the *ABC Weekly*". *Occasional Papers of the Speech and Language Research Centre*, 286-306.

2482 ---. 1989. "Community attitudes to Australian English". In Collins & Blair, 111-26.

2483 Richards, Jack C., *et al.* "The culture of the English language teacher: a Hong Kong example". *RELC Journal* 23:81-102.

2484 Richmond, Edmund B. 1989. "African English expressions in the Gambia". *WE* 8:223-8.

2485 Rickford, John R. 1983. "Standard and non-standard language attitudes in a creole continuum". (*SCL*, 16). Jamaica: SCL.

2486 ---. 1986. "'Me Tarzan, you Jane!' Adequacy, expressiveness, and the creole speaker". *JL* 22:281-310.

2487 ---. 1987a. "Decreolization paths for Guyanese singular pronouns". In *Gilbert, 130-8.

2488 ---. 1987b. *Dimensions of a Creole Continuum. History, Texts, & Linguistic Analysis of Guyanese Creole*. Stanford: UP. (Rev. in *EWW* 10:149-54).

2489 ---. 1988. "The Caribbean". In *Ammon, *et al.*, 1313-24.

2490 ---. 1991. "Sociolinguistic variation in Cane Walk: a quantitative case study". In *Cheshire, 609-16.

2491 --- & Elizabeth Closs Traugott. 1985. "Symbol of powerlessness and degeneracy, or symbol of solidarity and truth? Paradoxical attitudes toward pidgins and creoles". In *Greenbaum, 252-61.

2492 Roberts, Peter A. 1988. *West Indians and Their Language*. Cambridge: UP. (Rev. in *EWW* 9:345-7).

2493 Rohany, Hawa. 1991. "A comparative study of opinion-giving strategies in Malaysian and British English". Ph.D., University of Essex. DAI 53:3 (1992), 794-A. (Summary in *EWW* 14:2).

2494 Romaine, Suzanne. 1988. "Some differences between spoken and written Tok Pisin". *EWW* 9:243-69.

2495 ---. 1989a. "English and Tok Pisin in Papua New Guinea". *WE* 8:5-23.

2496 ---. 1989b. "Lexical change and variation in Tok Pisin". In *Walsh, 268-79.

2497 ---. 1989c. "Grammaticalization as a source of language change: two case studies from the history of English and Tok Pisin". In S. Romaine & N. Vincent, eds. *Grammatical Categories and Grammaticalization*. London: Philological Society.

2498 ---. 1990a. "Pidgin English adversity". In *Ricks & Michaels, 195-203.

2499 ---. 1990b. "Variability and anglicization in the distinction between *p/f* in young children's Tok Pisin". In *Edmondson, *et al.*, 173-86.
2500 ---, ed. 1991a. *Language in Australia*. Cambridge: UP. (Rev. in *EWW* 13:138-42).
2501 ---. 1991b. "The Pacific". In *Cheshire, 619-36.
2502 ---. 1992a. *Language, Education, and Development*. Urban and rural Tok Pisin in Papua New Guinea. Oxford: Clarendon.
2503 ---. 1992b. "English: from village to global village". In *Machan & Scott, 253-60.
2504 ---, *et al.* 1985. *Papers in Pidgin and Creole Linguistics No. 4*. (PacL A-72). Canberra: ANU.
2505 Roy, John D. 1984. "An investigation of the processes of language variation and change in a speech community in Barbados". Ph.D., Columbia University. (Summary in *EWW* 6:290-2).
2506 ---. 1986. "The structure of tense and aspect in Barbadian English Creole". In Görlach & Holm, 141-56.
2507 Rubagumya, Casmir M. 1986. "Language planning in the Tanzanian educational system: problems and prospects". *JMMD* 7:283-300.
2508 ---, ed. 1990. *Language in Education in Africa: A Tanzanian Perspective*. Cleveland: Multilingual Matters. (Rev. in *EWW* 12:157-60).
2509 Rubal-López, Alma. 1991. "English-language spread: Predicting three criteria". Ph.D., Yeshiva University. DAI 53:3 (1992), 964-A. (Summary in *EWW* 14:2).
2510 Runsewe, Oluremi I. 1986. "Communication in General Nigerian English: an intonational study". Ph.D., University of Essex. (Summary in *EWW* 10:317-9).
2511 Saah, Kofi. 1986. "Language use and attitudes in Ghana". *AnL* 28:367-77.
2512 Sadanand, K. 1983. "The use of English in industries in Andhra Pradesh: a sociolinguistic study". Ph.D., Hyderabad: CIEFL.
2513 Sahgal, Anju. 1991. "Patterns of language use in a bilingual setting in India". In *Cheshire, 299-307.
2514 --- & Rama Kant Agnihotri. 1985. "Syntax - the common bond. Acceptability of syntactic deviances in Indian English". *EWW* 6:117-29.
2515 --- & ---. 1988. "Indian English phonology: a sociolinguistic perspective". *EWW* 9:51-64.
2516 Saleemi, Anjum P. 1985. "English in nonnative use: a second-language view". *ETF* 23. (Reprinted in Baumgardner 1993:29-36).
2517 ---. 1993. "Native and non-native grammars of English". In Baumgardner, 59-64.

2518 Sandefur, John. 1984. *Papers on Kriol: The Writing System and a Resource Guide*. (Working Papers of SIL-AAB, Series B, Volume 10). Darwin: Summer Institute of Linguistics.

2519 ---. 1985a. "English-based languages and dialects currently spoken by Aboriginal people: suggestions toward a consensus of terminology". *AJL* 5:67-79.

2520 ---. 1985b. "Dynamics of an Australian creole system". In Romaine, *et al.*, 195-214.

2521 ---. 1986. *Kriol of North Australia: A Language Coming of Age*. (Working Papers of SIL-AAB, A10). Darwin: Summer Institute of Linguistics. (Rev. in *EWW* 9:146-7).

2522 ---. 1991. "A sketch of the structure of Kriol". In Romaine, 204-12.

2523 --- & John Harris. 1986. "Variation in Australian Kriol". In J.A. Fishman, *et al.*, eds. *The Fergusonian Impact*. Vol. 2: *Sociolinguistics and the Sociology of Language*. Berlin: Mouton de Gruyter, 179-90.

2524 Sankoff, Gillian. 1990. "The grammaticalization of tense and aspect in Tok Pisin and Sranan". *LVC* 2(3):295-312.

2525 --- & Claudia Mazzie. 1991. "Determining noun phrases in Tok Pisin". *JPCL* 6:1-24.

2526 Sanyal, S.C. 1987. *English Language in India & Indo-Anglian Prose Style*. Elms Court, Ilfracombe: Stockwell.

2527 Saraf, R.S. 1987. *Teaching English in India*. Pune: Shri Vidya Prakashan.

2528 Saravana, Vanithamani. 1986 (1989?). "Variation in the English spoken by English-Tamil bilinguals in Singapore". Ph.D., Monash University, Clayton.

2529 Satyanath, Shobha. 1991. "Variation and change: (daz) in Guyanese". Ph.D., University of Pennsylvania. DAI 52:7 (1992), 2534-A. (Summary in *EWW* 13:291-2).

2530 Sawyerr, Elizabeth Morohundiya. 1992. "Perceptions of and attitudes toward Krio and its use in various domains". Ph.D., Howard University. DAI 53:8 (1993), 279-A. (Summary in *EWW* 14:2).

2531 Schmied, Josef. 1985a. *Englisch in Tansania. Sozio- und interlinguistische Probleme*. Heidelberg: Groos. (Rev. in *EWW* 7:163-4).

2532 ---. 1985b. "Attitudes towards English in Tanzania". *EWW* 6:237-69.

2533 ---. 1986. "English in Tanzanian education". BASS 5:63-114.

2534 ---. 1988. "Recognizing and accepting East African English grammar". In H. Williams, ed. *The Role of Grammar in the Teaching of English*. Proceedings of the British Council Conference, Nairobi 1988.

2535 ---, ed. 1989a. *English in East and Central Africa* 1. (BASS 15). Bayreuth: University. (Rev. in *EWW* 10:350-2).

2536 ---. 1989b. "English in East Africa: theoretical, methodological and practical issues". In Schmied, 7-37.

2537 ---. 1989c. "Second-language varieties across the Indian Ocean". In Schmied, 85-97.

2538 ---. 1989d. "Conference report: compiling a corpus of East African English". *ICAME Journal* 13:75-7.

2539 ---. 1989e. "Comparing Indian and East African English". In Dieter Riemenschneider, ed. *Critical Approaches to the New Literatures in English*. Essen: Blaue Eule, 131-41.

2540 ---, ed. 1990a. *Linguistics in the Service of Africa*. (BASS 18). Bayreuth: University. (Rev. in *EWW* 12:161-2).

2541 ---. 1990b. "A corpus of East African English: prospects and problems". In Schmied, 67-88.

2542 ---. 1990c. "Corpus linguistics and non-native varieties of English". *WE* 9:255-68.

2543 ---. 1990d. "Language use, attitudes, performance and sociolinguistic background: a study of English in Kenya, Tanzania, and Zambia". *EWW* 11:217-38.

2544 ---. 1990e. "Accepted language behavior as a basis for language teaching: a comparison of English in Kenya and Tanzania". In Rubagumya, 123-32.

2545 ---. 1991a. "National and subnational features in Kenyan English". In *Cheshire, 420-32.

2546 ---. 1991b. *English in Africa. An Introduction*. Harlow: Longman. (Rev. in *EWW* 13:314-6).

2547 ---, ed. 1992a. *English in East and Central Africa* 2. (BASS 24). Bayreuth: University. (Rev. in *EWW* 13:336-7).

2548 ---. 1992b. "The status of English in Kenya and Tanzania: a comparative study". In *Blank, II:117-27.

2549 Schneider, Edgar W. 1990. "The cline of creoleness in English-oriented creoles and semi-creoles of the Caribbean". *EWW* 11:79-113.

2550 Scollon, Ron & Suzanne Wong-Scollon. 1991. "Topic confusion in English-Asian discourse". *WE* 10:113-25.

2551 Searle, Chris. 1984. *Words Unchained. Language and Revolution in Grenada*. London: Zed Books.

2552 Sebba, Mark & Loreto Todd, eds. 1984. *Papers from the York Creole Conference, 24-27, September 1983*. (*York Papers in Linguistics* 11,

Special Issue). York: Department of Language, University of York. (Rev. in *EWW* 6:320-2).

2553 Semenets, Oleg E. 1984. *Social Processes and Language Reality. English in Asia and Africa.* Kiev: Vyscha Shkola Publishers. [in Ukrainian].

2554 ---. 1985. *Social Context and Language Development. Territorial and Social Differentiation of the English Language in the Developing Countries.* Kiev: UP. [in Ukrainian].

2555 ---, ed. 1988. *Social Linguistics and Social Practices. Aspects of Socio-cultural Variation of the Polyethnic English Language.* Kiev: UP. [in Ukrainian].

2556 --- & Ludmila A. Rusetskaya. 1991. "Research into regional and socio-cultural variation of English undertaken at Kiev". *EWW* 12:267-78.

2557 Sharpe, Margaret C. 1985. "Kriol - an Australian language resource". In Romaine, *et al.*, 177-94.

2558 ---, ed. 1989. *Language Contexts of Aboriginal Australians.* (*Armidale Papers*, 11).

2559 Shastri, S.V. 1985. "Towards a description of Indian English: a standard corpus in machine-readable form". *EWW* 6:275-8.

2560 ---. 1988. "The Kolhapur Corpus of Indian English and work done on its basis so far". *ICAME Journal* 12:15-26.

2561 ---. 1992. "Opaque and transparent features of Indian English". In *Leitner, 263-76.

2562 ---. fc. "Using computer corpora in the description of language with special reference to complementation in Indian English". In Baumgardner.

2563 Sheperd, Susan C. 1989. "The impact of the child's world on pairing form and function in Antiguan Creole and English". In Wieslaw Oleksy, ed. *Contrastive Pragmatics.* (Pragmatics & Beyond, New Series, 3). Amsterdam & Philadelphia: Benjamins, 113-27.

2564 Shi, Dingxu. 1993. "Learning Pidgin English through Chinese characters". In *Byrne & Holm, 459-65.

2565 Shields, Kathryn. 1984. "Jamaican Creole or Standard Jamaican English? Teacher language in the Jamaican context". In Sebba & Todd, 279-90.

2566 ---. 1989. "Standard English in Jamaica: a case of competing models". *EWW* 10:41-53.

2567 Shnukal, Anna. 1982. "You're gettin' somethink for nothing: two phonological variables of Australian English". *AJL* 2:197-212.

2568 ---. 1985a. "Multilingualism in the eastern Torres Strait Islands". In Clyne, 265-79.

2569 ---. 1985b. "Variation in Torres Strait Creole: a preliminary discussion". In Romaine, *et al.*, 155-75.

2570 ---. 1985c. "Torres Strait Creole: some non-linguistic constraints on dictionary-making". *Australian Review of Applied Linguistics*, Series S, 2:154-67.

2571 ---. 1988. *Broken: An Introduction to the Creole Language of Torres Strait*. (PacL C-107). Canberra: ANU. (Rev. in *EWW* 12:338-9).

2572 ---. 1989. "Variable subject relative pronoun absence in Australian English". In Collins & Blair, 70-7.

2573 ---. 1990. "Torres Strait Creole: historical perspectives and new directions". In M.A.K. Halliday, *et al.*, eds. *Learning, Keeping and Using Language. Selected Papers from the 8th World Congress of Applied Linguistics, Sydney, 16-21 August, 1987*. Vol 2. Amsterdam & Philadelphia: Benjamins, 163-73.

2574 ---. 1991. "Torres Strait Creole". In Romaine, 180-94.

2575 ---. 1992. "Meriam Mir lexicon in Torres Strait Creole". In Dutton, *et al.*, 385-403.

2576 Siachitema, Alice K. 1987. "Use and attitudes towards the English language in Lusaka". Ph.D., University of Edinburgh.

2577 ---. 1991. "The social significance of language use and language choice in a Zambian urban setting: An empirical study of three neighbourhoods in Lusaka". In *Cheshire, 474-90.

2578 Sibayan, Bonifacio P. 1985. *Status and Role of English and Pilipino in the Philippines*. Washington, D.C.: US Information Agency.

2579 --- & Andrew B. Gonzalez. 1990. "English language teaching in the Philippines: a succession of movements". In *Britton, *et al.*, 269-96.

2579a Sidhwa, Bapsi. 1993. "New English creative writing: A Pakistani writer's perspective". In Baumgardner, 205-13.

2580 Siegel, Jeff. 1986. "Pidgin English in Fiji: a sociolinguistic history". *Pacific Studies* 9:53-106.

2581 ---. 1987. *Language Contact in a Plantation Environment: A Sociolinguistic History of Fiji*. Cambridge: UP. (Rev. in *EWW* 9:147-8).

2582 ---. 1989. "English in Fiji". *WE* 8:47-58.

2583 ---. 1990. "Pidgin English in Nauru". *JPCL* 5:157-86.

2584 ---. 1991. "Variation in Fiji English". In *Cheshire, 664-74.

2585 ---. 1992. "The future of Tok Pisin: another look". In Dutton, *et al.*, 405-8.

2586 ---. 1993. "Pidgins and creoles in education in Australia and the Southwest Pacific". In *Byrne & Holm, 299-308.

2587 Singh, Frances B. 1987. "Power and politics in the content of grammar books: the example of India". *WE* 6:253-62.

2588 Singler, John Victor. 1984. "Variation in tense-aspect-modality in Liberian English". Ph.D., University of California at Los Angeles. (Summary in *EWW* 6:292).

2589 ---. 1987a. "The city, the mesolect, and innovation". *JPCL* 2:119-47.

2590 ---. 1987b. "Where did Liberian English *na* come from?". *EWW* 8:69-95.

2591 ---. 1988. "The place of variation in the formal expression of inflectional processes: evidence from Kru Pidgin English". In K. Ferrara, *et al.*, eds. *Linguistic Change and Contact: Proceedings of the Sixteenth Annual Conference on New Ways of Analyzing Variation in Language*. Austin: University of Texas, Department of Linguistics, 345-53.

2592 ---. 1989. "Plural marking in Liberian Settler English 1820-1980". *AS* 64:40-64.

2593 ---. 1991. "Social and linguistic constraints on plural marking in Liberian English". In *Cheshire, 545-62.

2594 Smith, Anne-Marie. 1986. "Papua New Guinea English". Ph.D., University of Papua New Guinea. (Summary in *EWW* 8:293-4).

2595 ---. 1988. "English in Papua New Guinea". *WE* 7:299-308.

2596 Smith, Brian D. 1991. "English in Indonesia". *ET* 26:39-43.

2597 Smith, Geoff P. 1990. "Creolized Tok Pisin: uniformity and variation". In Baldauf & Luke, 179-209.

2598 Smith, Ian. 1985. "Multilingualism and diffusion: a case study from Singapore English". *IJAL* 11:105-28.

2599 Smith, Larry E. 1986. "Cross-cultural understanding and English literatures from the Other Circles". *WE* 5:241-8.

2600 Smith, P. 1987. *Education and Colonial Control in Papua New Guinea: A Documentary History*. Melbourne: Longman Cheshire.

2601 Smolicz, J.J. 1986. "National language policy in the Philippines". In *Spolsky, 96-116.

2602 Smout, Kary D. 1988. "*Senkyoshigo*: a missionary English of Japan". *AS* 63:137-49.

2603 Soo, Kengsoon. 1990. "Malaysian English at the crossroads: some signposts". *JMMD* 11:199-214.

2604 Spencer, John. 1988. "Reflections on language and development in tropical Africa". In Josef Klegraf & Dietrich Nehls, eds. *Essays on the English Language and Applied Linguistics*. (Studies in Descriptive Linguistics, 18). Heidelberg: Groos, 479-88.

2605 ---. 1992. "Africa's contribution to the lexicon of English". In *Blank, II:110-16.

2606 Sridhar, Kamal K. 1982. "English in a South Indian urban context". In Braj B. Kachru, ed. *The Other Tongue. English Across Cultures.* Urbana: University of Illinois Press, 141-53. (Reprinted in Sridhar 1989:88-98).

2607 ---. 1985a. "Bilingualism in South Asia (India): national/regional profiles and verbal repertoires". *ARAL* 6:169-86. (Reprinted in Sridhar 1989:1-10).

2608 ---. 1985b. "Sociolinguistic theory and non-native varieties of English". *Lingua* 68:39-58. (Reprinted in Sridhar 1989:35-51).

2609 ---. 1989a. "Pragmatic differences between native and indigenized varieties: requesting in Indian English". In Sridhar, 99-116 and in *Walsh 1989:326-41.

2610 ---. 1989b. *English in Indian Bilingualism.* New Delhi: Manokar. (Rev. in *EWW* 12:334-6).

2611 ---. 1989c. "Language policy for education in multilingual India: issues and implementation". In *Proceedings of the Conference on Language Contact and Conflict, June 2-4.* Brussels: Center for Research on Multilingualism. (Reprinted in Sridhar, 11-34).

2612 ---. 1991. "Speech acts in an indigenised variety: sociocultural values and language variation". In *Cheshire, 308-18.

2613 ---. fc. "The pragmatics of South Asian English". In Baumgardner.

2614 --- & S.N. Sridhar. 1986. "Bridging the paradigm gap: second language acquisition theory and indigenized varieties of English". *WE* 5:3-14. (Reprinted in Sridhar 1989:52-65).

2615 --- & S.N. Sridhar. 1992a. "Indigenized Englishes as second languages: toward a functional theory of second language acquisition in multilingual contexts". In Rama Kant Agnihotri & Anju Sahgal, eds. *Research in Applied Linguistics.* New Delhi: Select Publishers.

2616 --- & S.N. Sridhar. 1992b. "The empire speaks back: English as a non-native language". In Peter Nelde, ed. *Plurilingua X: Bilingualism and Minorities.* Bruxelles: International Research Center on Multilingualism.

2617 Sridhar, S.N. 1992. "The ecology of bilingual competence: language interaction in the syntax of indigenized varieties of English". In *Smith & Sridhar, 141-50.

2618 [entry deleted]

2619 ---. fc. "Toward a syntax of South Asian English: Defining the lectal range". In Baumgardner.
2620 Steffensen, Margaret S. 1991. "Australian Creole English: the effect of cultural knowledge on language and memory". In *Cheshire, 256-67.
2621 Stein, Peter. 1992. "Zur Geschichte und gegenwärtigen Situation der englischen Sprache auf Mauritius". In *Blank, II:128-48.
2622 Strevens, Peter. 1992. "English as an international language: directions in the 1990s". In *Kachru, 27-47.
2623 Sure, Kembo. 1989. "Attitudes towards English among Kenyan students". In Schmied, 39-61.
2624 ---. 1991. "Language functions and language attitudes: a case of diglossia in Kenya". *EWW* 12:245-60.
2625 ---. 1992. "Richer or rotten? A study of borrowing from English to Dholuo". In Schmied, 21-45.
2626 Sussex, Roland. 1989. "The Americanisation of Australian English: prestige models in the media". In Collins & Blair, 158-70.
2627 Sutton, Peter. 1989. "Postvocalic R in an Australian English dialect". *AJL* 9:161-3.
2628 Swales, John. 1985. "English as the international language of research". *RELC Journal* 16:1-7.
2629 ---. 1988. "Discourse communities, genres and English as an international language". *WE* 7:211-20.
2630 Tagliamonte, Sali & Shana Poplack. 1988. "How Black English *Past* got to the present. Evidence from Samaná". *LinS* 17:513-33. [= 1665]
2631 Talaat, Mubina. 1993. "Lexical variation in Pakistani English". In Baumgardner, 51-8.
2632 Talib, Ismail. 1992. "Singaporean literature in English and a dictionary of Singaporean English". In Pakir, 188-201.
2633 Tan, Chor Hiang & Anthea Fraser Gupta. 1992. "Post-vocalic /r/ in Singapore English". *YPL* 16:139-52.
2634 Tay, Mary W.J. 1983. *Trends in Language, Literacy and Education in Singapore*. Singapore: Department of Statistics, Census Monograph 2.
2635 ---. 1986. "Lects and institutionalized varieties of English: the case of Singapore". *IDEAL* 1:93-107.
2636 ---. 1991. "Southeast Asia and Hongkong". In *Cheshire, 319-32.
2637 Taylor, Andrew. 1989. "Hong Kong's English newspapers". *ET* 20:18-24.

2638 Taylor, Brian, Gerhard Leitner & Elizabeth Phelps. fc. *A Bibliography of Writings on English in Australia and New Zealand and its Interaction with Indigenous and Migrant Languages.*

2639 Taylor, John R. 1991. "Remarks on the KIN-PIN vowels in South African English". *EWW* 12:75-85.

2640 Thomas, Andrew. 1990. "Language planning in Vanuatu". In Baldauf & Luke, 234-58.

2641 Thumboo, Edwin. 1986. "Language as power: Gabriel Okara's *The Voice* as a paradigm". *WE* 5:249-64.

2642 ---. 1988. "The literary dimension of the spread of English: creativity in a second language". In *Lowenberg, 361-401. (Reprinted in *Kachru 1992:255-82).

2643 Tickoo, M.L., ed. 1991. *Language and Standards: Issues, Attitudes, Case Studies*. Singapore: SEAMEO RLC.

2643a Tingley, Christopher. 1981. "Deviance in the English of Ghanaian newspapers". *EWW* 2:39-62.

2644 Todd, Loreto. 1984. "Language options for education in a multilingual society: Cameroon". In Ch. Kennedy, ed. *Language Planning and Language Education*. London: Allen & Unwin, 160-71.

2645 ---. 1985. "Lexical patterning in Cameroon Pidgin and Tok Pisin". In *Hancock, 116-33.

2646 ---, *et al.* 1978. *Papers in Pidgin and Creole Linguistics 1*. (PacL A-54). Canberra: ANU. (Rev. in *EWW* 5:108-11).

2647 --- & Martin Jumbam. 1992. "Kamtok: anatomy of a pidgin". *ET* 29:3-11.

2648 Tripathi, P.D. 1990. "English in Zambia". *ET* 23:34-8.

2649 Troy, Jakelin. 1990. *Australian Aboriginal Contact with the English Language in New South Wales: 1788 to 1845*. (PacL B-103). Canberra: ANU. (Rev. in *EWW* 12:167).

2650 Tryon, D.T. 1986. "Neologisms in Bislama (Vanuatu)". In J.A. Fishman, *et al.*, eds. *The Fergusonian Impact*. Vol. 2: *Sociolinguistics and the Sociology of Language*. Berlin: Mouton de Gruyter, 305-13.

2651 ---. 1987. *Bislama. An Introduction to the National Language of Vanuatu.* (PacL D-72). Canberra: ANU. (Rev. in *EWW* 10:180-1).

2652 Turner, George W. 1989. "Some problems in Australian English etymology". In Collins & Blair, 214-24.

2653 ---. 1991. "Australian English and general studies of English". In Clyne, 35-54.

2654 ---. fc. "English in Australia". In *Burchfield.

2655 Underwood, Robert. 1989. "English and Chamorro on Guam". *WE* 8:73-82.

2656 Urdang, Laurence. 1990. "On observing World English". *ET* 21:11-6.

2657 Valentine, Tamara M. 1991. "Getting the message across: discourse markers in Indian English". *WE* 10:325-34.

2658 Vaughan, Graham M. & Ingrid Huygens. 1990. "Sociolinguistic stereotyping in New Zealand". In Bell & Holmes, 49-66.

2659 Vavrus, Frances K. 1991. "When paradigms clash: the role of institutionalized varieties in language teacher education". *WE* 10:181-95.

2660 Verhaar, John W.M., ed. 1990. *Melanesian Pidgin and Tok Pisin. Proceedings of the 1st International Conference of Pidgins and Creoles in Melanesia.* Amsterdam: Benjamins. (Rev. in *EWW* 12:168-70).

2661 Verma, Yugeshwar P. fc. "Some features of Nepali newspaper English". In Baumgardner.

2662 Versteegh, Kees. 1991. "The substratum debate in creole linguistics". *Diachronica* 8:59-80.

2663 Viereck, Wolfgang. 1987a. "English as an international language". *Indogermanische Forschungen* 92:172-95.

2664 ---. 1987b. "Hugo Schuchardt. Kreolische Studien X: Über das Negerenglische in Westafrika - aus dem Nachlaß herausgegeben mit Einleitung und Anmerkungen". *Anglia* 105:1-27. [cf. 2085]

2664a ---. 1989. "Zur soziolinguistischen Situation in der englischsprachigen Karibik". In Karl Kohut, ed. *Rasse, Klasse und Kultur in der Karibik.* Frankfurt/M.: Verouert, 135-52.

2665 Watson-Gegeo, Karen Ann. 1987. "English in the Solomon Islands". *WE* 6:21-32.

2666 ---. 1989. "Introduction: English in the South Pacific". *WE* 8:1-3.

2667 Webb, Victor N. 1983. "On the South African English vowel system". *Stellenbosch Papers in Linguistics* 10:134-64.

2668 Webster, Jonathan. 1992. "Text analysis and lexicographical research: implications for Singapore English". In Pakir, 172-86.

2669 Weiner, Edmund. 1986. "The *New Oxford English Dictionary* and world English". *EWW* 7:259-66.

2670 ---. 1987. "The new *OED* and World English". *ET* 11:31-4.

2671 Wells, J.C. 1987. "Phonological relationships in Caribbean and West African English". *EWW* 8:61-8.

2672 Wierzbicka, Anna. 1986. "Does language reflect culture? Evidence from Australian English". *LinS* 15:349-73.

2673 Wilkes, G.A. 1985. *A Dictionary of Australian Colloquialisms*. Sydney: UP. (Rev. in *EWW* 11:164-5). (Revised ed. 1990).

2674 ---. 1986. *Exploring Australian English*. Sydney: Australian Broadcasting Corporation. ([2]1992).

2675 Williams, Jeffrey P. 1985. "Preliminaries to the study of the dialects of White West Indian English". *NWIG* 59:27-44.

2676 ---. 1987. "Anglo-Caribbean English: a study of its sociolinguistic history and the development of its aspectual markers". Ph.D., University of Texas at Austin. DAI 48:11 (1988), 2862-A. (Summary in *EWW* 9:310-1).

2677 ---. 1988. "The development of aspectual markers in Anglo-Caribbean English". *JPCL* 3:245-63.

2678 Winer, Lise. 1983. "Methodological considerations in the *Dictionary of Trinidadian English*". *Dictionaries* 5:36-57.

2679 ---. 1984a. "Early Trinidadian Creole: the *Spectator* Texts". *EWW* 5:181-210.

2680 ---. 1984b. "Factors affecting error rate in written English in an English Creole context: residence and school type". In Sebba & Todd, 323-33.

2681 ---. 1985. "Trini Talk: learning an English creole as a second language". In *Hancock, 44-67.

2682 ---. 1986. "Socio-cultural change and the language of calypso". *NWIG* 60:113-48.

2683 ---. 1989. "Trinbagonian". *ET* 18:17-22.

2684 ---. 1990a. "Orthographic standardization for Trinidad and Tobago: linguistic and sociopolitical considerations in an English creole community". *LPLP* 14:237-68.

2685 ---. 1990b. "Intelligibility of Reggae lyrics in North America: dread ina Babylon". *EWW* 11:33-58.

2686 ---. 1992. "Ethnic lexis in an English Creole dictionary". *Dictionaries* 13:65-74.

2687 ---. 1993. *Trinidad and Tobago*. (VEAW, T6). Amsterdam: Benjamins.

2688 ---. fc. "Folk etymology in Trinidad and Tobago English Creole". In N. Doane, *et al.*, eds. *Words of Honor: Essays Presented to Frederic G. Cassidy*. New York: Garland.

2689 --- & Edith Lily Aguilar. 1991. "Spanish influence in the lexicon of Trinidadian English Creole". *NWIG* 65:153-91.

2690 --- & Hans E.A. Boos. 1993. "Right throughs, rings and taws: Marbles terminology in Trinidad and Tobago". *LinS* 22:41-66.

2691 --- & Glenn G. Gilbert. 1987. "A 19th century report on the creole English of Tobago: the Uh-Schuchardt correspondence". *EWW* 8:235-62.

2692 Winford, Donald. 1984. "The linguistic variable and syntactic variation in creole continua". *Lingua* 62:267-88.

2693 ---. 1985a. "The concept of 'diglossia' in Caribbean creole situations". *LinS* 14:345-56.

2694 ---. 1985b. "The syntax of *fi* complements in Caribbean English creole". *Language* 61:588-624.

2695 ---. 1990. "Serial verb constructions and motion events in Caribbean English creoles". *Working Papers in Linguistics* 39:109-48.

2696 ---. 1991. "The Caribbean". In *Cheshire, 565-84.

2697 ---. 1993a. *Predication in Caribbean English Creoles*. (Creole Language Library, 10). Amsterdam/Philadelphia: Benjamins.

2698 ---. 1993b. "Directional serial verb constructions in Caribbean English creoles". In *Byrne & Holm, 183-203.

2699 Wong, Irene F.H. & Henry Thambyrajah. 1991. "The Malaysian sociolinguistic situation: an overview". In Kwan-Terry, 3-11.

2700 Wong, Lian-Aik. 1992. "A descriptive analysis of the varieties of Singapore English - as recreated by Singapore writers of fiction". Ph.D., Indiana University of Pennsylvania. DAI 53:6 (1992), 1897-A. (Summary in *EWW* 14:2).

2701 Wright, Susan. 1987. "'Now now' not 'just now': the interpretation of temporal deictic expressions in South African English". *African Studies* 46:163-77.

2702 ---. 1990. "Present pragmatics and past histories: some temporal expressions in South African English". *Multilingua* 9:201-30.

2703 Wurm, Stephen A. 1984a. "Influence of English and other metropolitan languages in the Pacific area: languages for intercultural communication in the Pacific". *EWW* 5:89-92.

2704 ---. 1984b. "Pidgin English in the Pacific area: remarks on its varieties and development". *Diogenes* 127:101-12.

2705 ---. 1988. "Papua New Guinea". In *Ammon, *et al.*, 1353-7.

2706 --- & Peter Mühlhäusler, eds. 1985. *Handbook of Tok Pisin (New Guinea Pidgin)*. (PacL C-70). Canberra: ANU. (Rev. in *EWW* 7:147-50).

2707 Wyke, Clement. 1991. *Sam Selvon's Dialectal Style and Fictional Strategy*. Vancouver: University of British Columbia Press.

2708 Yankson, Kofi E. 1990. *Chinua Achebe's Novels. A Sociolinguistic Perspective*. Uruowulu-Obosi (Nigeria): Pacific Publishers.

2709 Youssef, Valerie. 1990. "The development of linguistic skills in some Trinidadian children: an integrative approach to verb phrase development". Ph.D., University of the West Indies, St. Augustine.

2710 ---. 1991a. "The acquisition of varilingual competence". *EWW* 12:87-102.

2711 ---. 1991b. "Variation as a feature of language acquisition in the Trinidad context". *LVC* 3:75-101.

2712 Yraola-Westall, Elizabeth. 1986. "Tagalization of Spanish and English - A case study of code-switching and mixing". Ed.D., United States International University. DAI 47:4 (1986), 1309-A. (Summary in *EWW* 8:298-9).

2713 Yule, Valerie. 1988. "English spelling and pidgin". *ET* 15:29-35.

2714 Zanetti, B. 1991. "Towards a non-sexist language: a preliminary survey and analysis of singular 'they' use in New Zealand English". *New Zealand English Newsletter* 5:26-34.

2715 Zimmermann, W. 1984. "Language planning, language policy and education in Namibia". *International Education Journal* 1:181-96.

INDEX

In the VARIETIES OF ENGLISH AROUND THE WORLD (VEAW) series the following volumes have been published:

G1 LANHAM, L.W. & C.A. MACDONALD: *The Standard in South African English and its Social History*. Heidelberg (Groos), 1979, ^{2}/1984.

G2 DAY, R.R. (ed.): *ISSUES IN ENGLISH CREOLES: Papers from the 1975 Hawaii Conference*. Heidelberg (Groos), 1980.

G3 VIERECK, Wolfgang, Edgar SCHNEIDER & Manfred GÖRLACH (comps.): *A Bibliography of Writings on Varieties of English, 1965-1983*. Amsterdam, 1984.

G4 VIERECK, Wolfgang (ed.): *FOCUS ON: ENGLAND AND WALES*. Amsterdam, 1985.

G5 GÖRLACH, Manfred (ed.): *FOCUS ON: SCOTLAND*. Amsterdam, 1985.

G6 PETYT, K.M.: *'Dialect' and 'Accent' in Industrial West Yorkshire*. Amsterdam, 1985.

G7 PENFIELD, J. & J. ORNSTEIN-GALICIA: *Chicano English: an Ethnic Contact Dialect*. Amsterdam, 1985.

G8 GÖRLACH, Manfred & John A. HOLM (eds.): *FOCUS ON THE CARIBBEAN*. Amsterdam, 1986.

G9 GÖRLACH, Manfred: *Englishes. Studies in Varieties of English 1984-1988*. Amsterdam/Philadelphia, 1991.

G10 FISCHER, Andreas and Daniel AMMANN: *An Index to Dialect Maps of Great Britain*. Amsterdam/Philadelphia, 1991.

G11 CLARKE, Sandra (ed.): *Focus on Canada*. Amsterdam/Philadelphia, 1993.

G12 GLAUSER, Beat, Edgar W. SCHNEIDER and Manfred GÖRLACH: *A New Bibliography of Writings on Varieties of English, 1984-1992/93*. Amsterdam/Philadelphia, 1993.

T1 TODD, Loreto: *Cameroon*. Heidelberg (Groos), 1982.
Spoken examples on tape (ca. 56 min.)

T2 HOLM, John: *Central American English*. Heidelberg (Groos), 1982.
Spoken examples on tape (ca. 90 min.)

T3 MACAFEE, Caroline: *Glasgow*. Amsterdam, 1983.
Spoken examples on tape (60 min.)

T4 PLATT, John, Heidi WEBER & Mian Lian HO: *Singapore and Malaysia*. Amsterdam, 1983.

T5 WAKELIN, M.F.: *The Southwest of England*. Amsterdam, 1986.
Spoken examples on tape (ca. 60 min.)

T6 WINER, Lise: *Trinidad and Tobago* Amsterdam/Philadelphia, 1993.
Spoken examples on tape (ca. 60 min.)

